**Her heart gave a great lunge, its rhythm interrupted. For a moment it was as if the whole world stood still.**

"It's me, Mel. Let me in."

Shakers and movers would covet such a voice; beguiling and commanding at the same time. No way she could ignore him. No way he would give her the chance. Pulses racing she hit the button to open the security door. She was on the top floor. The lift would deliver him to her in moments. Her feet sprouted wings and she ran down the hallway into the master bedroom. Her hair was wildly tumbled; there was a hectic blush in her olive-skinned cheeks, her eyes seemed more brilliant than usual. She had changed out of her classic designer suit immediately she'd arrived home, pulling a caftan over her head. No time to renew her lipstick. She ran a moist tongue over the full contours of her mouth.

As usual he'd reduced her to a bundle of nerves. You'd think she would be well and truly over that. She, who had gained a reputation for being cool, calm and collected. Only she was hypersensitive to every last little thing about Dev Langdon.

# THE CATTLE KING'S BRIDE

BY
MARGARET WAY

First published in Great Britain 2012
by Mills & Boon, an imprint of Harlequin (UK) Limited,
Eton House, 18-24 Paradise Road, Richmond, Surrey TW9 1SR

© Margaret Way, Pty., Ltd. 2012

ISBN: 978 0 263 89431 8
ebook ISBN: 978 1 408 97106 2

923-0512

Harlequin (UK) policy is to use papers that are natural, renewable and recyclable products and made from wood grown in sustainable forests. The logging and manufacturing processes conform to the legal environmental regulations of the country of origin.

Printed and bound in Spain
by Blackprint CPI, Barcelona

**Margaret Way**, *a definite Leo, was born and raised in the* subtropical River City of Brisbane, capital of the Sunshine State of Queensland, Australia. A Conservatorium-trained pianist, teacher, accompanist and vocal coach, she found her musical career came to an unexpected end when she took up writing—initially as a fun thing to do. She currently lives in a harbourside apartment at beautiful Raby Bay, a thirty-minute drive from the state capital, where she loves dining *alfresco* on her plant-filled balcony, overlooking a translucent green marina filled with all manner of pleasure craft: from motor cruisers costing millions of dollars, and big, graceful yachts with carved masts standing tall against the cloudless blue sky, to little bay runabouts. No one and nothing is in a mad rush, and she finds the laid-back village atmosphere very conducive to her writing. With well over one hundred books to her credit, she still believes her best is yet to come.

# CHAPTER ONE

AMELIA's first call of the day was at 8:00 a.m., just as she was about to leave for work. The ear-splitting din of three phones ringing simultaneously, the main line, the extension and the fax, resounded through the apartment, shattering the morning's silence. Difficult to continue on one's way with that call to arms and pressed for time, she decided to ignore the triple summons. It would go to message and she would attend to it when she arrived home.

Her hand on the doorknob, something—call it a premonition—urged her to turn back. She felt in her bones that this wasn't going to be her usual day. Dropping her expensive handbag, she moved with care onto the white tiles of the kitchen floor—she was wearing stilettos—snatching up the phone.

"Mel here." Her usual engaging tones emerged a bit on the impatient side.

"Amelia, it's me," said the dulcet, slightly accented voice on the other end.

Anxiety settled in. "Mum! Is everything okay?" Cordless phone in hand, she dropped into a chair. The news wouldn't be good. Her mother wasn't given to phone calls. Mel was the one who did the calling and the emailing while her mother rang once a month. It was as though she had precious little free time. This early morning call had to be urgent. "It's Mr Langdon, isn't it?" Gregory Langdon, legendary cattle baron, was seventy-eight years old. His lifelong vigorous health had been failing rapidly over the past year.

"He's dying, Amelia." Sarina made no attempt to hide her powerful grief. "His doctor has given him a week at most. He wants you home."

Even given that kind of news, Amelia found herself bristling. *"Home?"* She gave a disbelieving snort, descending to a familiar dark place. "It was never a *home,* Mum. You were a domestic until Mr Langdon elevated you to housekeeper. I was always the housekeeper's cheeky kid. I've begged you over and over to come live with me, but you've chosen your own path." It was a tremendous hurt. She loved her mother. She earned an excellent salary; she was in a position to make life a whole lot better for them both.

Sarina Norton answered in her near emotionless way. "As I must, Amelia. You must steer your own way in life. You don't need to be burdened with me. Mr Langdon was very good to us. He gave us shelter after your father was killed."

No one could deny that. Not even Mel, although over the years their long stay on Kooraki had been the source of endless humiliation, with her mother the butt of scurrilous gossip. Her father, Mike Norton, the station foreman, had been killed in a cattle stampede when she was six. It had been regarded as a huge tragedy by everyone on the station. Mike Norton, the consummate horseman, had been thrown from his horse and trampled before his fellow stockmen were able to bring the bellowing, stampeding mob under control.

Such a terrible way to die. She had suffered nightmares for years and years, often waking with her own screams ringing in her ears. "Was that really so extraordinarily generous for a man of Mr Langdon's wealth to be good to us? He could have given you, a grieving widow with a small child, enough money to comfortably tide you over, before helping you get back to one of the cities. God knows Mrs Langdon hated us.

How did you tolerate that? I *never* did. Even as a child I used to rage at her. How could I not? The imperious Mistress of Kooraki Station took such pleasure in goading and humiliating you. Mrs Langdon hated us until the day she died."

"She hated us because Gregory loved us. You were a great favourite of Gregory's."

Amelia reacted. "*Gregory?* What's happened to the so-respectful Mr Langdon?"

Her mother remained silent. Her mother had long since turned silence into an art form.

Only silence wasn't Mel's thing. She liked everything and everyone up front. No secrets, no evasions. She had grown up with them hanging over her like a dark, ominous cloud. "So we're supposed to owe *Gregory* love and gratitude forever and ever. Is that it, Mum? That's ruthless old Cattle King Gregory Langdon getting in touch with his feminine side? He couldn't control his dreadful Mireille. She must have made him a totally lousy wife."

"Whatever, he *married* her. He must have loved her at one time."

"*Reality check here, Mum,*" Mel said cynically. "She was the heiress to the Devereaux fortune."

"And she was the mother of his son and heir," Sarina retorted with no change of tone. She showed none of the fire of her Italian heritage. "There was no chance of divorce in that family."

"More's the pity!" Mel lamented. "Surely divorce has to be preferable to allowing lives to be damaged. Everyone suffered in that family."

"Divorce wasn't an option, Amelia," Sarina, reared a devout Catholic—or so she claimed—repeated. "And, while we're on the subject, Gregory couldn't control his wife when he wasn't there. So I suggest you be fair. Gregory was an important man with huge responsibilities, many commitments.

Mrs Langdon may have always wanted us out of the way, but she never got her wish, did she?"

"Now that's a tricky one, Mum," Amelia answered grimly. "We both know plenty of people thought, even if they didn't dare say it to his face, you meant more to him than his own wife." Why not bring it out into the open? Mel thought defiantly. The gossip that had had to be endured had left its indelible mark on her. So much bad history! Shame had been part of her life on Kooraki. She had grown up doubting herself and her place in the world. Dev had once said during one of their famously heated exchanges that her emotional development had been impeded. Easy for him to talk. He had the Langdon-Devereaux name. What did she have?

She had never been able to ask her mother questions. If someone gave every indication they didn't want questions raised, you never did. Even a fatherless daughter left in the dark. Yet she loved her mother regardless and had been fiercely protective of her all her life. Sarina, not that far off fifty and looking nowhere near it, was a very beautiful woman. What must she have been like in her twenties? *Pretty much like you.*

"*We* meant more to him, Amelia," Sarina said. "Mr Langdon loved children. You were so full of life, so intelligent. He liked that. You were never afraid of him."

"Or of Mireille. I'm the definitive Leo, Mum. Surfeit of pride."

"I do know that, Amelia. You have to remember it was Langdon money that put you through school, then university."

"Maybe *Gregory* felt a tad guilty. Neither of us ever knew what exactly happened the day of the stampede. My father, from all accounts, was an exceptional horseman, an expert cattle handler. Yet he was thrown. For all we know, wicked old Mireille could have paid someone to spook the cattle and target Dad. Ever think of that? She was one ruthless woman.

She even went so far as to imply it could have been a David and Bathsheba situation, casting guilt on her own unfaithful husband. She was just so hateful."

There was another moment of utter silence as if her controlled mother had been caught off guard. "Amelia, I can't talk about it," Sarina said in a sealed off voice. "It's all in the past."

Mel inhaled a sharp breath. Her mother was in *denial about* so many things. She had long since faced the fact she only knew the parts of her mother Sarina was prepared to share. "The past is never dead, Mum. It follows us around. I *hated* taking Langdon charity."

"You've made that perfectly plain, Amelia. But you did take it. Please remember, beggars can't be choosers. Michael left me with very little. He hadn't been promoted to foreman long."

"Plenty of people told me what a great guy Dad was. I do remember him, Mum. I'll mourn him until the day I die. My dad!" She spoke strongly as though her claim was being contested.

"Do you think *I* don't miss him, Amelia?" her mother retorted, curiously dispassionate. "After I lost him I had to face the fact I had few employment skills. More significantly, I had a small child to bring up. I had to take what was offered. I'm glad I did, for all I suffered."

"For all *we* suffered, Mum. Don't leave me out. I don't know what would have happened if I hadn't been sent away to boarding school."

"Then please remember it was Mr Langdon who insisted you have a first-class education. You were *very* bright."

"I remember the way Dad used to read to me," Mel said with intense nostalgia. "Thinking back, I realise he was a born scholar in the true sense of the word. He craved knowledge. He was an admirable man."

"Yes, he was, Amelia," her mother agreed. "He had great plans for you, but I have to remind you, you wouldn't be where you are today without Gregory Langdon. Why, you were given access to one of the finest private libraries in the country right here on Kooraki."

"And wasn't dear Mireille savage about that?" Amelia did her own bit of reminding. Yet she had to consider the magnanimity of the gesture! A young girl, daughter of a servant, granted access to a magnificent library with wonderful books bound in gold-tooled leather with gilt-edged pages—the great books of the world, tomes on history, literature, poetry, architecture, the arts of the world. It was a library that had come together over generations of book-lovers and collectors. "What a cruel woman she was, poisoning every relationship. She even distanced her own son from his father. No wonder the grandson took off, but he never did say why."

"Dev, unlike his father, resisted control," Sarina said. "Gregory was a mountain of a man."

"That's not it, Mum," Mel flatly contradicted. "It was something more. Another unsolved mystery. Dev had to have had some private issue with his grandfather he wasn't prepared to talk about. Not surprising, really. They were one screwed up family."

"Too much goes on in your head, Amelia."

"Maybe, but I spent much of my life walking through a minefield. Right now I'm making a life for myself, Mum. I can't come—I'm sorry. I have a good job. I want to hold on to it. Mr Langdon may say he wants me, but no way the clan will. Dev mightn't turn up, either."

"I think otherwise," Sarina replied, quite strongly for her. "Ava and her husband are already here. Ava's marriage wouldn't appear to be a happy one, though she would never confide in me. Luke Selwyn is charming, but perhaps Ava isn't the woman he thought she was."

Mel reacted to the definite note of malice. "Please don't criticise Ava, Mum. Ava is a gentle, sensitive soul. In her own way she's had a tough time. Women have always been second-class citizens to Gregory Langdon. Sons matter, grandsons matter. Men are the natural born rulers of the world. If there's blame to be placed for a marriage breakdown it's on Luke. The charm—I certainly don't see it—is superficial at best. He's a shallow person, full of self-importance. He wasn't near good enough for Ava. Dev didn't like him and Dev is a good judge of his fellow man."

"But Ava *would* have him," Sarina said, again without empathy.

"She needed an escape route." Mel understood Ava's underlying motivation.

"Be that as it may! Dev has been contacted. He'll come and he isn't a forgiving man."

"Why would he be?" Mel's heart gave a familiar twist at the very sound of his name. "But it's his grandfather. They're *family,* Mum. I'm not. I have no place there."

"It was the first thing Dev asked. 'Is Mel about to obey the summons?'"

"And I can just imagine how he said it! That's exactly what it is. A summons, never a request."

Her mother provided an answer of sorts. "Gregory Langdon lived his whole life as the heir to, then the inheritor of a great station. Orders come easily to men like that. They don't really know anything else. Money. Power. The rich are very different, my dear. Dev is very different."

"I *know* that. His world view is simple. *Born to rule.*"

"You must make the effort, Amelia." There was a steely note in Sarina's voice. "Surely you're due a vacation? It has to be a year since your trip to New York. You and Dev are needed here. There is that bond between you."

A bond that up until now couldn't be broken.

*Two parts of a whole.* Dev had said that. Dev wanted her there.

*Jump, Mel, jump!*

What Dev wanted, Dev got. He lived in her heart and in her brain. Indeed, he was part of her. She had always loved him. She couldn't *stop* loving him, no matter how hard she tried, or the relationships she had tried to make work because *she knew at some subterranean level Dev was out of reach.* Only his dominance over her was beyond her control. Fate was unavoidable, predestined, she thought. She missed Dev more than anyone could possibly imagine, even if it was *she* who constantly held out against him and the tantalizing talk of marriage. She was lost in a maze of doubts and misgivings and she couldn't get out.

She had never told her mother that Dev had been with her on a brief visit to New York. She felt that the older woman would have vented her strong disapproval. Her mother, though ultra-restrained in her manner, had a curiously implacable streak and a blackness of mood that seized her from time to time. Odd that she would disapprove of her and Dev, considering the endless rumours about Sarina and Gregory Langdon.

Her brain churning, Mel hung up at the conclusion of the call. There was no denying Gregory Langdon had shown her affection as a child. Probably the fight in her had intrigued him. Would Gregory Langdon reinstate his splendid grandson? She had the absolute certainty that he would. Underneath the tyrannical hand, Gregory Langdon had been proud of Dev, loving him as he had never loved his own son, Dev's father, Erik. Besides, Gregory really didn't have an option. It was an open secret that Erik Langdon would never be up to the job. No way could Erik step into his father's shoes.

Dev could. She *knew* it would be wise to stay away from Kooraki for her own peace of mind. Stay away from Dev.

Stay away from the on-off passionate love affair neither of them seemed able to resolve. In Mel's view there were too many powerful forces aligned against it.

Dev—James Devereaux Langdon—in all probability his grandfather's heir.

Who was she?

*That woman's daughter.*

She would never escape the tag.

# CHAPTER TWO

GETTING through the day was surprisingly difficult. Even her boss at Greshams, the merchant bank, Andrew Frazier, had asked if she had anything on her mind. Obviously he had noted her abstraction and she owed him an explanation. He was her mentor and a kind of father figure, and she found herself confiding that Gregory Langdon, national icon, was dying. Andy knew all about the Langdons. She didn't mention she had been summoned to Gregory Langdon's deathbed. Only Andy, being Andy, asked.

Since she had been recruited straight from university with an Honours degree in Economics, Andrew Frazier had come to learn a lot about what went on under Amelia Norton's smooth, confident and very hard-working exterior.

"I don't *want* to go, Andrew. Nothing good can come from my going back to Kooraki."

Andrew steepled his fingers, looking across at his protégée. "But Langdon has asked for you and your mother wants you there?"

"Yes," she admitted wryly.

"Isn't the grandson the guy you're in love with?" Andy questioned, concerned about her. Amelia Norton was a very clever young woman, a glowing Italianate beauty, with considerable business skills, but he knew beneath the surface she wasn't happy or fulfilled.

"I should never have told you that, Andy," she said, dipping her dark head.

"Just answer the question. This love affair has been on the boil for years!"

The light of irony came into Mel's beautiful dark eyes. "A bit like Scarlett and Rhett."

"So what's the stumbling block?"

"Lots of things, Andrew. I don't want to get mixed up with the Langdon-Devereaux clan. Most of them are shareholders in Langdon Enterprises. I had to break free of all that. I have to *stay* free. Peace of mind is very important to me."

"I think it comes down to your fear of being dominated, Mel. I gather young Langdon is a very forceful guy."

"It's in the chromosomes," Mel said. "Nothing and no one, least of all me, could change that."

"You have fears he could possibly turn into his grandfather at some later stage of life?"

"Dev is a real piece of work," Mel said in a low voice. "A force of nature. He's as tough as they come. He'll take on anyone, including his own grandfather. No one does that. Absolutely no one."

"But surely you told me the old man was a virtual tyrant?"

"He was. He dominated Dev's dad, Erik, completely. With all that money and power, people tend to turn into despots."

"Are you sure you're giving your Dev a chance?" Andrew asked, disconcerting her. "I would have thought the last man *you'd* want would be a wimp." Such a man would never be able to handle her, Andrew thought to himself. "I thought we'd agreed your upbringing on Kooraki has a lot to do with your mind-set. The late Mrs Langdon being so unkind, your mother made to feel like a servant in the worst Victorian times."

"How I hated it, Andy!" Mel said, tears actually coming to her eyes. *"Hated it,"* she repeated.

"Yet Gregory Langdon saw to it you and your mother were protected. You told me yourself he paid for your education."

"You sound like you think I should go, Andy." Mel blinked furiously.

"That's your decision."

"So many mixed emotions!" Mel sighed. "There are so many cross-currents in that family. It's like a seething cauldron. Even between Dev and me. The cause, of course, is the collective hostility towards my mother. And me as an extension. Ava, Dev's sister, is the real princess. She's lovely."

"She'll be there?"

"Of course." Mel nodded. "Ava loves people, even when they don't deserve it."

"You're due for your annual vacation, aren't you?" Andrew Frazier saw his protégée was in two minds and needed helping out

"There's the underwriting of the Saracen deal."

"Burgess can finish what little there's left of that. I sense you think you should go, Mel. Your mother's wish matters. So does Gregory Langdon's. You owe him that much."

Mel met her mentor's shrewd, kindly eyes. "I would have to go tomorrow, Andy. His doctors give him no more than a week."

"Then get yourself organized, Amelia," Frazier advised. "If Langdon dies and you aren't there, I don't think you will be able to forgive yourself in the future."

At first she couldn't believe anyone was buzzing her at ten-thirty at night. She almost didn't bother going to the intercom. Probably some teenagers having their little bit of fun. It wouldn't be the first time. Only whoever was pushing the button to her apartment wasn't going anywhere fast. She had almost finished packing and a couple of items of clothing still lay on her bed. Thrusting her lush fall of hair over her shoulders, she walked down the hall to push a button. Immediately she received a clear video shot of who was standing in the entrance to her eight-unit block.

Her heart gave a great lunge, its rhythm interrupted. For a moment it was as if the whole world stood still.

"It's me, Mel. Let me in."

Shakers and movers would covet such a voice, beguiling and commanding at the same time. No way she could ignore him. No way he would give her the chance. Pulses racing, she hit the button to open the security door. She was on the top floor. The lift would deliver him to her in moments. Her feet sprouted wings and she ran down the hallway into the master bedroom. Her hair was wildly tumbled; there was a hectic blush in her olive-skinned cheeks, her eyes seemed more brilliant than usual. She had changed out of her classic Armani suit immediately after she'd arrived home, pulling a Pucci-style kaftan over her head. No time to renew her lipstick. She ran a moist tongue over the full contours of her mouth.

As usual, he'd reduced her to a bundle of nerves. You'd think she would be well and truly over that. She, who had gained a reputation for being cool, calm and collected. Only she was hypersensitive to every last little thing about Dev Langdon. She drew a couple of deep breaths to counteract the onset of nervous tension.

Fine black brows raised superciliously as she opened the door. Dev didn't hesitate. He moved inside with his familiar *athletic grace, dropping an overnight bag to the floor, where* it fell with a thud. "Are you going to hug me or what?"

Dev did mockery better than anyone. "Hugs would be only the start." She shut the door, staring pointedly at the expensive leather bag.

"Have to talk to you, Mel." He moved into the living room,

looking around appreciatively at the lovely, inviting interior. *Mel had real style!*

"About what?" She reacted sharply.

"Don't play the fool. You, of all people, it does not suit."

"So what are you doing here?" The worst of it was he looked marvellous. Tall, rangy, wide shoulders that emphasized the narrow expanse of his waist, lean hips, long legs. A shock of blond, thickly waving hair curled up at the collar of his denim bomber jacket. Jewels for eyes, a dazzling shade of aquamarine that glittered against the dark golden tan of his skin.

Here was a man sexy enough to take any woman by storm. "I'm here to pick you up, dear heart. Your mother contacted me. I've got Uncle Noel's Cessna. We leave first thing in the morning."

She leant heavily into sarcasm as her form of defence. "Are you proud of the way you give orders?" She ran a backward hand over her tumbled mane.

"Not proud of it at all," he said wryly. "It's inherited, I suppose."

"Not from your father."

He spun to face her. His chiselled features with his strong cheekbones had grown taut. "Enough about my dad."

"Let's move on to my mother," she countered. There were always shifts and starts, backing off, coming together, combustible electric currents, with her and Dev. Why not? They had serious unresolved issues between them.

"Try to keep focus, Mel," he said briskly. "My grandfather is dying. He wants to see you and me." He stood back so he could study her from head to toe. "You look beautiful, Mel," he said in a dark, caressing voice. "More beautiful every time I lay eyes on you. Which isn't often of late," he tacked on in an entirely different tone.

"I thought we'd agreed on time-out?"

He contradicted flatly, "*You're* the one who always insists on time-out. Just how much time-out do you want? You're so into your intensive search for identity, it's become an obsession. You'd better find yourself soon. Neither of us is getting any younger. Neither of us is able to jettison the other. I know *you've* tried."

"What about you?" she retorted hotly, falling into the trap. "Isn't Megan Kennedy still in the picture?" An image of that very glamorous brunette sprang to mind. "It's certainly a match the clan would approve."

"Except for a couple of strikes against it. One, I don't give a damn what the clan thinks. Two, although I like Megan—she's a fun girl and doesn't pretend otherwise—no chance I'm in love with her."

"But shouldn't we treat love as absolutely foolish, Dev? What's that saying? 'There is always some madness in love'?"

"Nietzsche." Dev came up with the name of the German philosopher. "He went on to say, 'But there is also always some reason in madness.'"

"Madness either way. Love fades, Dev. Other attributes have to come into play—friendship, shared backgrounds and beliefs, eligibility. Sex isn't the be-all and end-all."

Dev gave a sardonic laugh, his dazzling eyes whipping over her face and beautiful body beneath its thin silky covering. "*I* wouldn't marry a woman I didn't want in my bed. My kind of woman would have sole possession of my body, my heart and my soul. The trouble with you, Amelia, is you're not only at war with me, you're at war with yourself."

She didn't reply. Her anger was *warring* with a terrible longing.

Dev threw up his elegant hands, callused on the fingertips. "Look, I don't want to continue along these lines, Mel. I could do with a drink. I need to unravel."

"What about a power nap, then take off?" she suggested,

hardly trusting her own voice. Whatever the friction, there was the never-ending thrill of his presence. "Where are you staying, anyway?'

"Mel, darling, I'm staying right here."

"Joke?"

"Can't say I'm full of humour at the moment," he confessed, stabbing a hand into his thick hair. It was one heck of an asset, that hair, Mel thought, bleached by a hot sun to a lighter gold than the last time she had seen him. "You can put me up, can't you, Mel? I'm not expecting to share your bed."

"Smart thinking, Dev. You *won't*." It was her classic defence mechanism.

Only he gave her a devastating grin. "Can't you say, 'I've missed you'? 'It's good to see you, Dev.' Something with a bit of weight to it?"

"Sorry." She shook her head. "You've taken me by surprise. And at this time of night! You could have rung."

"And have you hang up? No way! Drink, Mel. Single malt Scotch if you've got it."

She moved away, anxious to break eye contact. "So Noel lent you the Cessna?" Noel was the Devereaux patriarch. Dev, his great-nephew and godson, was the apple of his eye. Noel Devereaux had two daughters, but no son to succeed him. He adored his girls, both married to the *right* people, but it was a son he had longed for. Now he had Dev, since Dev had packed up and stormed off Kooraki. There was no love lost between Gregory Langdon and Noel Devereaux, both rich, powerful men.

"I do most of the flying these days. Noel is a good guy."

"It must be a big help having *you* around the place," she pointed out dryly. "Word is, you virtually run Westhaven."

"So?"

"So I thought congratulations might be in order?"

"I'm not an employee, sweetheart." Dev's tone was laconic. "I'm family. Uncle Noel actually wants to hand over control."

"You mean retire?" she asked in genuine surprise.

He shrugged. "Not exactly, but Diane wants to travel. She wants them to spend much more time together—see more of their girls and their grandchildren. The time appears to be right for Noel to hand over the reins."

"To you, obviously."

"The girls aren't interested, neither are the husbands, very successful city men. It's control, anyway, not ownership."

She didn't risk another comment. "Can I get you something else?" He had come a long way. And for *her*. Though *it was as if she had little say in the matter.*

"A ham sandwich, maybe? Could I grab a cup of black coffee, as well? You doing okay, Mel?"

"Wonderfully well, thank you, Dev." She maintained a cool control.

"So look at me. I always know when you're telling big fat lies."

"No lie. I'm highly regarded at Greshams." Mel began to assemble the makings of a ham, cheese and wholegrain mustard sandwich. The coffee would take only a few moments. "I'll feed you, then I wish you'd find yourself a hotel, Dev."

He pressed his back into the plush leather sofa with an exaggerated sigh of comfort. "Sorry, Amelia. I'm staying here. I need some sleep. Speaking of sleep, it's not too late for you to say you'll sleep with me."

"Get it straight, Dev. I *won't*." Mel's answer was remarkably breezy considering how she felt. She walked back, handing him a good measure of Glenfiddich over a few ice cubes.

He raised his remarkable eyes to her. "Many thanks, dear heart."

Knowing him so well, she observed, "You're upset."

He took a long gulp of whisky before replying. "Why

wouldn't I be? I owe him. *You* owe him. He cared about you.
You were such a feisty little kid."

"So what went wrong, Dev?" she asked with some bitterness.

They were back on well-trodden ground. "We all know
that," Dev gritted out.

"Your grandmother hated my mother and me."

His expression darkened. "She *feared* your mother. I'd say
she had a certain respect for you, you little terror!"

"Well, she's gone now and soon your grandfather will
join her. They'll lie together in the family plot, if nothing
else. You're talking about running Westhaven. Surely you've
considered your grandfather could have planned on handing
Langdon Enterprises to you."

"After *our* bust-up?" he said, draining the rest of the
Scotch. "Many harsh words were spoken."

"You've never told me what it was all about." She tried to
fix his gaze but did not succeed.

How could he? Dev thought, leaning forward to place his
crystal tumbler on the table, with its small collection of art
books. Mel had more than enough to handle. Better he never
told her. It was all so sick and sad.

"Okay, so you won't!" she said, her nerves frayed. "But,
trust me on this, Dev. We both know your father has always found walking in your grandfather's shadow very heavy
going. It's not in his nature or his area of expertise to step
into Gregory's shoes."

Dev wasn't having any of it. "Dad will inherit as a matter
of course," he said as though it were written in stone. "My
father is the legitimate heir."

"Maybe, in the normal way, but your grandfather isn't
going to allow his hard-won empire to fall apart. He needs
someone to run it after he's gone. That someone is *you*."

Dev punched one fist into the other. "Dad has worked his butt off."

"I know."

Dev loved his mild-mannered father. He had always been very protective of him, even as a child. Erik Langdon was a long way from being incompetent, but it had proved impossible for him to emulate his dynamic father, a man with the Midas touch. Erik lacked the specific qualities it took to be the man at the very top of the chain. He had once gone on record as saying it was like trying to drive a vehicle uphill with the handbrake on. The Can-Do man had skipped a generation. It was Dev who had inherited all the skills necessary to succeed his tycoon grandfather.

"I'm sure your father will be justly rewarded," she said, as gently as she could, "but your grandfather won't cede him control. Want to bet I'm right?"

"Darling Mel, you *always* are," Dev drawled. "Let's get off the subject. Life is just one long series of hurdles for us."

"It happens when one gets caught up with wealthy, dysfunctional families." Mel matched him for sarcasm. "I'll get your sandwich. The coffee will only take a moment."

"You never intended to go, did you?"

She could have shown him her packing. Instead, she said, "I don't like letting my mother down."

"You've let *me* down, haven't you?" he flashed back. "How many times exactly have you told me you loved me?"

She took a deep breath. "I couldn't begin to count the number, Dev. But we live on two different levels. We have separate lives. You have an escape valve, being who you are. Soon you'll be the CEO of Langdon Enterprises, with huge responsibilities, always busy, always travelling thither and yon."

"Gimme a break, Mel!" His voice held a rasp. "You're a clever woman. You'd fit in supremely well."

Her laugh was raw. "Not with the clan, I wouldn't. They do have a hold on you, Dev. A few of them are major shareholders."

"So what? I can't solve your problems, Mel. Problems are keeping this God-awful distance between us," he said with intense frustration. "This damned love torment. The never-ending family stuff is the prime cause of our alienation."

"It's *your* family, Dev. Not mine. Such as it is. We've talked and we've walked all around our feelings. We're on a merry-go-round and we can't jump off. Any thought of marriage has turned into an impossible dream."

Dev leapt to his feet, his aquamarine eyes blazing with anger and outrage. "You know why? Because you're always applying the brakes. Think I don't know you fear being dominated? As though it could happen! What you *really* want is to bend my will to yours. It's the war of the sexes, with you the man-hater. You said you wanted to stand on your own two feet. I've gone along with that."

"Standing on my own two feet is central to everything." Mel tried to defend herself.

"But I applaud it, Mel," he cried in utter exasperation. "That's what you can't seem to grasp. I'm proud of you and how clever you are. You'd be a big asset to Langdon Enterprises, if you ever left Greshams. Anyone would think we were in competition, the way you behave. I don't understand what it is you want me to be. I can't grapple with all your expectations of the perfect man. I'm *me*. Far from perfect. Sometimes I think you're actually frightened of me. Not in a physical sense. You know I would never hurt you. But you do have this huge problem with male domination."

God knew it was true. "I grew up with it, didn't I, this little satellite orbiting a giant tyrannical figure. Your grandfather carried domination to the extreme. Always the iron fist."

"For goodness' sake, Mel," Dev protested, "he was *himself*. Stronger, cleverer, tougher than anyone else."

"You might be describing yourself." Mel shook her head bleakly.

Dev showed his fast-rising temper. "Now you're making me really angry. What is it you want me to be, Mel? Do you even know? I can't figure it out and I've come at it from every angle. As far as I can see, your biggest problem is *you*. Your exaggerated need for independence, self-reliance, like you don't need a man, as though a man could break you. I'm telling you it's paranoia!"

"Okay, maybe it is!" Pressure was expanding inside her, building up a huge head of steam. There were always bottled-up forces ready to explode when they came together, a consequence of their shared troubled history and her mother's illicit position in Gregory Langdon's life. "Let's stop now, Dev," she said more quietly. "I don't want to argue with you."

He sat down again, bending his blond head almost to his knees. "And I don't want to argue with you. But you are one strange woman, Mel."

"I expect I am," she said in a haunted voice. "You know your place in the world, Dev. All *I* know is I grew up without a father and a father's love and wisdom. What I know about my mother wouldn't fill half a page in a child's exercise book. She's the only child of Italian parents, Francis and Adriana Cavallaro, who migrated to Australia and settled in Sydney. It has a large Italian and Italian-descent population. There was no other family. My mother left home, a bit like Ava, to escape her father's very strict control. I never got to know *any* of my family. God knows why she decided to shift as far away as North Queensland. That's a long haul."

"Do we even know if that's *true?*" Dev muttered. "I wouldn't put it past your mother to have been wearing an impenetrable disguise all these years. When she came to

Kooraki no one would have questioned her background. Where she came from would have been considered irrelevant. She was simply Mike Norton's young wife."

"Terrible to think my mother's past could be an invention, a construct of lies. I hate blacked out spaces, secrets."

"Tell me about it," Dev said. "Most families have them. *You* are letting them plague you to death. You have to make a leap of faith. Faith in me. Your mother has her story but it's obvious she doesn't want you to know it, even if it would offer you comfort."

She gave him a despairing look. "Was her home life so bad she simply had to run away? Did she cast off her past like a snake sloughs off its skin? My dad would have known. But he's not around to tell me," she said with the deepest regret.

"One day your mother might confide in you, Mel." Dev tried to offer comfort, but he had no faith whatsoever in Sarina Norton, whom he knew as a devious woman and most likely an accomplished spinner of lies. "She's a secretive woman without your strengths. But she had no difficulty conning men into thinking they needed to protect her." He hadn't intended saying that. It just sprang out. His own view was that men needed protection from Sarina Norton.

"Con? Did you say con?" Mel asked, midway between wrath and shock.

"I did and that's my theory," Dev shot back unapologetically.

Mel was severely taken aback. Dev had never spoken harshly of her mother.

"Give it a bit of thought, Mel. Your mother is a born actress. If she'd made it to the big screen she would have won an award."

"What, playing the role of conning men?"

"I can't think of anyone better," Dev said bluntly. "Didn't

you ever watch her with the male staff? In fact any man that moved across her path."

Mel looked back at him, stunned. "What is this, Dev? Payback time? I didn't realize you so disliked my mother."

His expression hardened. "On the subject of your mother it pays to keep my mouth shut. I've never been out to hurt *you*, Mel."

Disturbing thoughts were sweeping into her mind. "But she thinks the world of you, Dev. How could you attack her, unless she tried to con *you*?" It didn't seem possible.

Dev picked a non-existent thread from his shirt. "Cons don't go down well with me, Mel."

"What sort of an answer is that?"

"Are we going to have a problem with it?" he asked in a decidedly edgy voice.

Not, she realized, unless she was prepared to launch into an all-out fight. "Did it help or *harm* her, do you suppose, the fact that she was so beautiful?" Mel asked, always looking for some way to unravel the mystery that was her mother.

"Hell, she still is." There was a harsh note in Dev's voice. "Beautiful women have a lot of power. You know that. You have to accept your mother's nature, Mel. I know you wanted her to come live with you, but the reality was she wanted to stay on Kooraki."

Mel responded with real grief. "She chose Kooraki over me. She chose your grandfather over me, a man old enough to be her father, but what the hell? He was anything but your average bloke." With a defeated sigh, she picked up the laden tray. Dev stood up to take it from her, setting it down on the coffee table.

She let him eat in peace. She had poured two coffees. Now she sat opposite him, sipping at hers, the rich aroma tantalizing her nostrils and soothing her.

"That was good!" he exclaimed in satisfaction when he

was finished. "I haven't had anything since around ten this morning."

"Why is Mum so set on my attending?"

"Why are you so set against it?"

"All your grandfather thinks he has to do is give the order and we all fall into line. Well, most of us do," she said wryly. "Not you, of course, even when you were told you were being cut out of his will."

"Big deal!" Dev exclaimed. "I was prepared to risk it. I never felt good about telling my grandfather to go to hell, Mel. It was just something that had to be said. And there's another thing. Whether he meant it or not, he broke Dad's spirit."

"I can't understand why your father never stood up to him."

Dev's brief laugh was without humour. "Not everyone is a born fire-eater, Mel. Besides, he had to contend with a double whammy. Between my grandfather and my grandmother, Dad had a rough ride. My mother tolerated the situation as long as she could before she had to take off. Self-preservation. I used to dream of her coming back. Poor Ava was the worst affected. But at least we see our mother now. The truly amazing thing is they're still married. Neither of them filed for divorce. Both could have found new partners in record time."

"I expect your grandfather forbade it."

"Maybe he did." Dev shrugged. "He might have stopped Dad, but not Mum. She broke free. My parents should have moved away from Kooraki after they were married. They should have had a home of their own. I remember they were happy once. I believe they still have strong feelings for one another."

Mel thought so, too. "Will your mother come?"

Dev nodded. "If Gregory dies, there'll be the funeral."

"Is Ava happy?" Mel asked. Lovely, graceful Ava, the granddaughter shoved into the background.

Dev gave a brotherly howl of anguish. "We both know Ava

chose marriage as a way out. She had no real idea of what she was letting herself in for. She always claims she's happy, but I don't accept that. If I ever found out that husband of hers was ill-treating her in any way—not physically. He wouldn't dare—but trying to browbeat her, he'd better look out. And that's a promise."

*Mel had no doubts about that. She stood up.* "For your information, I did intend to go, Dev. I'm as good as packed. I'll have to cancel my morning flight."

"Better do it now," he said, rising to his feet and carrying the tray back into the kitchen. "I'm not exactly sure where I'm to sleep. Obviously the master bedroom is *verboten*. No need to lock the door, by the way. I don't bother women."

"No. It's generally the other way around."

"I'm a man like any other, Mel." He gave her a sweeping glance out of his aquamarine eyes. "Even for you I can't swear off sex entirely." There was a sardonic twist to his handsome mouth.

"No need to tell me," she said with an acid edge. "Someone *always manages to give me the latest gossip. I knew all about* your little fling with Megan Kennedy."

"Megan knew what she was getting into," he said, unperturbed. "We're still friends."

She rounded on him, temper flashing. "Isn't that lovely!" She hadn't forgotten how fearfully upset she had been, how hard it had been to hide it. The "Megan" affair had been her worst case of jealousy yet. She had to remind herself she'd had her own little flings that were predestined to fail.

"Might I remind you the pot can't call the kettle black?" he said suavely. "Now, where do I sleep?"

She waved an imperious arm. "There's the second bedroom, as you well know. The bed is made up."

"You only have to call out if you get lonely, Mel."

"My head only has to touch the pillow and it's lights out," she assured him.

# CHAPTER THREE

DESPITE her claim, Mel lay awake with the full moon casting its light across her bedroom. Maybe it was the coffee that was keeping her awake? That was the easy answer. The real answer? How could she sleep with Dev just down the hall? She knew what her problem was. She was sexually frustrated, assailed by desires she couldn't control with him around. She had to ask herself—could there possibly be another man in the world for her but James Devereaux Langdon?

Restlessly, she kicked at the top sheet, freeing her feet. She punched the pillows yet again, then turned on her left side, only she wasn't comfortable with the steady thud of her heart. Over to the right side, she checked the time. Twelve forty-five. She would be exhausted in the morning if she didn't succeed in putting Dev and her body's needs out of her mind. Ten minutes went by. Was there *no* way out of this? It was as though a tribal sorcerer had put a spell on her. There were one or two old sorcerers left on Kooraki. Magic and ritual with the Aboriginal people would never die out. Only she knew as well as anybody you couldn't get everything you wanted in this world. She had wanted a career. She had one. She had gained the respect of her peers and notice from the hierarchy. She was earning really good money.

*You made a big mistake letting Dev stay.*
He knew exactly how to push her buttons.

In the guest bedroom Dev was having an even worse time
of it, the area below his navel aflame. He was unbearably
aroused. He wanted to get up and go down the hall to her.
He gave a short frustrated laugh that he muffled against the
pillow. The last thing he should do was put Mel under even
more pressure, even if it was killing him keeping his hands
off her. Why was it he never had a problem with other women,
yet he had one big problem with Mel? He threw the top sheet
off, trying to rein in emotions so driving they threatened to
sweep away any misgivings. This constant pitch of desire he
had for Amelia could be classed as a type of lunacy.

His poor embattled grandmother had tried hard to convince him that Mel could have been Gregory's daughter.
It had upset him enormously at the time, but he had never
really believed it. His gut told him not. And his gut was right.
It was a pathetic and cruel attempt on his grandmother's part
to separate him from Mel. Yet he had understood his grandmother's raging jealousy. His grandfather *had* lost his heart.
But not to his lawfully wedded wife. It was there in his grandfather's eyes every time he looked at Sarina.

He had no idea when that love had been consummated.
Perhaps after the tragic death of Mel's father. Mike Norton
had been a leading hand on Maru Downs, a North Queensland
station in the Langdon chain. His grandfather's normal practice was to visit all the stations and the outstations checking
on operations. There he had met Sarina, Mike Norton's beautiful young wife.

His grandfather had offered Mike a job on Kooraki. No
question Mike had been foreman material, well up to the job
offered, but the intense allure of Norton's young wife could
have been the deciding factor. Was that what had happened?

His grandfather had been a man of strong passions. Sexual passion had a way of not allowing its victims to escape.

He should know.

Afterwards, she told herself she didn't really remember walking down the corridor to Dev's room. Maybe her mind was playing tricks, surrendering to a dream. It was not as though they didn't know one another's body intimately, but the thrill, the rapture, the sense of belonging had never lessened, never lost its power.

Dev heard the door handle turn. He swung onto his back, looking up to see Mel framed in the doorway. There was enough light from the full moon to see her clearly. She was wearing a pale coloured nightgown that shimmered like moonbeams.

He sat up, startled, supporting himself on one elbow. "Are you okay?"

She shook her dark head.

"What is it, Mel?"

She gave a little laugh that sounded like a sob. "I'm never okay. You know that." She moved across the room, then sat on the side of his bed, staring into his eyes.

"You can't do this, Mel," he protested, his whole body powerfully, painfully aroused.

"I want to sleep with you," she said, dragging the top sheet away from him. It exposed his naked hard-muscled chest with its tracery of golden hair.

His voice held a tense warning. "You get into this bed and we're going to have sex, Mel," he said. "You *know* that. So don't try the little-sister routine."

"No, no. I come to you for comfort, like I always used to." She hesitated for a fraught moment, then said, "How long did we think we might be closely related, Dev?"

He exploded, just as she knew he would. "For half a second! Well, me, anyway. Always the eternal anguish, Mel, the eternal question. You'd go to any lengths to drive me mad. Do you *seriously* believe I would have ever touched you had I believed it? Are you that crazy?"

She shook her head in shame.

"Am I supposed to give you a round of applause for that?"

"Don't be like that, Dev," she begged. "There was so much gossip."

"Mireille's poison." His verdict was harsh. "She had a great talent for implying sinister, cruel lies. Jealousy is one of the most powerful deadly sins. It gets people murdered every day of the week."

"Poison finds its way into the bloodstream. My mother bewitched him."

Dev put his two hands to his head, groaning. "Okay, so she did! And hasn't there been a tremendous emotional fall-out?" Angry and immensely frustrated, he put strong hands on her, pulling her down and then into the bed beside him. "Are we going to continue this interminable conversation?" He hooked one strong arm around her. "You, woman, drive me mad. I just want to draw a secure circle around the two of us so no one can get in. God knows we've lived our lives with controlling people. Both of us have resented it bitterly. As a consequence, you're in retreat from me in case I turn into the biggest controller of them all."

Her laugh was woefully off-key. "Let's face it, being the man in control is going to be your role, Dev. You'll find that out when your grandfather's will is read. Most of the time I was able to separate the truth from the sick rumours. But I was just a little kid, Dev. My father was dead. Mum and I had no protection from that all-important quarter. My father wouldn't have stood for—"

"I find the whole issue unbearable, Mel. I worry about

you. You're so clever, so seemingly confident, a beautiful woman. Anyone would say you've had the lot, yet a crucial part of you remains a lost little girl. Fragile."

"I am *not!*" she protested, hitting a hand to his shoulder.

He caught her hand, kissed it. "Most people don't see it. I do. So my grandfather and your mother loved one another. Is there anything wrong with love? Love might be madness, but it's glorious, as well. Look at you and me. It takes a real man to put up with you. God knows my granddad didn't get unconditional love and affection from my grandmother. She was the ultimate possessive woman. It helped to be an heiress in her own right. Gregory was her paid-for possession. She did pump a lot of her own money into Kooraki during the lean times."

"Then he married her for her money?"

"Maybe he thought she was a lot more docile than she really was. He wouldn't be the first man to take a wealthy bride. He sure isn't going to be the last. Countless women marry for money, social position, security. Nothing much has changed from the old-style marriage of convenience. It still goes on. The odd thing is that a lot of the time it works better than the madly in love scenario. Like us."

Mel didn't argue. She had observed that among her circle of high-flying friends. "I suppose neither side has high expectations of the other," she offered in explanation.

"For the life of me, I couldn't do it," Dev said. "But I'm not going to spend the rest of my life tippy-toeing around you, Mel. You reckon I'm a tough guy, right?"

*"Precisamente,"* she said. *"You're already tycoonish."*

"Tycoonish? Is there such a word? If there is, spare me!" he groaned. "A ruthless tycoon could have found a sure way to capture you. I could have made you mine. Made you pregnant. You would have had to marry me and not carry on with all the old-style, hopelessly outdated class distinctions."

"They'll never be outdated," she contradicted flatly. "It's human nature. God, Dev, I'd *love* to be pregnant," she cried. "My biological clock is ticking away. I want children. I love children. I want to hold our baby in my arms."

"Stop, oh, *stop!* I have a burning need to clarify this. You want *our* baby?"

"Of course I do."

"You mean I don't need to give up hope?" he shot back with extreme sarcasm.

"You know what they say—hope springs eternal."

"Quit the smart talk, Mel. I'm in no mood for it. You have a bizarre way of attaining your objectives. But then you probably deal in the larger concepts of life. I'm too busy."

"I know how hard you work," she said in a conciliatory tone.

"Can you tell me this? Are you planning on prolonging this sex-starved unmarried state for the foreseeable future?"

"It *is* exciting," she said, shivers running down her spine.

"Oh, yes. Unlike you, I don't consider it to be *cool*. You're using your beautiful body as a serious weapon, like right *now*. No, don't get angry." He placed a taut restraining arm across her breasts. "Think about it."

Mel loved the weight of his arm. She turned her head to stare up at him, the planes and angles of his dynamic face, the high sharp cheekbones, the width between the jaw bones that tapered to a strong chin with its distinctive Langdon cleft. "I can't *think* when I'm in bed with you."

"Who needs you to *think?*" He withdrew his arm. "It might be a wise move to go back to your own bed, Mel." He spoke in cool, sarcastic style. "What better thing is there to do in bed but sleep? It's all down to you. Go on. Get up."

"If I can."

"It's your practice to do what you damned well like. You're

free to walk away, Mel. I could point out there are plenty of women I know who wouldn't consider it."

"Tell me something I don't know," she said, still not moving. "I'm pretty hotly desired myself."

"I don't want to hear about it, thank you," he said in a flat, hard voice.

"I remember a time when you used to be nicer," she quavered. She didn't want to fight. Her need for him was fierce.

"God help me, don't I regret that now?" Dev suddenly lifted himself on his strong arms to loom over her. "You want me to make love to you, is that it, you crazy woman?"

Wasn't it her dread that she could drive him away with her fears and phobias? At one time she had seriously considered DNA testing, then backed off in shame. Gregory Langdon couldn't have been her father, although he had been on the scene. Mike Norton was her father. He had loved her. Could a man love a child he knew wasn't his? Maybe some men could. The child couldn't be blamed for the sins of the fathers.

"Well?" Dev growled.

She threw all her chaotic thoughts out of the window. "Yes, yes, yes, yes!" she cried. "A thousand times ye—"

He stopped her by lowering his body onto her, covering her, letting her feel his full weight—taut, hard body, the musculature, the rib cage so clearly defined the imprint was left on her body, her flesh satiny-soft and yielding to his potent maleness. His mouth came down near mercilessly on hers. But wasn't she starved for it, hot and aching with longing? She could never mistake Dev for anyone else, not even in the blackest night with her lack of vision total. Every part of her recognized and accepted him—the scent of him, the magical feel of him, her wild response. Her very flesh lit up in ecstasy for him. So did her heart, flowering in her chest.

Dev kissing her was the most ravishing feeling in the world. It was so intensely erotic, it transformed her not into

*an acquiescent, trembling creature, but a voluptuous woman.*
She cried out with pleasure. He was a masterful manipulator,
but the mastery was inherent in everything he did. How could
she relish the sexual excitement that came with the dominant
male, then tell him perversely that she feared domination?
She had to be a basket case.

Still kissing her, Dev moved off her, falling back onto his
side. "You drive me mad with wanting you," he rasped. "I
should really be thinking about going into therapy if I had the
time. I could take up something calming like arts and crafts,
maybe wood whittling."

"I'm sorry, Dev." She pressed close to his body, sighing
and breathing into his ear.

His mouth clamped on hers. "Damn you, Mel." His hand
slid a little roughly down the length of her abundant hair.
"Just tell me what you want and I'll give it to you."

A shiny tear fell onto her cheek. *"You."*

"You want *me,* not *us?*"

"Just love me, please," she begged.

"But I want *us,* Mel! Be warned. There's a caveat attached
to all this. I'm *not* going to wait for you forever." He spoke
forcefully, even as he was trying to keep the immensity of his
desire for her in check. There were still walls to be knocked
down with Mel. Even as a child, Mel had felt impelled to
rebel against Langdon authority. He knew his grandmother
had been hateful to Sarina. Mel, too, but it was Mel's determined nature that made her fight back.

His great hope was his grandfather's passing would put
an end to the chaos of the past with all its moral dilemmas.
Mel's fears were born out of extremes. He understood her. He
loved her. But it was hell. So much time and pain had passed
between them. There had to be a resolution.

Her body gave off heat and its own intoxicating fragrance.
He could feel the heat off her beautiful breasts and the heat

between her legs. He rested his hand there. "Listen, I adore the nightgown, Mel, but it has to come off."

"Just *do* it," she begged, moving her body to make things easier for him.

"That's an irresistible plea if ever I heard one," he mocked. "Okay, let's try it inch by inch." He drew her nightgown slowly up the length of her legs, past her taut stomach, her narrow waist, letting the silk-satin lie in folds under her breasts. Then he moved down to the bottom of the queen-size bed—too small for a man like him—taking her elegant feet in his hands.

Mel lay back, eyes closed, in a state of surrender. Her *short-term forays into other far less troubling relationships* had brought home to her she would never be satisfied with any other man but Dev. No one else seemed to know what she wanted. No one else could cause the throbbing in her breasts, the mad flutter like a million butterflies in her stomach, the little electrical charges all over, the tiny, keen knife-like thrusts between her legs. No one else could even bring her to orgasm. She had never been able to fake it. Odd that lack had never been noticed.

Dev was kissing her bare feet. The lick of his tongue and his kisses moved languorously up her trembling, increasingly restless legs. He pressed his lips to her flat stomach, the tip of his tongue tracing the whorls of her navel, then his mouth began its downward trail again to where her body was pulsing white-hot. She could hear his breath deepening and quickening. Her own breath was shortening. With exquisite smoothness, his index finger glided inside her—she was *so* ready for him. Her heart leapt like a wild bird bouncing off the walls of its cage.

*God! Oh, God! Oh, God!*

"Please, Dev, come inside me." She knew she was whimpering. The muscular contractions were growing so strong, she felt she might climax too soon.

"Just you wait a bit longer," Dev murmured, clearly taunting her. "Punishment isn't over yet. I want you to come alive for *me,* no one else."

Her flesh had melted. Her bones had turned to liquid lava. This was what Dev wanted, as much sensation as possible. "Dev, my heart is ready to explode." She was feverishly turning her head from side to side. Her long legs had fallen apart of their own accord.

"Just a little longer," he murmured.

"You *devil!*"

"Whose fault is that? With you, I have to take my pleasure when I can."

Moments later, judging it precisely, he removed her nightgown with care, then threw it unerringly towards a chair, where it landed in a silky pool. Her breasts were uncovered to his gaze, her hyper-sensitive coral-pink nipples tightly budded and standing erect.

There was a roaring in Mel's ears as he took one, then the other, into his mouth.

"Tell me you love me," he muttered, determined on causing her at least some of the pain she caused him.

She didn't answer. Her total focus was on wrapping her legs strongly around him, tightening them. She wanted to capture him, not knowing when exactly he had managed it, but he was as naked as her. Their nakedness felt absolutely right. It had from the very first time. Dev was her first lover. He had taken far more than her virginity. He had taken her lifelong allegiance.

"You know I love you." Her body was breaking out in a fine dew of perspiration, the exquisite agony of want. "You've marked me forever."

"I'd say we marked each other," he said harshly, not at all satisfied with her answer. "Say it. You-*love*-me."

"I-*love*-you." She tried to lift her head off the pillow, her voice barely above a ragged whisper. "Oh, *please,* Dev." Her body, so long starved of him, was frantic for release. Yet he wanted to circle her like an eagle.

He bent his head to lick away the trail of her hot tears, then descended into kissing her, savouring the lush texture of her lips, tasting the nectar within. Only then did his strong hands move beneath her satiny heart-shaped rear, cupping it, then lifting her body high so its delta was close-up and ready. He wanted to bury himself deep, ever deeper inside her so they fused.

Her little keening cry was the trigger. He came in a flooding roar. She came with him in her own burst of fire.

He wouldn't have changed places with any other man in the world.

He had waited and *waited* for Amelia. It had made many aspects of his life excruciatingly difficult. What Mel had to learn now was he would never let go. The waiting was over. *He would not stand for interference from anyone. That in-*cluded Mel. The king was near death. Long live his successor.

Gregory Langdon lay very still in his magnificent brass-studded mahogany bed that had been custom made for him decades before. His skeletal hands rested on the coverlet. The heavy curtains Sarina had almost drawn shut blocked the glare of sunlight from outside. His son, Erik, was downstairs. Ava, Erik's daughter, his beautiful granddaughter, had arrived with her no-account husband. He guessed the cracks were already appearing in that ill-advised marriage. He and Ava had quarrelled over the young man she had only imagined she loved. On the surface, Luke Selwyn had appeared a suitable suitor for his granddaughter's hand. His family had money—so he wasn't a fortune-hunter but over a period of time Selwyn's less-attractive qualities had begun to surface. He was basically a lightweight, a *floater* through life, all drive and ambition blunted by wealth.

In the end Gregory had made it very plain that he was violently opposed to the marriage, but gentle, sensitive Ava for once in her life had defied him and ignored the concerns of her brother. Dev had been against the marriage, as well. Dev was devoted to his younger sister and her to him.

He knew the rest of them had arrived—Langdons and a fair sprinkling of Devereaux. They thought the world of Dev, nicknamed after *their* family. They looked up to Dev and admired him.

Only so far—and he couldn't hold out much longer—no Dev and no Amelia. He drew a shallow breath, pain sweeping over him in a monstrous wave. He was dying. He accepted it. There was no place else to go. The pain would finally cease. But he couldn't die before Dev and Amelia arrived. He had resisted another jab of the needle that lessened the agony but befuddled his mind. Even dying, he needed to be in possession of his faculties. The pain didn't matter. He needed reconciliation even if he didn't deserve it. Dying was a terrible business. Better to die quickly than have an agonizing end drawn out. He had been such a vigorous man. Splendid health he had taken for granted. But finally the traumas of old age had unleashed themselves upon him. Black oblivion would come as a mercy.

At a slight sound, Gregory Langdon looked towards the bedroom door. *Probably the nurse. He didn't like her one* bit. A big, broad-shouldered, no nonsense woman, competent, but distressingly plain. He was used to having beautiful women around the place—Ava, Amelia, and the light of his life, Sarina. There had been no happy start, let alone a happy ending for him and Sarina. That was one miracle he couldn't command. The timing, right from the beginning, had been all *wrong*. He and Sarina, a married woman, had been a generation apart, not that it had mattered. Mireille had hated him and hated Sarina to the death. He couldn't condemn his wife for *all* her cruelties. He had married Mireille without love, but at his parents' constant urging. To give Mireille her due, she had genuinely tried to make him a good wife. Only a man should never marry a woman he didn't *want*.

He knew which woman he wanted the instant he set eyes on young Sarina Norton, so beautiful she took his breath away. He had never counted on a woman doing that. And Mireille was by no means his first woman. He would carry that vision of Sarina into the next life. If there was one. He wasn't a religious man. What we had was all we got. Let folk have their faith. It didn't do any harm. Then again, he could be in for a big surprise two minutes after lift-off. Some leap of faith there!

A woman's slender form floating towards him in a cloud.

An angel, his dark angel. "Sarina?" he called.

"I'm here, Gregory." Sarina moved across the carpeted expanse of the huge room to stand beside his bed. She took his emaciated hand in hers. "Are you sure you can stand the pain?" she asked, looking down at the wraith of the once-invincible Gregory Langdon.

Gregory carried her hand shakily to his mouth. "Tell me, Sarina. Are my grandson and Amelia coming?"

"They are, my dear one." Sarina choked back a sob. "They're due to fly in at noon."

"God, haven't I made a mess of my life?" Gregory groaned. "My son lived in fear of me. News to me, but my grandson accused me of it, anyway. Dev never went in fear of me. Neither did Amelia. Ava was always so quiet and shy. Dev and Amelia were more a pair than Dev and his own sister. Could I have a drop of water, please, Sarina?"

"Of course." Sarina went to the other side of the bed, pouring a little water into a spouted cup. Fears were rising in her. Gregory could well die before Dev and Amelia arrived. She prayed their flight hadn't been delayed. Noel Devereaux had allowed Dev the use of his plane to pick Amelia up. That had been a generous gesture. Gregory and Noel Devereaux had shared a complex past. They had never been friends.

Gregory Langdon was able to swallow a few drops of water. A little dribbled down his cleft chin. Sarina picked up a tissue and very gently dabbed at his chin and dry, cracked lips.

*Gregory!* Her gaze rested on him. She had thought him immortal. She bent to kiss his sunken cheek. She'd had feelings for Michael, the man she had chosen as her rescuer, but they were as nothing compared to the feelings Gregory Langdon had been able to arouse in her just by *looking*. Many years older, he was nevertheless the man who had taken full possession of her heart. One didn't choose these things. They *just happened. She and Gregory weren't the first to be taken* victims by fate. Then, as Gregory had begun to age, she had found her eyes resting on another. She had been shocked at that point—how bad could things get? She'd been desperate not to register her feelings, her *lust,* in her eyes. She loved Gregory. But her body had played a bitter trick on her. Her body needed a young man. She had begun to crave Gregory's grandson. Dev, who was bonded to her own daughter.

It had been hell locked up in close proximity to this extraordinary young man forbidden to her. Sometimes she had tortured herself with the notion that Gregory *knew*. She had been really frightened after the monumental row Gregory and Dev had. They were always rowing about something or other, but that time it had to have been really serious. Dev had left.

"Sit with me, Sarina," Gregory was whispering to her, snapping her back to the present. He was clearly in extreme pain.

Sarina drew up a chair. "They'll be here soon," she said in a voice of gentle solace. "I hate to see you suffering, Gregory. You don't want me to call the nurse?"

"No!" The words leapt from his throat, almost as forceful as in the old days. "It's *you* I want, Sarina. You opened up a whole new world for me. Life might have been perfect if we had met at another time, but we got it all wrong. I got too old for you, didn't I, my dark angel?"

She felt a flicker of fear. She was relying on her inheritance to escape. "No, Gregory."

He ignored that untruth. "I sensed it before it happened," he rasped. "But it's all in the past. I was totally out of order when I turned on my grandson. Half off my head with jealousy. That feeling of shame has never gone away. I was jealous, so *jealous,* even of my own grandson."

Fear was unfolding rapidly in her chest. "Don't let's talk about it now, Gregory," Sarina begged.

Gregory took a huge, shallow breath. "No. No point. Stay with me, Sarina."

"You know I will. To the end," Sarina vowed.

The flight to Kooraki took much longer than expected. Take-off had been delayed as a backlog of light aircraft was given clearance. A station hand drove them up to the house. Mel felt so sick and nervous she stumbled up the short flight of stone steps that led to the broad veranda.

Dev took hold of her arm, rubbing it gently. "I'm *here,* Mel." He looked down at her, his expression grave. "We can handle this together."

"What if we're too late, Dev?" She stared up at him, drawing on his strength.

"We did our best. Even my grandfather can't dictate his time of departure from the planet."

They had barely reached the entry to the Great Hall with its bold chequerboard marble floor when Sarina came at a rush towards them. Her olive skin was close to marble-white. Tears were pouring down her cheeks, unnoticed and unchecked. The astonishing thing was that she looked *furious*. "He's gone!" she cried, wringing her hands and making no attempt to embrace her daughter. "Whatever delayed you?" Her voice resounded in the double-storey space, hoarse with grief and open condemnation.

Dev shot Mel a look. "Don't say a word, Mel." His tone was quietly controlled but his eyes blazed. "The world never did revolve around my grandfather, Sarina. For your information, we had to wait in line for take-off. These things happen. You can take us up to his room now. We really don't need your censure."

Sarina sobered visibly. "Forgive me, but Amelia could have come days earlier." She knew she was in no position to take on the splendid, the commanding James Devereaux Landon, who even now made her blood run hot.

"She's here *now*," Dev clipped off. His stomach was churning as he sensed the violent sensations that were running through Sarina.

Sarina turned to lead the way. The reception rooms, living, dining, lay to either side entered through archways. The grand staircase with its beautiful metalwork as delicate as lace curved away to the right. Sunlight fell through the huge stained-glass windows on both storeys. A portrait of a beautiful dark haired, dark eyed woman faced them as they moved up from the first landing. It was a magnificent bravura painting circa eighteen-hundred that bore a resemblance to Sarina.

Maybe that was the reason Gregory Langdon had bought the painting. Dev had often wondered why his grandmother hadn't ordered the painting to be taken down but perhaps she had blinded herself to the likeness.

They were moving down the gallery to Gregory Langdon's suite of rooms when Ava emerged, hurrying towards them, arms outstretched. It couldn't have presented a more striking contrast to the way Sarina had greeted them. Ava wasn't smiling. It wasn't the time to smile, but there was love and warmth in her face. Relief, too, that they had come.

Ava was the real angel in the Langdon midst. A gentle person pitted against a high-octane family. Dev and Ava were alike enough to be twins—the blond hair, black-fringed aquamarine eyes, fine-chiselled features, the Langdon cleft chin, which was more a shallow dent in Ava's case. It was their personalities that couldn't have been more different. Dev had looked after Ava her whole life, and he was deeply upset when she had married Luke Selwyn.

Ava went to her brother first, throwing her arms around him and burying her head against his shoulder before turning to Mel.

"Too long since I've seen you, Mel," she said, tears in her eyes. Both young women went into a heartfelt hug.

"I've missed you, too," Mel said. "I'm so sorry it had to be on this occasion." She couldn't bring herself to say *sad*. Gregory Langdon might have been an incredible man, but he'd had difficulty in expressing his love for just about everyone. Except Sarina. No wonder it had incurred so much jealousy, hatred and despair.

"Who's with Granddad?" Dev asked his sister, putting a hand on her shoulder.

"Dad, of course. A few of the others."

Ava, though beautiful and gifted in so many directions— she painted beautifully, was a fine pianist—was just the daughter of the family, her given role to marry well. This was a man's world. No question. Mel was one female who had rebelled against it, even if she knew running a vast cattle station like Kooraki really was much too tough a job for any one woman.

"I won't go in," Mel said when they were outside Gregory Langdon's door. "I'm not family." Gregory was dead in any case. Her mother's attitude had upset her dreadfully. It was always Gregory Langdon in life and in death. Had Sarina loved her poor father at all?

Well, *had* she?

When had Sarina first fallen under Gregory Langdon's spell or was it vice versa? When had she become his mistress? That was a subject never to be approached. It was wrong, so wrong, the great wall of silence. It had always put a tense and very uncomfortable strain between her and Dev. It couldn't have happened, surely, when her mother and father lived on Maru Downs? It couldn't have happened when Mireille was alive. Mireille would have watched them both like a hawk.

Would they have *dared?*

*You bet they would.*

Dev didn't insist. He nodded to Mel, signifying her decision was okay with him, before putting his arm around his sister, leading her back into the bedroom. Mel and her mother were left alone.

*Speak to me, Mum. I'm here. I'm really here.*

Sarina kept her head down, her expression deeply introspective.

"That was a wonderful welcome, Mum." Mel broke the silence, trying to find pity in her heart.

Sarina's glossy dark head shot up. "How could you expect a welcome at a time like this?" She stared back at her daughter with huge black lustrous eyes.

"Oddly enough, I did. Just goes to show how little I

really know you. But then, all I know is what you *wanted* me to know. You turned into Gregory Langdon's creature."

Sarina made a most uncharacteristic move. She lashed out at her daughter, striking her across the face. "How dare you?" she cried. "I never want to hear such a thing again."

Mel didn't deign to touch a hand to her hot smarting cheek, thinking she actually heard her heart break. "I won't say it again, Mum. I've said it once and I meant it. You put both of us into a prison for which Gregory Langdon had the key. I, for one, am not sorry he's dead. He was a tyrant. And you became a hollow woman. Don't forget I'm *my* father's daughter. Someone has to speak for *him*."

Sarina looked genuinely shocked. All thought of Michael Norton, her dead husband, appeared lost to the past. "Why would you hate Gregory so?" She gave Mel a black look. "He did so much for you."

That provoked Mel's fiery response. "Even now you bypass my father for him. Open your eyes, Mum. He did it for *you.* You were his captive. He brought you to Kooraki. You were the real reason he gave Dad a promotion. He wanted you around. The man dominated your life. He tried to dominate mine but that wasn't on."

"Well, he's dead now, Amelia," her mother said starkly, fearing where her daughter might go with her accusations. The thing Sarina admired most in her daughter she also feared. Mel said what she thought. She didn't keep it locked away inside her as *she* had done all her life.

"Then I'd say neither of us will be welcome within these walls. We're *outsiders,* Mum."

Sarina blinked fiercely. "I know Gregory has looked after me."

"Of course! You got it right from the horse's mouth."

"When did you start to become so hard, so unforgiving, Amelia?" Sarina asked in a fierce whisper.

"When I overheard Mireille Langdon calling you a con-niving slut," Mel said jaggedly. "Remember how I attacked her. You had to pull me off. I was desperate for us to move out after that."

Sarina's beautiful face worked. *"Where?"* She kept her cry muffled, although the door of Gregory Langdon's bed-room was so thick and heavy it was virtually soundproof. "I was turned out of my parents' home," she cried emotionally. "How could I endure it all over again?"

A loud roaring filled Mel's head. "Finally the truth!" She threw up her hands. "How about that? *Turned out?* The story was you escaped. Mum, was that a total cover-up? I'm even beginning to wonder if every word that comes out of your mouth is a lie. Why were you turned out? For that matter, why did you make your way to North Queensland? Australia is a vast place. You could have shifted to anywhere in Victoria or New South Wales, not travel thousands of miles. You and your secrets! Going to take them to the grave, are you? You've made life so complicated. What to believe, what not to be-lieve. Yet you seem quite comfortable with your inventions. I find it horrible to think my own mother may be a pathologi-cal liar. You've never let *me* in. For all I know, you never let Dad in. But I bet you told Gregory Langdon your whole des-perately sorry story. In bed. How did you manage it? When did you manage it? Did he have you on Maru when Dad was away on a muster? Did Gregory send him away? I wouldn't be a bit surprised. Gregory was your great anchor in life, wasn't he? Not my dad, Michael."

*"No!"* Sarina burst out, making Mel recoil at the level of protest.

Her breathing had speeded up so much Mel had difficulty speaking, "No, what?" There was an iciness in the pit of her stomach. It was spreading to her limbs, her arms and her legs. She didn't think she could prevent herself from turning into a pillar of ice. "No, what, Mum?" she repeated in a choked voice. "You're not going to tell me Gregory Langdon was my father?" The cold waves had turned to a roaring tsunami. "I think I'll kill you if you do. Or kill myself."

Sarina was the very picture of outrage. "You're crazy—*crazy!*" she cried, vehemence in her black eyes. She turned away to slump into one of the baronial-style chairs that were lined up at intervals against the wall. "Gregory Langdon was *not* your father, Amelia. I insist you beg my forgiveness. And his. On your bended knees if you have to."

Mel's eyes locked on her mother's. "I'm too busy asking myself if I know you at all. I won't be begging forgiveness, Mum. Anything was possible with the two of you. *I'm* the one who deserved better. I spent my time fighting your battles for you. I was only a kid. Why couldn't you fight your own battles? There are plenty of strong women out there that do. Women left with half a dozen kids to rear alone. You would have received government assistance."

Sarina didn't deign to answer. When she did look up there was stony condemnation on her face. "Don't presume to judge me."

Mel emitted an incredulous laugh. "You're a shape-shifter, aren't you?"

"And what would *that* be?" Sarina asked with scorn, unfamiliar with the term.

"It's a person who can change into anything he or she needs to be to get what they want."

Sarina gave her small secret smile. "Would that you had such a talent. You have no heart, Amelia. There is something bitterly wrong with you."

"Well, it would have to be me, wouldn't it? Not *you*," Mel countered. She had such an *empty* hollow feeling inside her, not unmixed with dread.

"You show no respect. I can't condone that," Sarina said. "I have just lost the man I revered with all my heart."

Mel tried hard to subdue her anger. She looked long and hard at her beautiful mother. "God help you, Mum," she said, sadly shaking her head. "It seems to me you'll shed a whole lot more tears for Gregory Langdon than you ever did for my dad."

Sarina's full mouth twisted. "I did shed tears for Michael. You think you know about life, Amelia. You know *nothing*."

"And whose fault is that?" Mel asked quietly. "Why did you banish all the photographs? There were no wedding photos. No treasured mementos. The only photographs were of me. Anyone would call that strange. You told me it was your way of dealing with the pain of loss. Why is it I now doubt that? Dad was young. You were both young. God, Mum, you don't look anywhere near your age. Is that a lie, too? If you dressed differently and did your hair more stylishly you could almost be an older sister. What did you do that you had to distance yourself from your family and everything you had ever known? This is the stuff of fiction."

"Life *is* stranger than fiction, Amelia." Sarina jabbed a finger at her daughter as if to underscore her point. "I needed to cut all ties. It's easy enough to disappear if you need to. Outback life is like flying under the radar, anyway."

Mel felt a strong sense of unreality. How could you live with a person most of your life, love that person, then find out you didn't know them at all? Sarina had spun a web of lies around herself. Mel had never seen any wedding certificate. She had seen as a matter of course a copy of her own birth certificate. Michael Norton's name was on it as *Father,* Sarina Cavallaro-Norton, *Mother.* "Cover your face, Mum," she said sadly. "Cover it in shame."

Sarina only looked back at her daughter with her great brooding eyes. "I have no need to atone to you. So say no more. My life is not *your* life. Don't think it is. You have a life of your own."

A sense of hopelessness lay like a heavy burden on Mel's shoulders. "So I'm supposed to accept you're a made-up person?"

"Just leave it there!" Sarina reiterated in a fury. "If you have any love for me at all. I am not a bad woman. I am just a *different* woman."

"You didn't murder anyone, did you?" Mel asked, only half joking. She knew her mother's black moods when the shutters came down.

The heat of fury was in Sarina's flawless cheeks. It was as though Mel had touched on a nerve that was still raw and enormously painful. "How dare you? What I did was fall pregnant. There you have it!" she cried as though she had only confessed under torture. "My parents showed me no support or compassion for such a transgression. I was *adored* all my life, treated like a princess. Then they decided to hate me. My father looked at me with such disgust in his eyes. He turned on me savagely, became a stranger. I should have known he was half in love with me."

"Oh, Mum!" Mel visibly recoiled.

"Don't judge me!" Sarina cried. "His anger wasn't that of a father. It was that of a jilted lover."

For a moment Mel, herself, wanted to disappear in a puff of smoke. "Am I supposed to believe this?"

Sarina gave a mirthless laugh. "I don't care what you believe. I was frightened, but I didn't think it could be so bad. My mother never went against my father. Never spoke up for me or herself. Mireille Langdon, may she burn in hell, wasn't the first one to call me a slut. My own mother did. I will never forgive them for turning against me."

"Mum, you have to tell me more," Mel begged. "I'm not

judging you. Who, then, is my father? Not Michael?" A crushing sadness settled on her heart.

"He was less of a man than I thought," Sarina snorted.

"So you're confirming it wasn't Michael Norton?"

"What does it matter?" Sarina's voice was taut enough to snap. "One thing I know. I suffered terribly, but I never will again. I don't need to be questioned by you. You brought me nothing but trouble."

Mel's heart shrivelled. "That has to be the worst answer any daughter ever heard."

"You expect far too much of me, Amelia," Sarina said. "Suppose we leave it at that? I have no intention of going into details. Some things are best left alone."

# CHAPTER FOUR

MOURNERS came from near and far, by air and over land—family, friends, representatives of the big pastoral families, business partners, lawyers, a heavy sprinkling of VIPs all overdressed for the heat. Everyone, it seemed, wanted to pay their last respects to this extraordinary man who had built up a vast business empire.

Nothing could have kept Sarina away. She stood apart from the chief mourners, but so stunning in a form-fitting black dress, expensive shoes and black hat that no one could fail to spot her without gasping. Her lovely full mouth was compressed, but her black eyes were defiant—some said triumphant—as if to give notice to all and sundry: *I have a perfect right to be here.*

Mel looked on, heavy-hearted. It was as though her mother had a glamorous identical twin who had elected to stand in for her. She had spent many years trying to understand her ultra-reserved mother. Now she realized she hadn't scratched the surface. She too stood well back, experiencing that all-pervading sense of unreality. Sarina had swept the last rug out from under her feet in admitting Michael was not her father.

*Who, then?*

She meant to find out. She had been fobbed off and lied to long enough.

* * *

It was Ava who kept her company. She and Ava had always had an untroubled relationship. Lovely, graceful Ava was blessed with a soothing manner and a compassionate heart. But Mel, knowing her so well, realized Ava was caught in an unhappy marriage. She had gone into it so rashly. It took living with someone to find the flaws. Mel had uncovered one of Luke Selwyn's predominant flaws right at the beginning.

When Dev had arrived on Kooraki he had taken charge. Erik was beginning to think he no longer knew his place in the world. The dominant figure in his life was gone. He was devastated. There was no way he thought he could step into his father's shoes. At the graveside, he became aware of Elizabeth, his estranged wife's hand slipping into his.

He turned to look down at her, his expression revealing the immense comfort just her touch gave him.

*"We'll get through this, Erik. Keep strong."*

He couldn't reply for the lump in his throat. Elizabeth had said *we*. Surely he could take from that she still cared for him. Could he be blessed enough to win her back? Did he deserve to? There had only ever been one woman for him and that was Elizabeth. He should never have brought her back to Kooraki. That was the worst of it. He couldn't have gone against his father, who expected him to carry on as usual. In the end Elizabeth had grown to detest his parents. He had thought she had come to the funeral to offer support to their children, Dev and Ava. Now it appeared she was here to offer support to him if he wanted it.

He longed for it with all his heart. All that had stood between them was now gone. He would go down on his knees and beg Elizabeth to come back to him. He would do anything she wanted. He was quite prepared to give up Kooraki, had his father left him in charge. Only he knew his father too well. Gregory Langdon would have left the keys to his kingdom to the man capable of keeping that kingdom not only intact but enlarging it.

*He wasn't the man. Just admitting it made* him feel a great surge of relief.

"I've missed you so badly, Lisbet," he murmured as, hand in hand, they retreated to the Land Rover to drive back to the house. "It was all my fault." His emotions were so extreme, a big man, he found himself trembling.

"Dear Erik, please don't upset yourself. I was at fault, too. The two of us have been through such a lot, but by the grace of God I feel we've been given a second chance. I've prayed for it."

At that heartfelt disclosure he turned Elizabeth into his arms, holding her as though he would never let her go. "You know I won't hesitate to give up the reins. What *you* want is the only thing important to me."

Elizabeth laughed, even with tears standing in her eyes. "He's probably handed them to Dev, anyway, my dear."

He felt his own mouth twitch in response.

The mansion was crammed with people. Sombre for as long as it took, it had turned into more of a social catch-up. Most were eating and drinking, partaking of the lavish spread, as though expecting a world famine. There was no sign of her mother, Mel saw. Sarina had disappeared. She was no longer Kooraki's housekeeper. She wasn't even the person she had been. Sarina, with the expectation of a legacy, had morphed into someone else, someone independent, free of all the old restraints. Mel cringed inwardly at the thought of what Gregory Langdon had left her mother. She had the certainty it would be a sizeable sum. Above and beyond the usual services rendered. The gossip and the cruel jokes would start up again.

From time to time she felt Dev's eyes on her. They were tracking one another while remaining apart. She felt his strength reaching for her but she held back. She wasn't family. Ava, in a perfect black dress that contrasted with her camellia skin and golden hair drawn back in a French knot, moved from group to group, accepting condolences. A few strands had escaped when she had taken off her wide-brimmed hat. Now they glittered like golden filaments around her lovely fine-boned face. Her husband, Luke, moved with her, charming to all and sundry. It dawned on Mel that Luke was sending far too many glances in her direction. Luke, the womanizer even on his wedding day. He had actually tried to kiss her during the reception. She'd been quick to put the distressing incident down to the number of glasses of champagne he had downed. Her thought then, as now, was that Ava should never have married him. *Luke Selwyn wasn't a man of substance. Or integrity. Worse, he had a roving eye.*

The house was chock-a-block with flowers, all flown in. Banks of flowers and ornate wreaths had covered the casket. Such a heavy fragrance was in the house Mel found it overpowering. As the crowd had shifted and moved on, she had caught some of the whispers behind hands.

*What will she do now? What will happen to her now her protector's gone?*

The whispers would never go away. Her mother was just too beautiful and her stunning appearance today was a further eye-opener. It was given to few women to be able to utterly bewitch a man, a man of the calibre of Gregory Langdon. Not only bewitch him but hold him against all the odds. It was easy to fall in love. It was far more difficult to keep that love alive. Nothing would ever be the same again. Nothing would bring Gregory Langdon back. His glorious/inglorious reign, depending on one's point of view, was over.

Across the huge living room, Dev was talking to the O'Hare family. Flame-haired Siobhan O'Hare, the only daughter, was staring up at the strikingly handsome Dev as though there couldn't be a man alive to match him. Mel didn't blame her. Dev had always known and liked Siobhan. She was warm and friendly, eminently eligible as a prospective bride for Dev. The O'Hares were big landowners, with a pioneering history to match the Langdons and the Devereaux. Siobhan was very pretty, very bright, Outback born and reared, educated to university level in Sydney. Siobhan O'Hare was an ideal choice for James Devereaux Langdon. Mel knew just about everyone in the room would agree. Even *she* agreed. Her mother's long "association" with Gregory Langdon had put a taint on their relationship. Much as she loved Dev and battled with her anguished feelings, she wasn't the right match for him. Her dubious background had ensured that. Dev didn't need a wife who brought with her so much tawdry baggage.

Just as she was thinking of making a move upstairs, Dev joined her, after weaving deftly through the crowd. "How's it going?"

"Why do they do it?" Mel asked, deflecting a direct answer. "This is a wake, isn't it? Most of them look like they're at a party. Makes you think."

"It's the drink," Dev said. "Not safe to drink at funerals. Have you any idea where your mother is?"

How strange was that? "Lord, I'd be the last person to ask," she said wryly.

"Maybe she's packing as we speak." Dev gave her a tight smile.

Mel shrugged a shoulder, trying to hide the pain of utter disillusionment. "Could be. Your grandfather has left her provided for."

Dev nodded agreement. "I'm thinking a couple of million."

"And that paid for how many sexual encounters, do you suppose?"

"I would say Sarina put a high price on her own worth.

Anyway, what's a couple of million when you're worth a couple of billion all up?"

"Dear God!" Mel's voice was constricted with strain.

In his formal dark clothes he looked stunningly handsome. The thick waves of his beautiful blond hair caught and held the light. "Maybe I'd better prepare you," he said.

She felt a rush of trepidation. "Prepare me for what?"

"Like I need to tell you? My grandfather cared for you, Mel."

"You mean he cared for Sarina's daughter."

"If you want to think of it that way. My grandfather has looked after Sarina. Fine. I don't have a problem with that. It's my educated guess he has looked after you, as well. Which means you need to sit in on the will reading."

Mel had no option but to appear calm. She was aware people were looking their way, unaware the air around them appeared to others to be charged with electric energy. Most people had greeted Mel in friendly fashion, congratulating her on finding a place with the top-notch merchant bank, Greshams. To others she would always be *That Woman's Daughter.*

"I'm not coming to any will reading, Dev," she said flatly.

He took her arm. "I'll be right there beside you."

*"No."* She shook her head. "Do you have any idea if my mother will attend? She hasn't confided in me. I don't know who she is any more." For a brief moment she considered telling him what her mother had said. But it was neither the time nor the place.

"Did we *ever* know?" Dev shocked her by saying. "What a difference a death makes! Today, the day of my grandfather's funeral, your mother has chosen to look absolutely stunning."

"She was just masquerading as a housekeeper."

"You mother's lifelong strategy has been pulling the wool over your eyes, Mel. Keeping us all in the dark, for that matter. She's been an excellent housekeeper. No one can deny that. She trained the household staff so well they've been able to handle things today in her absence. With no warning, she simply quit."

"Maybe your father was informed?" Mel hoped that was the case.

"No," Dev confirmed.

Mel stared down at the magnificent antique Ziegler Sultanabad rug, focusing on the beautiful muted colours and the exquisite motifs as though fascinated. "I can't get my head around what's happening here. My mother is actually *two* people. Could it be late-onset schizophrenia?"

Dev stared down at her beautiful face, seeing how very upset she was behind the calm. "It usually strikes *young* people, Mel. I can't imagine a crueller condition, the structure of your brain split virtually overnight. Your mother is as sane as they come. She's exactly who she chooses to be at any given time. I think, with my grandfather gone, she's finally coming out into the open."

Mel exhaled an anguished breath. "What a searing assessment." She was feeling more and more out of place here, among these people with their privileged backgrounds. She should never have come. She should have stuck to her guns. "What will she do now?" she asked bleakly. "It breaks my heart, but she doesn't want *me*. She never wanted me. She told me she fell pregnant by *mistake*." Mel lifted her dark head to stare into Dev's jewelled eyes. "That's me—a mistake."

"Stupid woman!" Dev swore beneath his breath. "She's probably jealous of you, Mel."

"*Has it ever struck you, Dev, my mother looks ten years younger than her age? I've always put it down to her beautiful Italian skin.*"

"*Your* flawless skin." Today, beautifully made-up and

dressed so elegantly, Sarina Norton would have passed for a woman in her late thirties.

"I'm going upstairs now." Determination firmed Mel's classic features. "I can't stay here. When news gets out your grandfather left my mother a lot of money it will only confirm the rumours. It's as well my mother appears set to embark on a new life."

"Now she's free of her chains," Dev said satirically. "But don't *you* think of leaving, Mel. I won't let you."

"Really?" She rounded on him, her dark eyes flashing fire. "And how do you propose to stop me?"

"You'll find out if you try to leave before the will is read. We need to know where we are, Mel."

"I know where *I* am." Mel threw up her lustrous head. "I'm the Outsider. Always was. Always will be. I can only take on *what I can handle, Dev. You have to forget me.*"

His handsome face set into a dark golden mask. "Are you mad?"

"On the contrary, I'm being realistic. It will be all the better for you, Dev. Marry Siobhan O'Hare. You like her. I like her. Everyone likes her. She's actually *ideal*."

Dev gave her a long hard look. "Except, *actually,* I don't feel anything remotely like love for her."

"Love isn't the total package." Mel was afraid she would make a spectacle of herself by bursting into tears. "Think *about it, Dev. For all we've shared, I'm not right for you.* Siobhan *is.* She hasn't taken her eyes off us. Doesn't that tell you something? She and her family have high hopes."

"Then there's disappointing news in store for them," he said with diamond-hard intent. "Siobhan might think she fancies me, but she'll recover as soon as she meets the right guy." He detained Mel by taking her arm. "Please don't run away, Mel. Not yet. My mother wants to talk to you. She thought of herself as an Outsider, as well."

"Your family would have sucked the life out of anybody," Mel retorted. "Of course I'll speak to your mother. She was always kind to us."

"Then let me take you to her. Dad can't let her out of his sight now she's here. He still loves her, you know. He never stopped."

"What price love?" Mel asked in a deeply resigned voice.

Mel tried to shake all her disturbing thoughts out of her head as they approached Elizabeth Langdon. Dev handed her over, then left the two women to a few valuable minutes alone. Elizabeth, a refined, attractive woman, impeccably dressed with lovely chestnut hair and dark amber eyes, looked at Mel with genuine affection. "You're staying on for a while, aren't you, dear?"

"I'm not exactly sure, Mrs Langdon."

"Elizabeth, please," the older woman insisted. "A few days, surely?"

"Probably," Mel answered.

Elizabeth patted her arm supportively. "I'd like to hear all about what you've been doing before I go back. You always were a clever girl, Mel. And the way you used to stand up to my mother-in-law!" She gave a low gurgle. "That was truly memorable. I've never forgotten it. So young and you had more courage than I did."

"Maybe it's because I *was* so young," Mel suggested with an answering smile. "It's so good to see you again, Elizabeth. I wasn't sure if you were coming."

"I'm here to support my children, my darling Ava in particular. Dev has always stood on his own two feet. Now I see my husband needs support. We never did get a divorce," she confided softly.

"I'm certain he's most grateful for your presence," Mel said, knowing it was true.

"What's happened to your mother?" Elizabeth asked with a tiny frown. "I don't see her anywhere."

"I think she's being discreet," Mel managed.

"Difficult when you're such an outstandingly beautiful woman," Elizabeth said rather dryly. "First time I've seen Sarina in years, yet she grows amazingly *younger*." To Elizabeth, Sarina Norton had always been an enigma. Inititally she had felt sorry for the widowed Sarina, but she could *never* read her. Never get behind the inscrutable mask. Her little daughter, however, had been blazingly upfront. "She should get well away from here," Elizabeth advised in a serious but kindly voice.

"I'm pretty sure that's her intention," said Mel.

Mel didn't know what her mother's intentions were. Sarina had wanted her here for Gregory Langdon's sake only. She wasn't prepared to talk. Even now she would be bitterly regretting what information had been shocked out of her about her early life. Truly, Sarina had gone through her life like a performer in a play. Michael Norton had committed himself to looking after her and her newborn daughter. Michael Norton had given them both love. Sarina's story wasn't closed. It was wide open as far as Mel was concerned.

She walked the long gallery to her mother's room, desperate for finality. She needed to know who her biological father was. Anyone would accept that, but it simply hadn't occurred to Sarina. She had to be pathologically self-centred, taking little account of the feelings of others.

Outside her mother's door, she rapped hard, feeling the tight pressure in her chest. Things between her and her mother had changed forever. Sarina would have little difficulty cutting ties.

Sarina took so long to come to the door, Mel thought there was no point in hanging around. For all she knew, her mother, away from the intense scrutiny of others, could be crying her heart out. It was all *wrong*. She had only one child, and a smart-thinking child. She had no memory of seeing her mother in tears in the long weeks and months following Michael's tragic death. She had always supposed her mother had hidden her tears, preferring to grieve in private. How wrong could one be?

She was turning away when the door opened. Her mother stood there, still in her expensive black dress, the coldest expression on her beautiful face. It might have been an unwelcome stranger come to her door. This upset Mel immensely. Never in a million years had she anticipated her mother could be like this. She had thought their relationship was loving.

*The loving was all on your side.*

"What is it, Amelia?" Sarina looked determined to keep it short.

"May I come in, Mum?" Mel heard and didn't like the pleading note in her voice. "I need to talk more with you. You must understand that."

"It does no good." Still Sarina stood back, allowing Mel to enter the large room. It had been redecorated at some expense, Mel saw at once. Her mother had a spacious bedroom with an en suite bathroom and adjoining sitting room. Here, in her private quarters, Sarina had made a bold statement. The décor had a rich, almost opulent, feel with striking colour combinations at great variance with the pastel tones of old. Sarina had used desert colours, burnt orange, sienna, gold, cobalt and a deep coral red. There was a striking painting on the wall, a desert landscape by a famous Outback artist. Gregory Langdon must have given it to her. No way could her mother have afforded it. He must have given her all sorts of things, Mel suddenly realized. But all trace of tears had been wiped from Sarina's matt cheeks.

"May I sit down?" Mel found herself asking of her own mother.

Her mother gave her an odd look. "Of course. You must know I'm extremely upset with you, Amelia."

"I'm sorry about that, but I've given you no good reason to be."

"No *reason,* after the abominable things you said to me?" Sarina reacted as though Mel had committed treason. "You called me—your mother—a *liar.*"

"But you *don't* tell the truth, do you?" Mel countered. "I'm a grown woman holding down a pretty important job, yet you continue to treat me like a child. Everything has been on the 'need-to-know or no-need-to-know' basis. Anyone would think you were in a witness-protection program. It's got to the point where I'm prepared to believe anything. You've hidden yourself away on Kooraki all these long years. What are you afraid of? Or was it simply you loved Gregory Langdon? You couldn't bear to be parted from him. And he, *you.* That was the big scandal of our lives, but an *open* secret. Perhaps you can find it in your heart to tell me your plans for the future? I'm aware they may not include me. If that's the case, why don't you come right out and say it?"

Sarina settled herself into a deep-seated armchair upholstered in an exotic print that appeared to match the *real* Sarina's personality. There was a particular scent in the room, a mix of perfume and some kind of incense.

"How is your relationship with Dev going?" Sarina asked instead, her tone oddly intrusive. "Don't ever expect him to marry you, Amelia. I know he *has* you but he'll never marry you."

Mel was genuinely shocked. Was her mother deliberately setting out to hurt her? What was her strategy? "Excuse me, Mum, but you sound like you'd mind a great deal if he *did.*" She held her mother's dark gaze with her own.

"It won't happen," Sarina stated flatly, as though privy to inside information.

Maybe she was. Maybe Gregory Langdon had given his grandson a shortlist of eligible young women to consider. Megan Kennedy and Siobhan O'Hare were certain to be included on that list.

"We're not talking about me, Mum," Mel pointed out as calmly as she could. "We're talking about you. I can sort out my own life. No way would I ever become anyone's *mistress!*" It was out before she could withdraw it, a retaliatory blow that hung heavily in the air. Perhaps her lack of insight into her mother's unfathomable personality could be attributed to the amount of time she had spent away from her—boarding school at twelve, the years at university, then her job. For the first time in her life Mel felt her mother could abandon her just as easily as she had abandoned her early life.

Sarina's dark eyes glittered coldly. "You can leave, Amelia. This is my room. I'm stuck in it until I leave."

"Perhaps that's because you quit without notice," Mel pointed out.

Sarina stood up, gesturing hard. "I don't want you here in this frame of mind."

"So now I'm an intruder." Mel had to cast off her feelings of being bereft. "Who *are* you, Mum? You're as skilled at concealment as a chameleon. Please believe I wish you every good thing in life. I hope you get all you feel has been denied you. You're a beautiful woman and, as you already seem to know, a *rich* one. If you can ever let go of Gregory Langdon's memory, you may wish to marry again. It doesn't seem like you want to share the rest of your life with *me*. After all, you always chose Gregory Langdon over me, anyway. What I came to find out is—are you attending the will reading?"

Sarina didn't hesitate. It was as though all the humiliations, the torments she had suffered in the past, hidden behind a falsely serene manner, came roaring to the fore. "I'm looking forward to it, Amelia," she said with great satisfaction. "Any link I've had with the Langdons is broken. With Gregory gone, they no longer exist. I'm free at last to be the woman I was meant to be. I'll be moving out of here as soon as possible. I'd advise you to do the same. These people don't want us. I know Dev has always been your fantasy, your super-hero, but it will *never* work out. You won't have him. You'd be wise to heed what I say. He might use you, but marriage is out of the question. You will *never* be Mrs James Devereaux Langdon. You will never be his choice for a bride."

It was clear to Mel that her mother was gaining consider-able satisfaction from saying this. "You wouldn't *want* him to marry me?" she challenged.

Sarina's great dark eyes flashed. "My poor naïve child, he *won't*."

"Which doesn't stop me from loving him. I'm always going to love Dev."

"Then it's going to be very painful for you to watch him marry someone else." The flare of hostility was unmistak-able. "By the way, Gregory provided for you," she added as though Mel didn't deserve it.

Mel stood up. "I don't want any legacy from Gregory Langdon." Her body was braced as though expecting more blows. "I'll give it away. There are plenty of deserving chari-ties."

Sarina's laugh held outright scorn. "Who gives away money? Accept it, Amelia. One can do *nothing* without money. Take it. Then leave this place. There's nothing for you here."

"Nothing for you, either," Mel retorted. "I tried to tell you years ago but you would not be told. I'm smarter than you, Mum. And stronger. I'd rather live a solitary life than subju-gate myself to a man's will."

Incredibly, Sarina's black gaze appeared *amused*. "It's been a long time, Amelia, but payback time has arrived. Unlike you, I'm not too proud to take Langdon money. I *earned* it."

"And we all know *how*."

Mel walked in a daze to her own room at the far end of the gallery. Hard to come to terms with the fact that her mother didn't really care about her. Even worse to contemplate, Sarina could well be a pathological liar. There was no concrete evidence to back up her new revelations. If Gregory Langdon wasn't her father any more than Michael was, then who? A man who had abandoned the young woman he had made pregnant? A man to despise.

Mel put up a hand as she became aware there were tears streaking down her cheeks. She hadn't even known she was crying. She never cried. She had always tried to be brave, fighting her own and her mother's battles. Now she had to accept Sarina was two people.

# CHAPTER FIVE

THROUGH the open French windows leading out onto her room's balcony, Mel witnessed the steady exodus of mourners. *She took refuge behind the sheer fall of curtains watching* Dev accompanying the O'Hares to one of the station vehicles. A small fleet was on hand to transport those who had arrived in their own planes and those who had chartered flights to the station airstrip. The O'Hares' huge sheep and cattle station was some hundred miles to the north-east, more towards the centre of the vast State of Queensland.

She saw Dev shake Patrick O'Hare's hand. Next he bent his handsome blond head to kiss Mrs O'Hare's cheek, before turning to the petite flame-haired Siobhan. It was at that point Mel covered her face with her hands. Her heart crashed inside her. She loved Dev so much. No other woman would love him as much as she did, but she had the terrible feeling her life was about to implode. She would lose him, if she ever really had him. Her mother's taunt came back.

*You will never be his choice for a bride.*

Gregory Langdon had married a highly eligible woman he had never loved—a marriage of convenience uniting two powerful families. Dev could make the hard decision to do the same. Siobhan was such an attractive, happy and confident young woman, he could well find himself falling in love with her given a little time. A marriage between the Langdons and the O'Hares could bring big benefits to both sides. Siobhan had no big question mark hanging over her. Right throughout history, passion had carried people away. But in the end physical passion wasn't enough to base a life on.

Mel turned away, finding the zip at the back of her black dress. The will would be read in the library, a room exceptionally generous in size, beautifully proportioned, with very fine crown mouldings and twin chandeliers hanging from ornate plaster roses. It was a room that could easily accommodate a crowd, let alone a dozen people. Her mother was to be one of them. She shuddered at the thought. Sarina Norton, Kooraki's housekeeper for close on twelve years, had overnight shed her former persona, transforming herself into a force to be reckoned with.

God knew how much Gregory Langdon had left her. Mel wanted *nothing* from his will herself. Whatever it was he had left her she would donate it. Breast cancer research, premmie babies, a donation to the Royal Flying Doctor Service. She would take steps to do good with Gregory Langdon's money, though she couldn't brush aside the fact that he had been a philanthropist on a grand scale.

It might take a while but when the coast was clear she would head down to the stables and take one of the horses out. Just gallop and gallop and keep going until she came to the edge of the world. She desperately needed to be alone. The knock on her door startled her, she was so lost in her thoughts. Ava, perhaps? They were friends. Her dress half sliding off her, she pulled it back up, adjusting it on her shoulders, before redoing the zip.

Only it wasn't lovely, compassionate Ava standing in the doorway. It was Dev. There was an expression on his face she had never seen before. It was as though he had realized he was going to be handed the reins of power. Even before the will was read he had stepped into the role.

"What is this, Mel?" He crossed the room to her, catching her by the shoulders, staring down at her so intensely he might have being trying to fix her image for all time. "You look very distressed." Her eyes were glittering with unshed tears and her warm golden skin looked unnaturally pale.

"That's because I am." Mel's voice splintered. "I shouldn't have come here, Dev. My mother has entered a new phase of her life that doesn't include me. What do you want? I'm not attending any will reading. I couldn't bear it."

"Who's forcing you, Mel?" There was a decided edge to his voice. Above average height, she had taken off her high-heeled shoes. Now he loomed over her, six foot plus, his sculpted body lean and hard. "You've spoken to your mother again."

"I don't want to talk about it, Dev. She's not here, in any case. Her twin stayed on. The twin is going to take the money, then leave. I'm sure you won't see her again."

"It's not going to be as easy as all that." Dev's voice turned hard.

"What do you mean?" She felt another worry. "Is there something else I should know?"

"Your mother won't leave *with* the money," he said crisply. "Settlement could take time. A lot of time, maybe. I don't think we'll be in any rush."

Mel pulled away from him. "You really dislike her, don't you? I suppose you never liked her."

"Why would I?" Dev retorted, eyes brilliant. "She regarded my grandparents' marriage as a mere inconvenience."

"What about *him?*" Mel exploded.

"They both went off the deep end. What do you expect of me, anyway? I have no saintly attributes. I'm a Langdon. My grandmother mightn't have been anyone's idea of a nice gentlewoman, but she had good reason to be jealous of Sarina. Jealousy is a very powerful emotion. People *kill* when caught in its grip. The knowledge her husband preferred a servant over her must have stuck in Mireille's throat. She would have thought she had no option but to try to drive your mother away."

"Only she had no hope of doing it. Your grandfather was all powerful, manipulating us all. My mother and I were *forced* on your grandmother."

"Indeed, you were," Dev confirmed bluntly. "Sarina would never have been able to escape my grandfather's grasp if he wanted her."

She could feel the tide of anger sweeping up in her. "History isn't going to repeat itself, Dev." Her lustrous dark eyes flashed.

"Oh, cut the melodrama, Mel." Dev was all hard impatience. "In many ways you've put me through hell. It's the humiliated *child* in you taking a stand, the *I'm not going to be my mother* thing. You're *nothing* like your mother, Mel. You're an entirely different person. You have fire and pride, beauty and intelligence in combination. Only you have to see *who* you are before it's too late."

The message, delivered in a deeply frustrated and deadly serious voice, resounded in her ears. "So there it is—the ultimatum. I've been expecting it. Why have we never been unable to let each other go, Dev?"

"It's perfectly simple," he said acidly. "I must be out of my tiny mind!" When he spoke again, his tone was modified. "I know what you've had to go through, Mel. God knows I've been patient and I'm not a patient man. When did I fall in love with you? Maybe when you were seven and I was nine? Even then I wanted to protect you."

"So you had two little sisters, Ava and me?" Her voice was woefully off-key.

The blaze in his eyes gave fair warning. "Don't go there, Mel," he said in a deadly quiet voice. "My grandfather might have desired Sarina from the moment he set eyes on her but you can't damn a man for his desires. You can't damn him for wanting some happiness in life. Who are you to judge him? Well? Go on. Answer the question," he challenged with a good lick of censure.

Mel sat down, her nerves horrendously on edge. "It's easy to conjure up darkness from a heavy veil of secrecy, Dev. I know *you* had your doubts at one time."

A ray of sunlight fell across the room, dipping his blond head in gold. "To harbour passing doubts isn't unnatural, Mel," he said testily. "To hold onto them *is*. I want you to come downstairs. I want you to sit with me while the will is read. I know it will be painful, but I don't want you to hide away up here. My grandfather gave many things to you, most importantly your education. You've never had to struggle. You didn't have to haul yourself up the ladder. You were supported. You owe my grandfather, even if you try to shut that fact away. You've always shown courage, even fearlessness. Do it now."

"Under orders?" She threw up her dark head to stare at him, so superbly, arrogantly *male*.

"A request, Mel," he said.

Mel didn't answer. She rose, a graceful figure, her hands going to her long, thick hair. She had pulled the pins out of her aching head. Now she needed to rearrange her hair in a coil.

"Leave it," Dev said. Her beauty, her endless allure and her vulnerability was breaking over him, ripples spreading out strongly from his centre, threatening the control he needed to maintain. By some miracle, things might come right. Mel had struggled so long to reconcile all her conflicts, her heartbreaks. The situation with his grandfather and Sarina had dragged them all down, Mel more than anyone. But she had to understand he had reached his limit. There was no place for indecision left in his life.

Showdown time, Mel thought.

Feelings in the library were running dangerously high. Mel *received quiet acknowledgements. Nods here and there. None* of them appeared as distant as she had anticipated. Maybe the clan had a more benign view of her than they had of her mother. Despite her entrenched defences, she found herself relieved.

When the revelation came that Sarina Norton, Kooraki's former housekeeper, had been bequeathed twenty million dollars it came like a massive king hit. For long moments one could have heard a pin drop in the huge book-lined room, such was the seismic shock. Even the expression on Dev's handsome face was grim. Two million dollars had been his estimate and Mel had the idea he'd thought that way too high. Mel felt her own prickle of horror and disbelief. Twenty million dollars! So that confirmed it. Gregory Langdon and Sarina Norton, young enough to be his daughter, had been lovers. There was no longer any room for doubt. The cover-up was exposed.

"Dear God!" A muffled exclamation broke from one, seconded by another, then another.

Mel's limbs were locked in tension and a kind of shame. Her mother, at the far end of the second row of chairs, looked neither left nor right. She sat with aristocratic grace amid the wealthy Langdon clan, who sat as though petrified. Mel had taken her place well to the back. She had agreed to come. Sometimes she thought she would do anything for Dev. But she had refused to sit beside him. Not even within touching distance. Dev, who could pick up on all her signals, knew better than to try to persuade her otherwise.

Another bombshell, but nowhere approaching the same magnitude. She, Amelia Gabriela Norton, had been left two million dollars. Far more money than she could ever have saved in her life. No way was she jumping for joy. She hadn't asked for it. She didn't want it. Her charities would. To no one's surprise, James Devereaux Langdon had been handed the reins of power. In truth, they all had secretly nominated him the right man for the job.

Erik Langdon, one of the few genuinely grieving Gregory Langdon's death, far from letting fly with multiple resentments, as some of the clan might have expected, looked unperturbed by his late father's decision. He sat calmly with his estranged wife, although that no longer appeared to be the case as they were holding hands. Erik Langdon had inherited more than enough to last him a dozen lifetimes. He didn't have to bear the burden of heading up Langdon Enterprises, even with all the people they had working for them, the accountants, the bookkeepers, the high-priced lawyers, the various boards and their members. It was not a life he had been suited for. On the other hand, it had been easy to tell from an early age that Dev had been cut out for the job. Hadn't Gregory been grooming him for years until that final roaring, raging split about which both men had kept silent?

In many ways Gregory Langdon and his grandson were alike, Erik thought, tightening his grasp on his wife's elegant long fingered hand. They were the movers and shakers. Not him, though he couldn't think he was all that incompetent. He wasn't. Only he hadn't come up to his father's exalted standards. He was one of the lesser mortals. It didn't matter now. His parents were gone. He had other plans. Plans for himself and his long-suffering wife. No other woman he had met compared with Elizabeth. He didn't blame her for shifting far away from Kooraki. His mother, Mireille, had been a spectacular troublemaker, the worst in their feuding families, the Langdons and the Devereaux, with a particularly cruel tongue. He almost had it in his heart to understand the path his father had taken. It was like they said. If you couldn't find love at home you'd find it elsewhere. His father had been a very sexual man. A man of strong passions. And he had wanted Sarina Norton, that strange unknowable woman.

Did Sarina, who he had spent years addressing as Mrs Norton, feel guilt or shame at the wrong she had done her young daughter? Erik wondered. Amelia had been a highly intelligent child with a real understanding of what was going on around her. Beautiful, enigmatic Sarina Norton had been a huge embarrassment to them all and worst of all to her child. Amelia had suffered real damage. No child should ever be under constant attack. It was Sarina Norton's fault. She could have left. She would have received help. His mother would have paid her anything to go away. But she had elected to stay. Now they all knew why.

Erik and Elizabeth heard with pleasure their lovely Ava, who had married so unwisely, was now one of the richest young women in the country. Would that affect her marriage? Elizabeth wondered. The marriage wasn't a great success, though Ava never complained nor spoke ill of her husband. The handsome husband, Luke, was pleasant enough, although totally eclipsed by Dev. The Selwyns were well-to-do people, quite the socialites. It seemed no amount of money could buy Ava the happiness she craved and she had deserved much better in life. Erik felt both he and Elizabeth had failed one another and ultimately their children. On his part, it was a lack of strength, the courage, the backbone, to take a stand against his father's overwhelming presence. Time now to measure up.

Erik Langdon turned to his wife. "Everything okay, dear?" He could see clearly that she was upset.

Her head hovered close to his broad shoulder. "May

Gregory rest in peace," she said very quietly. "But I can't think a one of us wants him back."

"Not even Sarina," Erik whispered.

"She always put Gregory above her own daughter," Elizabeth murmured sadly. "Do you suppose she feels guilty about that?"

Erik didn't hesitate. He answered with an emphatic, "No!"

Luke Selwyn waited for the opportunity to catch up with the beautiful Amelia. She was a gorgeous creature, so glamorous with exotic looks, full-lipped mouth, come-to-bed eyes and a slow sexy smile. She was the polar opposite of his angelic, near-breakable Ava. He still carried the titillating memory of the little tussle he'd had with Amelia at his wedding reception, just holding her sleek body in his arms. For some reason, even given the time and the place, he had been desperate to kiss her, if only for a moment. He knew about her and James Langdon. Even he could feel the sparks around them but he was certain Langdon would never marry her. She was the housekeeper's daughter—a housekeeper, now an extremely rich woman. History had its courtesans. They were a species who would always survive and prosper. But beautiful Amelia had no real status in the clan's eyes. He knew a great many young women were seriously attracted to Langdon. When he married, he would marry well. Maybe the O'Hare girl.

"Wait up a moment, Amelia," he called, moving quickly to the foot of the curving staircase. He was determined to have a moment alone with her, though he knew he had to be careful. Langdon could just knock his block off. Langdon, the king of the castle! Amelia seemed to be a bit of a craze with him. Her story ran parallel to her mother's. Luke had often fantasized about Amelia. She was *hot* when his Ava was cool to the point of frigid. Who knew, Amelia might be able to slot him in somewhere? Langdon was on Kooraki. She worked in

Sydney with Greshams. Greshams was very hard to get into. She had to be smart. A smart girl could juggle any number of men.

Mel tried hard to control her irritation. Why on earth was Luke running after her? He would only be stirring up trouble. She knew he found her attractive. It actually made her feel sick the way he made a beeline for her whenever they happened to meet up at functions, dinner parties or the odd occasion when he invited himself to lunch with Ava and her. Her instincts told her he was fully prepared to betray Ava with a little something on the side. Maybe he had brainwashed himself into thinking she might be agreeable. Men of all ages thought no woman they were interested in could turn them down.

*Keep it low-key. A few civil words, then be on your way.*

His tone was low, openly admiring. "You look wonderful!" Luke mounted two of the steps.

"You look well, too, Luke," she responded coolly. "Is there something you wanted to see me about?"

"Well, I rarely get to see you." He smiled. "I'd love to catch up. That's all." While he spoke, his green and gold-flecked eyes were moving over her in a way she really disliked. "Maybe you could come back downstairs so we can talk."

"I think not," Mel said, roused by the sound of voices inside the library. "You and I haven't much to talk about, Luke." She kept a watchful eye over his head for either Dev or Ava, though she knew both had been deep in conversation with their parents when she had left the room.

"Sure we do," he responded with a bright smile. He had excellent white teeth, cosmetically enhanced. "Why don't you visit us more often?" he asked. "Ava and I really value your friendship."

"Ava and I like to catch up without you," Amelia said briskly. "Ava's not a fool, Luke. Far from it. She knows about your roving eye."

He appeared flustered. "You never told her?"

"What do you take me for?" Mel retorted, her voice sharp with contempt. "There's no use your pursuing me, Luke. We both know what this is all about. You fancy me."

"God, yes!" he groaned. "We could be careful." He snaked out a hand to take her wrist, his thumb savouring the satin texture of her skin.

She peeled his hand away, feeling repulsed. The urge to slap his smug face was so irresistible, she had a job controlling herself.

"Your father has the reputation around town for being a womanizer. Following in his footsteps, are we?" she asked, raising supercilious brows.

Luke only laughed. His good-looking face assumed a knowing expression. "Name me any top businessman in the city who doesn't have his bit on the side. It's the way of the world, Amelia. You know that. Doesn't your precious Dev have his affairs? It was really hotting up there with Megan Kennedy. I was told that for a fact. Only something went wrong. I figure he's going for the little redhead these days. What's her name, Siobhan O'Hare? Or don't you know what's going on, my beautiful dear thing? You're on the market, aren't you? There aren't going to be any miracles for you, Amelia. My wife and I do discuss family matters, or did you think we didn't? I know you and Dev have had a thing going for years, but it's never *simple,* is it? In the family's eyes, you and little Siobhan aren't in the same class."

Mel couldn't control her emotional reaction. "Goodbye, Luke," she said with tight control.

"Ah, Amelia, now you're cross with me. I didn't have to

spell it out, did I? You know the score." He kept following her up the stairs.

Mel swirled round. "Get lost, Luke. You disgust me."

*"I can live with it," Luke persisted, lost in an agony of lust.* His gaze slipped down over her. He loved the way her black dress curved around her body like the petals of a tulip. Her breasts were so beautiful. Any man's eyes would linger on their shape and fullness. He could feel himself hardening, pent up and excited. "Can I help it if I want you?"

"Any woman is for sale?" Mel was on the point of pushing him back down the stairs.

He gave a throaty chuckle, sickeningly, amazingly confident. "You're not as indifferent to me as you like to make out, Amelia. Don't go silent on me. We go back a long way." He caught her arm.

"Personally, I prefer to forget that," she said sharply, unaware she was grinding her teeth.

*"Yeah, well—" Luke's face contorted. "We didn't get far,* did we? I was drunk—"

He got no further as a man's voice sliced through the air with all the menace of a hurled knife.

"Let her go, Selwyn."

Luke flushed alarmingly. He was instantly aware of his precarious position. He released his grip on Mel, exaggerating his jump back from her, only to lose his balance. He wobbled dangerously before bracing an arm on the balustrade. Even then he landed with a stagger on a lower step of the stairs.

"That was super, Luke!" Mel said with contempt. "Do it again."

Only it was no time for levity. Dev was walking towards them, an electrifying figure, six foot three of hard muscle with the physical strength Luke Selwyn couldn't hope to match. The expression on his face said *furious.*

With difficulty, Luke Selwyn swivelled to face his brother-in-law, hastily arranging his handsome features into what he hoped was a reassuring smile. "Slow down, man. I was just having a few words with Amelia. Don't get to see her often."

"So what were you saying she didn't like?" Dev snapped back, blue-green eyes slitted, his voice so hard Luke felt desperate to be on his way.

"Nothing really, Dev."

Mel, too, experienced a wave of alarm. Dev's expression was so formidable anything could happen. He moved nearer Luke, his right fist clenched. Mel gave a stifled gasp. "Everything's okay, Dev." She was aware of the flush of blood beneath his dark golden skin. She couldn't believe this was happening. Dev looked perilously close to knocking his brother-in-law to the floor.

Luke must have felt the same because he was focusing all his attention on getting away. "Sorry if you got the wrong idea, Dev."

"You would be the one to be sorry," Dev ground out.

It was appallingly clear to Mel that Dev didn't seem to be looking for an alternative to beating his brother-in-law up. The only one who could probably put a stop to this was Ava, Mel thought. She rushed down the stairs. She had to calm the situation. Then, like a miracle, Ava appeared, regarding the fixed tableau with anxious, even appalled eyes.

For a long moment there was an aching *stillness,* then Ava spoke. "Whatever is the matter?" She stared at each one in turn, the expression on her lovely face strained.

Luke took the heaven-sent opportunity to rush to his wife's side, while Mel offered a halfway plausible explanation, keeping her tone light. "Luke came a mite too close to taking a tumble down the stairs."

"Gave me a bit of a fright," Luke blurted, looking the very picture of white-faced innocence. "That's never happened to me before."

Was Ava going to swallow it? Mel asked herself, holding her breath. Ava was no one's fool.

"Always a first time," Ava retorted, sounding all of a sudden extremely brisk. "Okay, then. I'm going up to our room. Come with me, Luke. Your face *has* gone pale."

"Shock," he said with more a rictus than a smile on his handsome face. "It's a wonder I didn't twist my ankle."

"That would have been rough," Dev cut in suavely. "Better watch it next time."

Ava shot a swift searching look at her brother, then she took her husband's arm, steering him towards the staircase. "Can we meet up in an hour, Mel?" she asked over her shoulder.

"Sure. Come to my room. We can have coffee on the balcony."

"I'll be there," Ava confirmed.

Dev waited until his sister and her husband had disappeared before asking the inevitable question. "What was that all about?" His brows were drawn together.

Mel tried for flippancy. "Beats the hell out of me!"

"That guy is unbelievable," Dev said grimly.

"That he is. I thought for a moment there you were going to challenge him to a sword fight."

Dev wasn't in the mood for jokes. "He always did fancy you," he said, rocketing back into anger.

*"Please!"* Mel shuddered.

"I know all the signs," Dev continued. "Lust."

Mel tried to keep calm. "I won't take that personally."

He looked at her, making a big effort to calm his feelings. "You're a powerfully sensual woman, Mel. You create excitement."

"Thanks a lot. So it's *my* fault?" Her volatile temper sparked.

"Of course." This time he answered smoothly, with a hint

of humour. He lifted her face to his, planting a staggeringly erotic kiss on her mouth.

"Dev, I'm *thinking someone might come.*" Startled, her senses swirling, she drew back.

"*I* thought about it. So?" His jewellike eyes glittered. It came to Mel, not for the first time, one needed great eyes to be truly charismatic.

"So there's enough talk as it is." She lifted a finger to her pulsing mouth. She didn't think she could exist without Dev's kisses but she wasn't about to tell him that. She had to keep her passions well below the surface. Become adept at it like her mother. "I'm trying to be as unobtrusive as possible."

He laughed briefly. "You don't do unobtrusive, Mel."

"I don't flaunt myself, either," she shot back.

"Selwyn thinks you do." His voice held a faint taunt. "It's like a damned soap opera around here."

"And it's not a joke, Dev."

"Who said anything about a joke?"

"You're forever winding me up."

He gave her the smile that was her undoing. "God knows that's easy enough. You don't just jump to conclusions, Mel. You take quantum leaps."

Who knew better than he? "I think I'm functioning reasonably well, thank you."

"You're functioning *extremely* well, but you do admit you have problems, Mel. Consequently, *we* have problems. Life for us has been one seething cauldron of emotion."

"Families *are* the great cauldron for brewing up trouble," she reminded him. "Especially your family."

Dev's handsome face darkened. "Don't forget Sarina." He had a mad impulse to say more but held himself in tight check. Sarina Norton, that strange woman, had always had her own agenda. "You couldn't beat Granddad for delivering seismic shocks. He looked after Sarina *exceedingly* well.

Apparently, the going wages of sin these days is twenty million dollars. But hey, it's good to progress in life," he tacked on satirically.

"You don't beat about the bush, do you?"

"Do I ever?"

The air around them had heated up. Nothing new. "Rumour has now become *fact*. It's abundantly clear to us all my mother looked after your grandfather pretty well."

"Looking after a man will do it every time," Dev offered very dryly.

"Is that what you want from the woman in your life, Dev?" She stared up at him.

"I always thought *you* were the woman in my life," he answered, as cool as you pleased. "Are you or aren't you?"

She looked away. "Maybe I've got to be a habit."

"Absolutely fine with me," Dev responded in his maddening fashion. "I have to say your mother is a piece of work. She didn't even officially quit. She just downed tools."

Mel couldn't suppress a moan. "I don't know what to say to that except I'm sorry. But really, what did you expect? You don't often meet a housekeeper who knows in advance she'll have millions in the piggy bank. There's a lesson in it for us all. It pays to keep your mouth shut. Now I'm continuing upstairs, Dev. We're well on the way to having one of our monumental blues. I'd say in the next few seconds."

"A blue works for me." Dev took a gentle but firm hold of her arm. "However, I appeal to you not to start one. Especially with a house full of people. You're not the only one to find this whole situation both embarrassing and humiliating. Then today of all days, with Ava only a short distance away in the library, the lecher Selwyn decides to chat you up."

Mel relaxed slightly. "He's the sort who likes to chat women up," she said. "Luke thinks he's a real stud. It's the high-end ego thing. Mercifully, you don't have it."

"Excuse me!" Dev looked affronted.

Mel could only manage a wry laugh. For all he had going for him, Dev had absolutely no narcissistic leanings. "Put it down to the fact he'd had a few drinks," she said. "There's no need for concern."

"But there *is!*" Dev insisted. "Let's go outside."

"Why?" She made a show of resistance, just for the hell of it.

"I *said* so. Look, Mel, in a minute or so they'll come streaming out of the library. I don't want to be here." He began to steer her away. "Selwyn knows what will happen if he bothers you again, but it's Ava I'm worried about. The sooner Ava gets rid of him the better. There's time. She's young. She can start again."

"I'm sure *he* doesn't want that," Mel said, believing it to be true.

"He doesn't love her," Dev muttered grimly.

Mel sighed. "I don't know if he's capable of it. But I do know he's peacock proud of her. Ava is very beautiful—"

"And she's very *rich,*" Dev added with a blaze of temper. "She wants to talk to you. You have a chance to find out if being married to Selwyn is what she really wants. If she wants out, then she simply has to say so. He won't be getting his hands on her money. Grandfather insisted on an ironclad pre-nuptial agreement. I don't want to see my beautiful sister locked into an unhappy marriage. I've seen first-hand what unhappy marriages can do. At least there isn't a child to worry about. There's been quite enough unhappiness," he stated bluntly.

"Another good reason to hate the rich," she only half joked.

"Granddad's solicitor is the only one not in shock," he said wryly.

"I imagine he's used to shocks. It must happen a lot when

wills are read. I'm so glad your grandfather looked after Ava. A woman needs her own money."

Dev gave a short laugh. "I agree. You stand on your own two feet, Mel. Ava has always admired you for that. She envies your achievements."

Mel shook her head. "I haven't set the world on fire. I'm no brain surgeon. By the way, I don't intend keeping the money your grandfather left me."

"Disgusted, are you, with your lot?"

Mel ignored the taunt. "I'm going to give it to organizations that really need it. I have charities I support."

Dev frowned. "But it's not much, surely, Mel? Think about it," he said seriously. "You can always make donations as you see fit."

"And I see fit to give away the lot. Why is it the truly rich don't seem to know they're rich?'

"I suppose they don't know any different. Dad didn't seem perturbed Granddad handed over the reins to me."

"I guess *he* saw it coming. We both know your father looked on the top job as an intolerable burden. Now he can live the life he wants. Your mother wants to come back to him. He certainly wants her."

"So at least one good thing has come out of all this."

They had moved out of the Garden Room, filled with a cornucopia of luxuriant plants and golden canes in huge planters, into a private walled garden. The heady swirl of fragrances acted as stimuli for the senses. Butterflies and dragonflies in a kaleidoscope of colours hovered over the abundance of blooms, near drowning in the nectar. The sky, even at late afternoon, was still a glorious dense blue, trailing silky white ribbons of cirrus cloud. Above them a great wedge-tailed eagle patrolled his domain. The sun beat down hot. A magnificent electric-pink bougainvillea streamed gracefully over the top of the trellis and through its walls, golden sunlight shafting through it here and there. Dev broke off a papery pink flower and pushed it into the gleaming dark coil at Mel's nape. "The amount of time we've wasted," he mused with deep regret.

"I don't blame you if you're tired of it all, Dev. The conflicts have affected me far more than you. You came from a position of strength. I didn't. We've both admitted we had a passing fear we could be related by blood."

"Do you think I don't know how much that's preyed on your mind?" Dev said. "Gregory, for all his sins, was *not* your father. None of us believed it. Not even my grandmother, no matter what she implied. One thing alone, the timing was way too tight. Are we to believe his passion for Sarina was so overwhelming he took her, a newly married young woman, virtually on sight?"

"There have been such cases," she said with a dismal laugh. "You mustn't forget how many dreadful encounters I had with Mireille. My mother seemed impervious to the endless humiliations Mireille heaped on her. I wasn't. And I was only a child."

"A child who possessed a high degree of fearlessness and integrity. If you really want to lay every last fear to rest we can always undergo DNA testing. Just say the word."

"And thereby slay the dragon."

"It would deal with your last vestige of doubt."

"I don't have any," she said, shaking her head.

"Neither do I."

"It was just one of my neuroses."

"My grandmother had a lot to answer for," he said grimly. "She tried to poison your mind."

"In my formative years, too."

Deep, deep in her subconscious, a memory abruptly surfaced. A memory she had safely buried. Now it returned.

Mireille Langdon was dead, but she could see her very plainly. Familiar fear and anger bloomed in her chest.

*"You stay right where you are, you insolent little girl,"* Mireille thundered, *her handsome face livid, working with rage. "How dare you speak to me in that fashion?"*

*She was frightened but she wasn't going to back down. "How dare you say terrible things about my mother?" Mel cried, straining just to breathe.*

*"Your mother!" Mireille threw back her dark head and laughed. "That conniving slut. Her face and her body might be beautiful but her soul is black. One of these days she's going to push me too far, mark my words, child. I could get rid of Norton, the poor cuckold, who sprang out of nowhere and was given promotion. Without him, you and your mother would have to pack up and go. I can guarantee it. Let it be known Mireille Langdon is mistress here. Your mother is a servant. No, don't you dare come at me with arms flailing, little girl,"* Mireille warned. *"I admire you in a way,"* she said with a terrible despairing sigh. *"You've all the guts your immoral mother hasn't,"* she snarled, *her spirit in the merciless grip of the malevolent green-eyed monster. "My husband isn't the only one with power, you will see. I am a Devereaux. I don't stand alone."*

Dev's voice jolted her back into the present. She couldn't credit now the way she had physically attacked Mireille Langdon when she was only a child. But someone had to defend her mother. She had taken on the role of champion. Not needed it would now appear. Sarina had struck her own powerful bargain.

"You're coming down to dinner?" Dev was asking.

"With the clan?"

"Not a one of them classier than you, Mel."

"*But I'm the enemy, aren't I? Or the daughter of the enemy.* Pretty much the same thing. The millions Mum got, they could have shared. They represent millions lost."

Dev rested both hands on her shoulders. "I'm not losing any sleep over it, Mel. My advice to you is get over it. Change your therapist."

"Therapist?" *she scoffed.* "*I don't have one. I don't actu-*ally know anybody who does."

"Talking to the right person, someone with experience and wisdom, could help get things out of your system." It was said with more than a hint of seriousness. "Maybe a few sessions?"

"You think a *few* would cure me?"

"Maybe we never say goodbye to the child within us," he mused, keeping his arm around her and walking on.

"Why would we? Childhood affects every last one of us. Good memories. Bad memories. Love or rejection. The stand families take can result in bitterness and estrangements right down the years. Relationships founder because they're not deemed *right.* I know in your family's eyes I'm not right for you. Even *I* don't think I'm right for you. The media could get hold of my mother's story. That involves me." She was aware of the widening implications.

"Well, twenty mill was right out of the ballpark, Mel," he said caustically.

"You're the CEO now, Dev. Would you consider contest-ing the will?"

"And wash our dirty linen in public?"

"I take that as a no, then, shall I?"

His arm tightened. "Mel, the last thing I want is to hurt *you.* That was worded badly but you know what I mean. Your mother can take the money and disappear for all I care. She had a right to a slice of the pie, but not a fortune."

"The biggest reward your grandfather could offer." Mel sighed. "It all makes me feel very sick. And sad."

"Don't think it doesn't sadden me, too. But everything is a nine-day wonder, Mel. Bigger stories sweep in to take priority. Did your mother drop the slightest hint when she'd be leaving? It's not as though she can call a cab."

"She's not the woman to confide," Mel said, feeling utterly betrayed. "She's advised me to leave. She didn't say with *her*."

"She's not, alas, a contender for Mother of the Year," Dev returned dryly. "She should be aware she's not dealing with Dad any more. She's dealing with *me*."

Mel's expression was accepting of that. "She doesn't need any prompting from me to see that. I'm sure she'll beg a word."

"Terrific! I can't wait."

They had almost reached the very romantic-looking white latticework pavilion at the end of the arcade. Mogul in appearance, it had been one of their favourite trysting places in the old days. To be alone in the witching hours. To make love.

*I'm with you. With you. And my blood is singing.*

Dev always said the most beautiful things. She had often told him he should have been a poet. She had no doubt of his love.

*Then.*

"Come to dinner, Mel. I think we can be certain your mother won't be joining us."

"I can't think she was expecting an invitation." Mel's tone matched his for dryness. "She'll know everyone is furious about her mind-blowing legacy."

"Like she can't handle it?" Dev asked with scorn. "Your Madonna-faced mother is in reality one tough cookie. I'd been thinking set limits, Mel, but that got blasted away. But

I suppose, when it comes down to it, it was my grandfather's money. It was his wish she have it."

Mel gave way to her entrenched bitterness. "Why, if he loved her, didn't he marry her when your grandmother died? It was such a reason for shame. My shame, *her* shame. My mother hung in there."

"Maybe she knew the big payout was coming?" Dev's tone was as dry as ash. "We have to face it, Mel. Your mother always had her own agenda. Being a loyal and loving daughter, you've been in denial. There wasn't going to be the fairytale ending. My grandfather thought it best not to marry her." As he spoke, he was acutely aware of the rigidity in Mel's body, the warring feelings that continued to hold her in their grip.

"She fitted better as a mistress. He was Gregory Langdon, cattle king. She was Kooraki's housekeeper. As Jane Austen would have put it, beneath his station. My mother has a few secrets she thought worth keeping."

"Maybe they're so secret she has a hard time remembering them," Dev shot back.

She wasn't ready to confide in him yet. It was a touch hard when she had no real conviction her mother had been telling the truth. She stared off to the pavilion. How many times had she and Dev declared their undying love? That was when their mouths weren't stopped by passionate kisses. The pavilion, to this day, was covered with a beautiful old-fashioned coppery-pink rambler with strongly fragrant blooms. She thought she would carry that particular scent to her grave.

"Hard for anyone to lay low when they've just come into twenty million dollars. The press *will* find out, sooner or later."

"None of this will touch you, I promise," Dev said.

"Even you can't guarantee that, Dev."

"I'll certainly try. But discovery, disclosure is in the nature of things. Even royalty can't evade it. Our job is to rise above it. Get on with things. Be glad of what we've got."

"Marcus Aurelius, Roman Emperor, said pretty much the same thing almost two thousand years ago. To paraphrase: get out of bed, take up your duty, appreciate what is around you."

"Which only goes to prove great minds think alike," Dev said, his tone smooth as silk. "I want you to join us tonight, Mel."

"So all things must happen in accordance with your will?"

Slowly he turned her to look at him. "Sure you're not a man-hater, Mel?"

"Sometimes." She stared into his beautiful iridescent eyes. "It *is* a war between the sexes."

His smile was sharp. "Well, I, for one, long for it to be over." He fanned the fingers of his right hand across her throat. "Especially when you feel you have to win."

"Only sometimes," she breathed, mesmerized by the man.

"You're winning now." He bent his head, kissing her long and hard for the pleasure and the pain of it. Lingeringly, he ran his mouth over the satiny column of her neck, his hands moving inevitably to the full contours of her breasts.

She stayed him, her hands over his, her eyes brilliantly alive with emotion. "Was it sex that bonded my mother to Gregory? Is it sex that bonds you to me?"

He let her go so abruptly she staggered, flinging out a steadying hand to the trelliswork, stark frustration etched on his face.

"I'll forget you said that. It's high time you felt a whole lot better about yourself, Mel. Until then, talk is futile."

# CHAPTER SIX

BY the time Ava joined her, Mel had managed to compose herself. Dev hadn't come after her. He might well have come to the end of his tether. Who would blame him? It was she who had kept their tempestuous relationship in check. Life had set her down in a maze so intricate it required a heroic *effort to find a way to break out. Yet few people were able to* resolve every issue. She thought she'd been close to a turning point, only her mother's mind-blowing legacy had put paid to that. Her mother mightn't care that she could be exposed to public scrutiny, but *Mel* cared a great deal. Few people knew her background. Now there was the distinct possibility they all would.

She longed for a father. A strong man who would have stood by her. A father she could turn to. Her stomach was tied in knots. She wouldn't have a moment's peace until she found out who had worn that crown. That Michael Norton wasn't her father could be a complete lie. Had Michael truly understood the woman he had married? No answer to that. He had gone and left her and the world behind.

Now she was battling to cope with an additional burden, the memory so recently dredged up. Was it possible Michael's death was somehow Mireille's doing? The thought didn't altogether shock her. Mireille had indeed wielded power and Koorakai was an enclosed kingdom.

\* \* \*

When Ava arrived, looking grave, they moved out onto the balcony. Mel had ordered coffee for two. It had been sent up on a beautifully set silver tray. Her mother had got some things right training the staff. It occurred to her, as it had so often in the past, her mother must have had a gracious upbringing. There was the way she looked, the way she spoke, the things she *knew,* as if she had been accustomed to a fairly privileged lifestyle herself. A huge family rift over a shock pregnancy fitted a familiar scenario. Her mother, too young, had fallen pregnant to an unsuitable man outside the sanctity of marriage? Her strict Italian father, who until that point had adored his beautiful daughter, then banished her as the daughter who had dishonoured her family?

When and where had Sarina and Michael met? She couldn't erase Mireille's comtemptuous *cuckold* from her mind. At the time she didn't even know what a cuckold was. She'd had to look it up. All the questions she could have asked Michael had gone with him to the grave. She had learned she was a 'premmie baby.' Mireille had informed her of that as though it was some kind of a stigma. Another thing Sarina had kept to herself. Again, at that time she hadn't properly understood what 'premmie' meant. For some reason Mireille had always spoken to her as though she were well on the way to being a woman instead of a child.

Ava took a chair opposite Mel, a small circular wrought-iron table between them. "What a day! Something wrong?" She took a closer look at her friend.

Mel looked away across the garden, with the rising fragrance of flowers almost an unbearable pleasure. The great tree canopies over the years had formed natural archways, preserving the shade for massed plantings of the giant-leafed dark green alocasias with their distinctive ebony stems. She turned back to Ava, who was twisting her wedding ring around and around on her finger. "Nothing out of the way. Had a few words with Dev. Neither of us can help it. We always get into our arguments. Some of them can be pretty fiery."

"So sparks fly around you?" Ava spoke as though that was something to be greatly desired. "They always did. But you're soulmates, Mel. What was it about? Can you tell me?"

Mel laughed without humour. "My mother, need I say? I know everyone was shocked today. Myself included."

Ava didn't rush to answer. "We'll get over it, Mel," she said finally. "You take everything so hard. You've taken on your mother's problems all your life. Problems a lot bigger than yourself. You are *not* your mother."

"Only the sins of the mothers can and do fall on the children, Ava."

"Okay, but you're mad to carry any sense of shame, Mel. It had nothing to do with you." Ava had often thought Mel had put something of a brake on her mother's plans. "Give it a little time, Mel," she advised. "It will all blow over."

"That's what Dev says." Mel shrugged. "Anyway, enough about me. What about you? You're not happy, are you?" Mel asked the searching question as she placed Ava's cup of coffee in front of her.

"Thank you." Ava gave vent to a heartfelt sigh. "I thought I'd be finding freedom in my marriage, Mel, but it hasn't turned out that way. I was the trophy wife, a Langdon. Luke is a greedy person. He's immensely self-centred. And he has the potential to be unfaithful, if he hasn't been already. I know he was trying to chat you up," she added with a pained grimace. "I'm not a fool. I'm so sorry about that. Luke thinks he's God's gift to women, just like his father, who has the old 'many a good tune is played on an old fiddle' type of mentality. Luke wants to keep me in a gilded cage. Like a canary, I have to sing his song. I don't have an ally in his parents. As far as they're concerned, he's *perfect,* the handsome dutiful son. If he's got a bit of a roving eye, so what? All men have. It's expected of them. Luke loves me in his way, only his kind of love is suffocating."

"I can see that." Mel took a sip of the rich, fragrant coffee.

"I'm expected now to fall pregnant. Over two years married. High time to hear the patter of tiny feet."

"Only something is holding you back. You don't see Luke as the father?"

"God help me, no," Ava confessed, bowing her shining head as if she felt guilt. "I can speak to you, Mel. You understand. There has been no divorce in our family. Even Mum and Dad didn't file for divorce."

"Because they continued to care so much about each other."

"Yes, isn't that lovely?" Ava's lovely face brightened. "Dad doesn't care about the will. He and Mum have big plans. They intend to travel."

"I wish them all the happiness in the world," Mel said with perfect sincerity. "As for you, we have a new order now, Ava. Dev is not your grandfather."

"Thank God for that!" Ava gave a shaky laugh. "Dev only wants my happiness. I should have listened to him. There were many questions I should have asked, yet I charged full steam ahead."

"Smart women can make bad choices, Ava."

Ava nodded agreement. "I feel like Luke is snuffing the life out of me. But it's all my own fault. I should have listened. I was such a fool."

"We're all fools from time to time," Mel brooded. "We can see where we went wrong with the benefit of hindsight. Sometimes circumstance gives us no choice. Or we don't know in advance how things are going to turn out."

"You're being too kind to me, Mel." Ava lifted her beautifully modelled head. Like Mel, she had arranged her hair in a shining updated chignon. "The writing was already on the wall. You were my bridesmaid. You saw it. A romantic dream in tatters."

"So what's the plan?" Mel, being Mel, took the direct approach.

Ava moaned. "It's going to cause a furore, but I intend to file for a divorce as soon as I get home. Mireille, were she alive, would be furious with me. 'You made your bed, now lie in it.' Can't you just hear her saying it?"

"*She* surely had to and it nearly destroyed her," Mel retorted, unable to forgive Mireille Langdon for the treatment she had meted out to an innocent child. Her mother, however, had been far from innocent.

"Have any of us recovered?" Ava asked.

Mel remained silent. *She* certainly hadn't.

"You're coming down to dinner, aren't you, Mel?" Ava picked up a cupcake, simply for something to do. She didn't want it.

"You must know how your family feels, Ava."

"And you the feisty one! You who used to tell my grandmother off when you were knee high to a grasshopper? You're not a gutless person, Mel. Please come."

*Dinner in the formal dining room passed without incident.* She was acknowledged with courtesy by everyone, aware she was receiving lots of covert stares when they thought she wasn't looking. She was drawn into the general conversation, though it was obvious to her that her mother's shock inheritance, *most improper, loomed large in everyone's mind. The* subject wasn't touched on. She knew Dev would not have tolerated it.

It had taken a lot for her to get dressed and come down to join them. She had brought a choice of two suitable dresses, both silk, one a lovely shade of violet, the other black patterned in silver. She settled on the violet, fixing her hair, half up, half down, then hooking sapphire and diamond earrings into her pierced ears. The earrings had been very expensive; her reward to herself for pulling off a lauded business coup.

As a mark of respect to Gregory Langdon, neither Erik nor Dev took his magnificent carver chair at the head of the long gleaming mahogany table that could seat forty when extra leaves were added. The chandeliers weren't turned on, but still the table was a blaze of candlelight. Three tall silver candelabra were set at intervals. Someone had placed a too tall silver vase of exquisite pink liliums as a centrepiece. Its height and the spread of the lovely flowers acted more or less as a screening device. She could see the people she wanted to see anyway.

She watched Dev talking, giving a half smile at times, charming to everyone but with a pronounced gravitas. His blond hair gleamed pure gold in the candlelight, as did Ava's. Both were seated opposite her. During their long talk, Ava had confided many painful personal things. It was obvious she had run out of the necessary mental and emotional strength. The marriage wasn't working. She was more of a symbol than a wife.

*"Luke has been intent on controlling me from day one."*

Luke was always playing to the grandstand, Mel thought. Ava said it had got to the stage when she could hardly tell the difference between what she had left behind and what she had signed on for. There was a great irony in that. Mel was grateful Luke hadn't come down to dinner, claiming he felt too distressed to eat. What a lie! More likely he found his brother-in-law just too intimidating.

Standing well back in the shadows at the far end of the room, Mel could see a few of her mother's well-trained staff, ready to spring to attention at a moment's notice. After the ex-

cellent three-course dinner, followed by coffee—Mel had noticed both she and Ava had hardly eaten anything—members
of the family began to excuse themselves, one after the other.
A charter flight had been organised for eight o'clock the following morning. It would take them all to Sydney. An early
night was in order, as well as providing a legitimate excuse
to escape an uncomfortable situation.

In the end Mel was left alone with the new Master of
Kooraki. "Thanks for joining us, Mel."

"Don't thank me. I did it for Ava."

"Is there no end to your goodness?" He sat studying her.
Her dress was beautiful, with its deep V-neckline showing
just the right amount of cleavage. He had never seen her in
that particular shade before. It set off the satiny warmth of
her flawless olive skin. "Love the earrings," he said. "A little
trifle from your mentor?"

She could feel her face flush. "Don't be ridiculous. I bought
them myself."

"A beautiful woman should never have to buy her own
jewellery."

"You mean when she's having an affair?"

"*Your* words now, Mel," he said with shimmering eyes.
They really were a wondrous colour. "I think it's about time
I paid a call to your mother," he shocked her by saying.

"What, *now?*" Mel's face was a study in alarm.

Dev took an exaggerated glance at his watch. "It's only
nine-thirty. We have the rest of the night. Why don't you pop
up and check she's dressed? A little discretion is called for.
She might have to change out of her negligee. I bet she's got
a few."

"Something wrong with that?" she reacted angrily. She
had spent her life defending her mother.

"God, no! Many the time you've lured me onto the rocks

with your gorgeous night apparel," he said, his expression sardonic.

"Not that I got to keep it on long."

His face settled into an expression of patience. "Are you going or not, Mel? Either way, I'm speaking to your mother tonight. She's not calling the shots."

"Easy to see who your grandfather was," Mel responded in a flash. "You're not going to turn into him *right now,* are you?"

"If that's what it takes, Mel," he told her very crisply, indeed.

"Futile to argue. Give me ten minutes."

"*Five,* then I'm coming up."

She almost ran the length of the gallery. No gentle tap on the door. This wasn't the time for her mother to barricade herself in.

Sarina finally appeared, wearing an exotic silk kaftan, the material patterned in brilliantly coloured tropical flowers. "I hope you don't intend making a habit of pounding on my door, Amelia. What's the matter now?"

Mel's response was sharper than any she had given her mother. "Good thing you're dressed. Dev wants a word with you. He'll be up in five minutes."

"*Wha-a-t?*"

Sarina appeared to buckle at the knees. Mel took hold of her mother's slender arm, unconsciously massaging it. "Look, Mum, it's okay. But you can't get away with the Greta Garbo act. Dev wants to know your plans. You can't just hide. You've already insulted the family by quitting your job."

Sarina didn't bat an eyelid. "I have nothing to apologize to the Langdons for," she said loftily.

"I think you do. Wouldn't you call it a breach of contract or something, giving up without notice?"

Sarina's beautiful face hardened. "That's my business, not yours. I want you to go, Amelia. I don't want you here when Dev comes."

"Well, I want to be here, Mum." Mel was prepared to stand firm. "I might be the only person in the entire world on your side."

Sarina looked back at her in such a way Mel felt a chill in her blood. Who *was* this woman? It was obvious her early life had scarred her. No time to think about that now. Sarina was wearing her long lustrous hair loose so it rippled down her back. She was still made up. Her exotic kaftan only complemented what was of late her slightly *wild* beauty. Whatever age she was, her beauty hadn't dimmed.

"Go, Amelia," Sarina said. "I don't need you." She stared back at Mel, who was too stricken to hide her distress. "Go on now."

"It might be best, Mel." Dev spoke from the open doorway. His jewelled gaze was fixed not on Mel but Sarina, who coloured up fiercely.

Mel nodded to him. "Yes," she said dolefully. "I'm only in the way." As she shifted her gaze from Dev back to her mother, she was surprised by the most extraordinary expression on her mother's face. That expression struck Mel mute. Sarina was staring at Dev with absolute *fascination*. She had seen that exact expression on women's faces when they looked at Dev. The one thing in the world she had not allowed for was seeing it on her mother. Sarina, who was still young and beautiful. As a further madness, had she fallen for Dev? Was Sarina the reason Dev and his grandfather had fallen out so violently?

The idea was *revolting*. Had Gregory, who had occupied Sarina's attentions for well over a decade, grown too old and sick? Had Dev then filled Sarina's hungry eyes?

It was *wicked*.

"Mel, what's the matter?" Dev asked her sharply. The look on Mel's face bespoke shock and something more. Disgust. As though some boundary had been crossed that should never have been.

Mel drew back, fearing the possibility she could be making another one of her quantum leaps.

*I mean it can't be real. It's indecent.*

"Mel?" Dev's gaze was searching.

"I'm staying," Mel abruptly announced.

Sarina took her place in an armchair, habitual calm back in place. "You're not wanted, Amelia."

"I never have been," Mel retorted.

"Stay if you want to, Mel." It was the voice of the man in command.

"Might as well come along for the ride," she returned in an ironic voice. How could she ever begin to fly when her wings were continually cruelly clipped?

The meeting was over. It was brief. Sarina would fly back with the others in the morning. She had graciously consented to give Dev the name of the hotel where she would be staying until she was ready to launch herself on an unsuspecting world. "The world is now your mother's oyster," Dev observed dryly, not bothering to mask his contempt.

Mel said nothing.

"I suppose most people would think that when handed twenty million dollars. Your mother is leaving Kooraki forever. Don't worry about her, Mel. Sarina knows how to look after herself. I wouldn't be surprised if it's not too long before she captures an adoring husband. Think of all the bewitching years with my grandfather."

"Sure she hasn't bewitched you?" It burst from her with violence. It was a wonder she didn't shout at the top of her voice.

"Now, that's disgusting!" Dev caught her arm, pinning her gaze. "You ought to be ashamed of yourself. What the hell are you on about now?"

"Evil!" Mel spoke with loathing, her voice cracking with emotion. "Pure evil. What was the cause of the big break with your grandfather? It drove you away from Kooraki to live with your great uncle. What was it, Dev? It had to be *something* very serious."

Dev looked with fury, his jewelled eyes blazing. "It's too ridiculous to even talk about. Let's get away from here. We could be overheard." He took hold of her arm, propelling her along the gallery.

Ava must have heard their raised voices because she emerged from her old room, still fully dressed. "Is something wrong? You both look upset." Easy to sense the rift between them. Both were breathing irregularly.

"It's the time for upset, isn't it, Ava?" Dev retorted. "We're all upset. We let *people torture us. I say put an end to it.*"

"Hear, hear! *I* intend to," Ava spoke forcefully.

"Atta girl!" Dev saluted his sister. "Get some sleep. You know I'm always here for you, Ava."

"You're the best brother in the world," she maintained. "Problem with Sarina?" she asked, watching Mel's face. Sarina had been obliged to spend her time bailed up in her room. She had forfeited her position for good and all.

Dev answered for her. "Exhausting as it is to admit it, yes. But Mel and I are going to sort it out."

"Right, Mel?" Ava asked, her beautiful eyes never once leaving her friend's face.

Mel managed a smile. "You're a good friend to me, Ava. You always have been. Dev and I are used to our fiery little chats. You know that. Everything's okay. I'll see you in the morning."

Ava was unconvinced. She could see the sparks flying off

them both like static, but what could she do? "Then I'll leave you to it. Love you both." She blew a kiss.

"Love you, Ava."

Dev and Mel spoke as one while all the while their biggest concerns were elsewhere.

As they neared the staircase, Mel said with fiery determination, "I'm going to bed, Dev. I don't want to talk."

He actually manhandled her, pressing her back against the wall. It was futile to struggle. "You started this, Mel. Histrionics won't save you. What's on your mind? Have the decency to spit it out."

Mel clenched her fists, feeling all of a sudden very sick. "I need to know why you left Kooraki. Was it because of my mother? Did you covet her, too?"

Dev's hands fell away. "Believe that, you'll believe anything." Disgust threw an iron mask over his arresting features.

"So tell me what it was about," she begged. "It has never been mentioned."

"I can't talk about it, Mel, I'm afraid," he said shortly. "I'm just too mad. Mad that *you, of all people, could* ask me such a *revolting* question. Your mother is *trash!*"

No one, not even Dev, was going to get away with that. Even if it were true. She hit him then, using all her strength and she was very fit.

He caught her hand in midair, his eyes ablaze. "Go to bed, Mel," he ordered in a voice harsh enough to make her blanch. "If I were the brute you seem to believe I am, I'd give you a backhander that would knock you off your feet. How's that?"

"Oh, God, forgive me. I'm sorry." There seemed to be a mist before her eyes as Mel fell back on childhood prayers, ironically taught to her by her mother.

"No, Mel, *I'm* sorry," Dev said, perversely kissing her punishingly hard on the mouth. "Sorry for the years I've spent loving you." He turned his back on her, making without a backward glance for the stairs.

Inside her room, Mel collapsed onto the day bed, burying her face in her hands. She had been so much at the mercy of her mother. Nevertheless, it had cut her to the heart to hear Dev call Sarina *trash*. What had provoked it? Dev had never used strong language about her mother. Sadly, she wasn't in any position to dispute the charge. Her mother was getting away with murder, as the saying went. A good thing she was leaving in the morning.

*It's your last opportunity to have it out. She won't be expecting a return visit. You'll have the element of surprise. Don't let her just walk away.*

Dev had most probably locked himself in his study, disgusted with her. Everyone else had gone to bed. It was a comfort to know all the doors of the homestead were made out of solid, sound-muffling mahogany.

She was surprised to find her mother's door unlocked. Maybe Sarina was expecting a nocturnal visitor, she thought with cynicism. Sarina did have a dangerous allure, and God knew she had used it. She turned the knob. There was silence in the room, but she could hear the shower running strongly.

Mel moved over to an armchair, ready for confrontation.

Sarina entered the bedroom with a white towel wound around her head.

"Peekaboo!" said Mel, totally without humour.

"My God!" Sarina actually jumped when she saw her daughter, sitting for all the world like a judge in session. "You startled me," she said, roused to anger.

"Who would care?" All love for her mother seemed to have dissolved.

Sarina shrugged. "So what's up *now*, Amelia? Think I'm going to tell you more with Dev not around? It's not going to

happen. I want to go to bed. You're always on about something. You've been like this since you were a child."

"What a burden I must have been to you, Mum," Mel said.
"I'm surprised you didn't have your pregnancy terminated."

"Too late!" Sarina declared cruelly, throwing off the hand
towel.

"Shame on you. Shame, shame, shame. You're one hell of
a sick woman, Sarina."

Sarina pointed the finger of scorn at her daughter. "More
of a woman than you, my dear."

"But I've got Dev," Mel taunted. "*You* haven't. Got the hots
for him, Mum? Isn't that a bit pathetic, not to say vaguely in-
cestuous? Did Gregory get too old to perform like the mighty
stallion he once was?"

Sarina didn't appear at all fazed. "At his best he would
never rival Dev."

"Oh, stop it." Mel gave a contemptuous laugh. "Even now
you're trying on another of your big-time lies."

Sarina ruffled a careless hand through her lustrous long
hair. "You're getting to be very boring, Amelia. Dev thinks
so, too."

Mel was amazed that such calm had descended on her.
"How does a human being get all bent out of shape? Dev is
in no way attracted to you, Mum. He despises you."

Sarina's great eyes flashed. "As if I'm crazy enough to
believe you! You're full of your own malice."

"No, Mum." Mel shook her head. "But you're crazy enough
to believe anything."

Sarina drew close to her daughter, speaking vehemently.
"At least I've never slept with my own flesh and blood."

Condemnation burst from Mel's throat. She leapt to her
feet. "That's the stake through the heart, is it? You'd stop at
*nothing to separate Dev and me. Are you going to change*
tack now and tell me Gregory Langdon was my father?"

"To hell with you!" Sarina threw up her hands, nostrils flaring in rage. "Michael Norton certainly wasn't," she barked.

It wasn't possible to be more wounded than she was. "Only who would believe you? You chop and change as you please. It's even possible you don't *know* who my father was! You could be delusional, you know that?"

"I have an ugly past." Sarina spat her fury.

"You must have. Something turned you into a compulsive liar."

"It has been suggested before." Bizarrely, Sarina laughed.

"Dear Gregory, I suppose. Maybe poor deceived Michael? Well, here's the deal, Sarina. Look into my eyes and tell me the truth for once in your miserable scheming life."

"Deal, what deal? What have you to deal with?" A faraway look came into Sarina's great eyes. "My story is my own."

"And that's the best you can do?"

Sarina rounded on her, prepared to lash out. "You're wasting your time, Amelia. Anyway, it's better for you not to know."

"Only I can't go along with that. Neither would anyone with a right to know. Gregory Langdon wasn't my father. A devil in hell prompted you to say that. Dev and I don't need any DNA testing to confirm it. You're eaten up with jealousy and it shows. You can't bear to think Dev might marry me when Gregory wouldn't marry you. That's it, isn't it? Shock tactics. *Jealousy and envy has you all fired up, ready to say anything to break us up."*

Sarina stood with one hand on her hip. Her black hair was drying and tumbling all around her face. She looked beautiful and half crazy. "You'll break up without me, my girl. I know that only too well."

Mel studied her mother's face and slender body. "How old are you, Mum?" she asked. "You have to be much younger than you've always claimed. How old were you when you had me? Sixteen, seventeen? Savage old Mireille was kind enough to inform me I was a premature baby delivered by a nurse from the Royal Flying Doctor Service. All the years of ugly rumours masquerading as fact were indeed fact. Mireille called Michael a cuckold. I didn't even know what it meant. Mireille could have had Michael destroyed. Ever think of that? She hated you so much she was prepared to do anything to see us off Kooraki, who knows, with Michael in a wheel-chair. Or worse, dead."

"You go too far." Sarina gave her a foul look. "But then you have your own demons. Michael's death was an accident. Gregory would have seen to it that we didn't leave. Gregory wanted me from the first moment he laid eyes on me."

"I suppose that has to be true," Mel said dully. "You were pregnant then, a young girl, a first baby, not showing. I sup-pose you put it over poor Michael. You'd have found it easy manipulating men. Even the great Gregory Langdon. Michael loved me. He believed I was his child. You're such a liar, I probably am."

"Well, you won't know now," Sarina said sweetly. "There are many mysteries in life, Amelia. Best to accept it. Only you're the sort of woman who likes banging her head against a brick wall. There's no way I'm going to explain myself to you. My cup overfloweth with money—lots of money." She laughed.

Mel looked at her mother with great forbearance. "Haven't you forgotten Dev could hold up your inheritance? He's the executor of Gregory's will. Then there's the press."

"Press?" Sarina's eyes widened as her hand flew to her throat.

"Good Lord, Mum, they're going to be very interested in you. A genuine rags to riches story. If you won't speak about your past, the media will drag it up. They're not short on investigative journalists, you know."

For the first time Sarina appeared flustered, then she rallied. "Who would care? I'll be out of the country."

"That's if Dev releases the money."

Sarina put her hands over her ears as though she didn't want to hear a word more. "I did my best, Amelia. I kept you. You should be eternally grateful. I won't have you digging into my past. I won't allow it. It's water under the bridge. Accept it. Dev won't marry you any more than Gregory would marry me. But a man has to have his sexual needs fulfilled. That's where we came in. Dev has always had, shall I say, a soft spot for me. I'll be able to talk him into releasing my money early. Now, go, Amelia. You've always been awkward to have around, with your never-ending questions."

Mel rose to her feet. "They *will* be answered," she said, certainty written all over her. "Take it on board, mother dear. You haven't seen the last of us, Dev and me."

# CHAPTER SEVEN

THE birds woke Mel around 5:00 a.m., a dawn symphony struck up from the highest branches in the wild bush. It was played with wondrous abandon by a multitude of voices in all registers. The strings reigned supreme, followed by the flutes, then the reeds, bolstered here and there by contrasting bass voices. It was inspirational to the ear and psychologically effective. Lying there listening, Mel felt better balanced to get on with her life.

Her sleep had been riven with nightmares. The ghosts of the past—Mireille, the wicked witch had figured largely; Sarina with all her dark harmonies fully revealed. Sarina had not only fooled her daughter, she had fooled everyone. Maybe even Gregory Langdon. Although, on her own admission, someone had called Sarina a liar. But it was all over now. Mel felt there was little hope of reconciliation. Sarina hadn't been cut out for motherhood. Not all women were. Even robbed of Dev, the man she loved, she would still want the truth. It was instinctive in every human being who discovered they knew little or nothing about their early life, or indeed about their true parentage. Sadness and disillusionment weren't easy to bear. They were binding chains that had to be broken.

She threw on her riding gear, then made her way through the silent house, taking a back entrance to the stables complex. A good gallop in the crisp morning air would clear her head and settle her nerves. She didn't expect the lads to be about yet, but she could saddle up her own horse. The finest horses were stabled at night and turned out by day. Ordinary horses were only brought inside in the depths of cold. It was unnatural, in any case, to keep a horse in a confined space for any length of time.

Unexpectedly, as she crossed the courtyard, she could hear voices coming from the tack room—male voices, one very loud, hectoring, full of wrath, jabbering in a tribal dialect. Two younger voices were trying to get a word in. Clearly there was an argument in progress. Did life ever run smooth? She had no intention of turning about. Perhaps she could settle it?

She strode into the room where dozens of bridles hung from their racks, the reins looped through the nosebands, saddles aplenty with all the accessories. The room smelt of all the usual things—horses, hay, leather, liniments. And something else, something *rank*.

The two part Aboriginal stable lads turned to her, clearly frightened, not to say terrified by a menacing presence.

"Good morning." She gave them a quick encouraging nod before turning to the ancient man, who stood his ground. He looked scary enough to spook anybody.

She knew him. It was years since she had last laid eyes on him. It was Tjungurra, the sorcerer, who was widely believed to have caused deaths. Tjungurra, the *kurdaitcha* man, whose role it had been to punish all transgressors. He was naked except for a pair of torn and dirty shorts, his emaciated chest hideously disfigured by deep ugly scars that had tribal significance. Bunches of dried leaves were tied to his arms. On his snow-white head, the hair wildly tangled, he wore a filthy scarlet headscarf. Brilliantly coloured parrot feathers hung from his long beard. In the old days no one would have dared cross Tjungurra. Tribal people continued to believe in sorcery and Tjungurra had undoubtedly been a *kurdaitcha* man.

The lads, from their fearful expressions, clearly thought he was still operative. Even more alarming, the rheumy black eyes fixed on Mel appeared to hold *hatred*.

"What are you doing here, Tjungurra?" she asked in a crisp but unthreatening voice. She faced the old horror front on, aware the lads were casting uneasy looks in her direction.

For answer, Tjungurra lifted his bony arm, balled a hand into a fist, then shook it at her, jabbering away in his native dialect. He appeared filled with rage. She could only pick up on one word in the torrent that spewed from his lips. She looked back at the old man, startled.

"I'm Amelia," she said. *"Amelia,"* she stressed, pointing to herself. "Sarina is my mother. Are you talking about my mother?"

"Leave 'im be, Miz Mel," one of the lads was brave enough to warn her, even if his voice emerged as a croak.

Tjungurra turned on him and the lad actually shrieked. Even Mel's nerve endings were trembling. "Speak English," she ordered. "What is it you want?"

The old man dared to move closer, causing an escalation in tension.

*Why is he here? Is this really happening?*

"Sarina," he jabbered hoarsely. *"Saa...ree...naa..."* He drew out the syllables like a length of rope.

It was a lovely name on most people's lips, but there was no music in the way the old man spoke it. It sounded more like a curse.

There was a hard twisting inside of Mel. "How did my father die?" She couldn't control it. She started to shout at the old man. "Tell me or I'll have you locked up. Locked away in a jail. You'd die there, caged like a wild animal. The old woman isn't alive to protect you. She can't take care of you."

The old man threw her a poisonous look, apparently just starting to warm up. He yanked a single brilliant parrot feather out of his beard.

"You don't frighten me, old man." One of the lads had surreptitiously put a whip into her hand. Now she brought it out, cracked it, causing the sorcerer to fall back, though he continued to point the feather at her as though he were a spear thrower.

No one had heard Dev come to the door. They all jumped at the sound of his voice. His tall, powerfully lean figure was silhouetted against the backdrop of brilliant morning light.

Mel spoke impetuously. "Look who's here, Dev. The wicked old man who killed my father."

"Mel!" he remonstrated, knowing how volatile she was.

"He did. He *did*," she shouted, with no way of knowing if it were true. There was a sharp pain in her right temple as though one of her rare migraines was about to start.

Dev reached her in a few strides, getting a firm grip on her arm. "I'm here, Mel. Get control." There was such toughness and authority about him even a sorcerer would think twice about messing with such a man. Moreover, a Langdon. The nomadic Tjungurra had crisscrossed Kooraki all his life.

It appeared Mel's accusations hadn't frightened the old sorcerer. Grinning evilly, he began to move about in a mockery of a dance, though it was soon apparent the movement caused him severe pain in the back and hips.

Dev's order to stop was more effective than Mel's crack of the whip. Instantly the old sorcerer broke off his weird ritual. Dev advanced on him, towering over him, speaking in Tjungurra's own dialect.

"Make him tell you, Dev," Mel implored, filled with an enormous conviction that Mireille Langdon had sought the help of the *kurdaitcha* man. She had it now. Mireille had wanted Michael Norton badly injured or dead. Had she cared? A jealous wife, a faithless husband, the woman who had stolen the faithless man's spirit. Michael Norton had been determined to be the most vulnerable. The easiest and most accessible to become the victim.

Dev looked over the old man's white head into Mel's eyes. "There's no way to make him speak, Mel. He'd die before he'd ever do that."

"Time for him to die!" Mel cried. "What's he doing here, anyway? Has he come for Sarina? Your grandfather is dead. He's heard about it, of course. The old drum system. That's why he's turned up. Is it revenge time? He mentioned her. I'm sure he thought I was her. He's probably gaga, the old murderer."

"I'll have him shifted away," Dev promised her.

"Where is far enough?" Mel cried. "The South Pole?"

With a gesture of his hand, Dev had the lads leave. They moved off in record time. They didn't want to deal with any of it. Least of all the *kurdaitcha* man.

"Someone spooked the cattle that day, Dev," Mel said, believing in her deepest heart that it had been this menacing old full-blooded Aboriginal.

Dev shook his head. "There was no evidence of that."

"*Was?* You know about this?" Her voice rose towards the rafters.

"For God's sake, Mel. It was over twenty years ago. I was a kid like you."

"*Never* like me! You're a Langdon. Even a *kurdaitcha* man would hesitate to kill a Langdon outright. Mike Norton, sure. We know the old monster used to make poison powder. I wonder why Mireille didn't get him to make up a batch for the house."

Dev's dynamic face went taut with strain. "Leave it there, Mel."

"I won't!" she defied him. "Were there sanctions imposed on this dreadful old creature? He would have feared Gregory like everyone else. Gregory wouldn't have had a problem having him killed or worse, locked up for life." Her whole body was shivering although it was hot. "Look at the old devil. He's aligning himself with you."

"He has to," Dev said briefly, his voice tight with control. "His power has long waned. He has no magic against me or mine. Go back to the house, Mel. We'll talk together later on. The plane leaves at eight o'clock sharp. We're rid of your mother once and for all."

Mel pointed to the old sorcerer as if she were pointing the bone. "He killed him. He caused him to be killed. Poor Michael, the innocent victim." She broke down, starting to sob. "You knew all this, Dev," she accused him. "You've known or had your suspicions for years about this bloodthirsty old man. But you had to protect the Langdon name. You people who think you're unaccountable, living like feudal lords in your own private kingdom. The likes of me can go to hell."

"Mel!" Dev implored, summoning up every scrap of his huge reserve of self-control. "We'll talk about this when you calm down." He would think of something to defuse the emotion.

"To hell with you!" Mel was on a roll. She rushed to the door, but not before she saw the old sorcerer nodding vigorously, a hideous grin of glee on his face.

Back at the homestead, she realized there was nothing else for it. Sarina, as *persona non grata,* was more or less confined to her room. Every step Mel took, she felt more and more drawn into Sarina's horrible sticky web.

"Knock, knock, who's there!" Sarina stood in the open doorway, coiled like a spring ready to snap.

"I'm getting awfully bored with this, Amelia. I'm not telling you anything more. I thought I made that clear."

"Don't Amelia me!" Mel pushed her mother back into the room. "Dressed for the trip, are we? Versace silk shirt, beautifully cut designer pants. How elegant you look! You could be any beautiful woman who has known nothing but a life of wealth and privilege. *Except you're a total fraud.*"

Sarina made a derisive sound. "I have to be downstairs in twenty minutes, Amelia." Clearly she thought her daughter a pushover.

"Tough! Let 'em wait! Sit down, mother dear. You don't feel uncomfortable, travelling with the enemy?"

"I sit at the back. I am blind to them."

"You're blind to everything," Mel said. "I'd been intent on a morning ride to clear my head, only I met up with a guy looking for you."

*"Me?"* Sarina looked startled.

*"You'll remember him, I'm sure."*

Sarina dropped into a chair, winding her arms around herself. "Who is it?"

"You surprise me, even now. *Is* there someone looking for you?"

"Amelia, there's no time," Sarina protested sharply.

"Take a guess."

Sarina's magnificent eyes suddenly rimmed with tears. "Why are you so cruel?"

"Won't work, Mum. You'd remember him. Tjungurra?"

Sarina didn't say anything for a moment. She looked mystified.

"The old witch doctor, the *kurdaitcha* man," Mel prompted.

"That old cannibal, looking for *me?*" Sarina asked in

amazement. "Whatever for? I never had anything to do with such a creature."

"Well, he's come looking for you," Mel said. "Heard the old lion is dead. Michael is dead. There's only *you*. I even had a bit of a scare. He thought I *was* you."

Sarina took a sharp breath. "Well, you certainly look like me." She put up her hands, rubbing her fingers across her temples. "What is this?" She appeared genuinely bewildered. But who would know? Her mother might be one of the greatest actresses in the world, but Mel's gut instinct told her that she really didn't know.

"It's a good thing you're getting out of here, Mum," she said. "You're hated. The evil old bird even came in ritual dress. I believe he was responsible for the stampede that killed Michael. It would be easy for him. He was over twenty years younger. I further believe Mireille put him up to it. She was in league with the devil. Langdon was too powerful to touch. You were locked away in the homestead, pretty well inaccessible. Easy to lie in wait for Michael. Your shocking affair with Gregory Langdon led to an innocent man's death," she cried in fierce and passionate challenge.

Sarina suddenly appeared massively uneasy. "Sheer speculation! You always did have an over-vivid imagination, Amelia."

"*I* have?" Mel cried. "That's rich, coming from you."

"I know absolutely nothing about this," Sarina swore. "It's not even something I can accept. Michael's death was investigated. It was a tragic accident."

Mel shook her head. "Mireille and Tjungurra were in it together."

Sarina bristled with anger. "Where's the proof? You're a sad, disturbed soul, Amelia."

"I have been, but not any more. I've been the victim of a conspiracy."

Sarina reacted with fury. "This is bizarre! I would *never* have been party to having Michael harmed. He was a good man, good to me. He helped me get away."

"But he wasn't my father?"

Colour rose to Sarina's face. "No, Amelia, I've told you he wasn't."

That hit her like a body blow.

Sarina spoke as though she had at long last laid down a heavy burden. "Michael came to my rescue after my lover abandoned me. The man promised me he was going to leave his wife. He swore he loved me. Never, ever believe a man loves you, Amelia. He may lust after you. *Love,* never. My father and my lover were responsible for what happened to me. I hate men. They're users. They can discard women like old shoes. Women don't matter. He gave me money instead."

Mel tried very hard to keep calm. "So the burning question—who *was* he?"

"Let me finish." Sarina had to gulp for air. "He was much respected in the town. A science teacher. I was a schoolgirl. He used to give me a ride home sometimes from school. Such a gentleman."

Mel couldn't answer for a moment, then she said, "Mum, I can't bear to hear. Just tell me the name of the town. I'll find out, anyway. Don't make an enemy of me. You've got enough already. Wonder of wonders, I'm still an ally."

"You *are* my daughter," Sarina reminded Mel with monumental self-regard. "The name of the town is Silverton."

Mel didn't have a clue. "Am I supposed to know where that is?"

"North Queensland." Sarina rested her head in her hands.

Mel took a deep breath, trying to shake off her feeling of unreality. "But you always said your family lived in Sydney, thousands of miles away from North Queensland."

Sarina gave a sour laugh. "I was more comfortable with Sydney, that's all. Love hurts, Amelia."

"Everything hurts!" Mel burst out. "Love kills. Betrayal kills. It killed Michael. And Mireille was prepared to have it done. But *you* were the one who exposed him to danger."

Sarina swept to her feet, a twisted smile on her beautiful face. "I expect God will punish me. That's if there is one. I don't think highly of myself, Amelia. I am what I am."

"Mum, anyone could say that. But you say it as though your actions can't be explained otherwise. I suppose you couldn't really love me because I was *that* man's child. The man who abandoned you. So you're what, Mum—forty-three, forty-four?"

"Something like that." Sarina looked away. "Beauty can be a curse, Amelia. A curse when you're young. A curse as you age and begin to suffer the ravages of time."

"Well, that hasn't happened to you so far, Mum," Mel said acidly. "You look terrific and hey, you're rich!"

Sarina walked to the door and leaned a hand against it for support. "Don't go looking for that man, Amelia," she warned. "I can spare you that, at least. He won't want to know you if he's even alive. He was nearly twice my age then. He laid waste to my youth, to my life. My own father did the rest." Sarina spoke with so much passion she might have been reliving that traumatic time.

"Secrets, secrets, you've guarded them well. Your family lived in Silverton. It's probably where you met Michael. And what of my grandparents?"

"They were punished," said Sarina, her normally dulcet tones as hard as flint.

Mel got a grip on her mother's shoulder. "Punished, how?"

"They're dead, Amelia. Killed in a car crash."

A doubting voice inside Mel's head kicked in. "Did that just pop into your mind? I'm going to check all this out, Mum. I'm sorry for what happened to you. You were little more than a child. It was way too soon to have a baby. But you could have been a good mother to me—instead, you turned your back."

Sarina continued to lean her hand against the door. "How could I comfort you, when I was in desperate need of comfort myself?"

Mel nodded, trying very hard to understand. "Tell me, did you love Gregory Langdon or did you simply use him?"

"He was mesmerized by me," Sarina said, straightening and throwing up her head like a movie queen. "I grew to have strong feelings for him, but, yes, I used him at first to accomplish my goal. Poor Michael aside, I'd have done anything to avenge myself on men. They betray us. Dev is a far, far better man than Gregory could ever have been, but he won't marry you, Amelia. Listen, because I'm only trying to save you."

"Too late, Mum. Neither Dev nor I seem able to let go."

"Are you mad, then?" Sarina rounded on her daughter, great eyes flashing. "You've been warned. In the end you'll find your dreams will dissolve. *Just like mine*."

Great clumps of fiery red earth clustered with wild flowers, were thrown up as the mare's hoofs thundered across the desert plains. The eroded hills in the distance glowed a salmon pink. By high noon they would have warmed to cinnabar, then furnace-red, heralding a glorious rose-gold sunset. The great prehistoric monuments of the Red Centre underwent spectacular colour changes during the course of a day. Uluru, venerated by the Lorijitas and known to them as *Oolera,* was a sacred dreaming place created by the all-powerful spirits. It rose over a thousand feet above the desert sands with the great mass of it buried below the sands, a single mighty boulder, the largest monolith in the world. Farther away rose the Olgas, Kata Tjunta, with its fascinating domes and turrets.

Gradually Mel calmed. Silhouetted darkly above her head a lone wedge-tailed eagle was performing its daily ritual, wheeling in higher and higher semicircles. The eagle was sacred to the desert tribes. The budgerigar accompanied her on her ride, clouds of parrot green and gold. She carried the wild beauty of Kooraki, the immensity of it, in her soul. The mare was heading almost of its own accord towards one of the most beautiful lagoons on the station and Kooraki boasted a great many. The waters, the darkest green of a rainforest, some turquoise-sheened, floated cargoes of exquisite water lilies all year round. Each lagoon, pond, billabong and swamp on the station carried its lovely flotilla generally of a single colour—the sacred blue lotus, pink, cream, white or yellow, the stunning blooms rising above their thick green pads. They made a heart-stirring sight.

At the top of the acacia-lined bank she tethered the mare, then half walked, half skittered down the slope, crushing pretty little purple plants almost flush with the soil underfoot. With a final leap, she came down on the pale ochre sand that formed a broad beach around the deep lagoon. Here the sacred blue lotus decorated the lagoon's reed-shadowed borders. Many a time she and Dev had made love in the cool green shadows to the back of her, sheltered by the overhanging feathery boughs of the acacias, heavy in golden blossom and scent. Their coming together right from the very first time had been as natural as life itself.

Dev crouching over her...kissing her...caressing her... Even thinking about it now rocked her body with sensations. Dev was a fantastic lover. Once he had told her his feeling of rapture was so intense he could die from it. She had felt the same way. Dev was her soul, boy and man. He had shaped all the days of her life. She knew she could never love anyone again who was not Dev.

*Only what had he done with wicked old Tjungurra?*

She knew he wasn't going to deliver the old witch doctor to the police. Blood was thicker than water. Dev was a Langdon. His first loyalty would be to his family, even to the memory of his dreadful grandmother.

Mel sank on the sand and softly wept. The thought of Michael and the manner of his dying had haunted her for years. Never in a million light years would she have suspected the old *kurdaitcha* man of playing a part in Michael's tragic "accident." The fact that the old man had turned up had seriously rattled her faith in Dev. At some stage Tjungurra must have been considered. He had been treated with a mixture of reverence and fear. But both she and Dev had been children at the time. Now, years later? Had someone confided their suspicions to Dev? It could even have been his grandfather who'd had to deal with the fallout and a raging wife half off her head with jealousy. It was a huge comfort that her mother had no idea. Sarina had genuinely cared about Michael as being the man apart.

Her breath was coming ragged in her throat. The breeze dried her tears. It was like silk against her flushed skin. For long moments she stared at the wide glittering expanse of water, the surface as smooth as poured glass. There was no one around for miles. The men would be working at the Ten Mile. A dip would cool her off and soothe her frazzled nerves.

She stood up, stripping off her clothes until she was down to her bra and briefs. She had to get on with life. She had to go in search of her biological father. *Silverton.* It wasn't one of the big sugar towns. She had a vague idea the district was a producer of tropical fruit, mango plantations. Sarina wasn't the first love-struck teenager to fall in love with a much older man, married or not. She would track this man down. Maybe give him one hell of a fright, she looked so much like Sarina, the young girl he had abandoned.

The lagoon beckoned. Though the sun was hot, the water

was surprisingly cold. Bending her supple body, she splashed her face, her arms and her breasts, before diving in. She swam well. As a girl, she had won many medals for her school in the inter-schools swimming contests. Gregory Langdon had paid for her excellent education at one of the country's top girls' schools.

*Thank you, Gregory, you old tyrant.*

She felt no gratitude. Only shame.

Dev found her lying on the sand, half asleep. Her breathing was shallow but relaxed. God, she was beautiful. He stood for a time watching her. But when he allowed his shadow to fall over her, her eyes flew open, hand up, shading them, as she gave a soft exclamation.

"How long have you been standing there?" she asked with a frown, starting to sit up.

"Just arrived," he said laconically. "Enjoy your swim?"

"It helped." Mel drew up her long slender legs, hugging her knees. God knew, Dev was intimate with her naked body, yet as his jewellike eyes smouldered and touched on different places she felt a hard knot of desire beginning to twist and twirl around inside her.

Only nothing romantic was about to happen. Not after the shattering events of that morning.

"So what did you do with your old witch doctor?" she challenged, looking straight at him.

"Standard thing. Killed him." Dev lowered his lean length to the sand beside her.

"Your grandmother had Michael killed," she said bleakly. "How do you feel about that?"

He turned to touch her face. "Heavy-hearted, Mel, if it were true."

"Another one of my quantum leaps?" she asked bitterly.

"Your antennae could be way off. The old man frightened the life out of the stable lads. They were terrified."

"I saw that," she said shortly. "What was he jabbering about, anyway? I did catch one word—*Sarina*."

"Apparently he thought you were her," Dev told her with a sharp exhalation of breath. "He tells me he's dying."

"Good!" Mel exclaimed at once. "He must be a thousand years old anyway. How many times did he see Sarina? He never came anywhere near the house. Sure he didn't come seeking redemption? Or did he plan to plunge his spearthrower into the heart of that wicked unfaithful woman?"

"Mel, Tjungurra has come back to Kooraki to *die*. He would be hard-pressed to fight off a child, let alone sink his spear in anyone. His long walkabout took what remaining strength he had from his body."

"So you're saying you're going to allow him to die on Kooraki?" she asked in angry disbelief.

"That's what I'm saying, Mel." His tone firmed. "This is Tjungurra's ancestral land. His tribe was here tens of thousands of years before the white man arrived. He'll do no one any harm, be certain of that. His people will help ease him out of life. He faces judgement, too, Mel. I think he's scared he won't make his way up to the stars. All Aboriginals are stargazers."

"We share that, don't we?" She cast him another challenging look. "How many times did we lie staring up at the stars, you filling my head with stories about Orion, the mighty hunter with his jewelled belt, the marvel of the Milky Way, that great river of stars, home of all those who lead good lives? That leaves quite a few people we know out. You were the one to show me the pointers to the Cross, Beta Centari, Alpha Centari. You shared all the stories you'd learned from the Aboriginals about our constellation. Your mother used to wear a very beautiful jewelled brooch representing the Southern Cross."

Dev nodded. "I remember it. Each jewel was different—a diamond, a sapphire, a ruby and an emerald. Dad gave it to her when they were courting."

"They never had their own life, did they?" she lamented. "Your father should have moved you all away."

"He was trapped, Mel. Can't you understand that? He was the heir. He was convinced his first duty was to Grandfather, which was to say Kooraki."

"And boy, didn't he suffer!" Mel exclaimed dismally. "Your mother. Ava, too. You managed to keep above it all but even you had endless fights with your grandfather. I know better than to ask you what the last big fight was about." No stopping the bitterness.

"Seriously, Mel, you wouldn't want to know. It was rubbish, anyway." Dev's expression had grown taut, his mood edgy.

"So, I don't get the chance to decide that for myself. Impossible to keep my mother out of it. I'm not a fool, Dev." Mel stood up, reaching for her jeans. She stepped into them, zipping them up.

Dev held her cotton shirt in his hand. "What a beautiful body you have."

"Shirt, please." There was a great brittleness to her movements.

He passed it to her without another word. She didn't bother tucking it in.

Dev raked a hand through his tousled blond waves. They blended in with the golden sunlight. "What more did you manage to get out of your mother?" he asked abruptly.

"More? What gives you that idea?"

"You're keeping something from me. I know you, Mel."

She pulled her thick mane out of its topknot, shaking it

loose. "Imagine that! You can keep things back. I can't." She stared out over the glittering water, where iridescent winged creatures were whirring before taking flight again.

Dev didn't respond as she expected, but when she turned her head to look at him, his hand shot out to encircle her arm. "Keep still," he murmured.

She obeyed without question. The reason for his action was immediately apparent. A pair of brolgas, the Australian blue cranes, long-legged, long-necked, were coming in to land on the sandy beach of the opposite bank. They bounced lightly, elegantly.

Mel drew in her breath, seizing on this rare moment of peace. "How about that?" she breathed.

"Sit down, Mel," he urged. "This is a privilege we can never take for granted."

She sank onto the warm sand beside him. Maybe this was a good omen. One couldn't survive without hope.

Within moments the taller brolga, close on five feet with the identifying scarlet patch across its face, bowed, grey wings with darker wing tips outstretched, waiting on its mate to bow gracefully in return. This was the start of the celebrated brolga ceremonial dance.

Mel bypassed the tension that was strung out between them. She reacted in the way she had done since childhood. She put out her hand, feeling Dev's close warmly around hers. They sat in silence, watching the birds begin their famous courting ritual of wonderful vertical leaps, amazing side steps, graceful dips. It was quite extraordinary, the rituals of nature, the wildlife, the beauty and mystery of it all.

The dance gradually came to an end. They would have applauded, only they knew they would startle the cranes and the wealth of bird life that was all but invisible in the blossoming trees.

"Peace does exist," Dev said very quietly. "Even if it's sometimes hard to find. How beautiful is our world!"

She acknowledged it. "I love it as much as you do. If only we could start over."

Dev shook his head. "Impossible. We have to take whatever life hands out. You know my view. There's no point expending time and energy on regrets for the past. We live in the present. We look to the future. Only way to go."

"I've never been as secure as you."

He lay his hand with tenderness against her hot, flushed cheek. "All this torment has been bound up with your mother, but she's off our hands."

Mel felt the bitter taste of that on her tongue. "You won't believe what she had to say."

"Try me." His voice took on a hard edge. "I knew it was something."

Mel picked up a lovely coral-pink shell that was half embedded in the sand. "That dear man, Michael Norton, wasn't my father." Her beautiful face poignantly expressed her sorrow.

After the initial shock, Dev wasn't all that surprised. "I'm sorry, Mel. I can feel your pain. But go on."

Mel calmed herself. "It still hasn't sunk in. My mother claims to have fallen pregnant to a married man, her teacher, when she was still at school. You can imagine how beautiful she was. He took advantage of her. Her family turned against her, her father especially. They disowned her. Or so she says. I can never completely believe my mother. Not when she's undergone a metamorphosis right in front of my eyes. But life *has* damaged her. Her home town was Silverton. Heard of it?"

Dev shot her a frowning look. "Of course I've heard of it. It's a prosperous little town in far North Queensland—processed dried fruit, mango plantations. That's probably where she met Mike. He came to us from Maru Downs. Silverton would be one of the closest towns to the station."

Mel took a hard swallow. "I'd always believed her people were in Sydney, with its huge Italian population."

"Your mother obviously found it easier to lie," Dev said. "There's a sizeable Italian population in North Queensland. Our sugar industry owes a great debt to immigrant Italian families. They were the ones who worked the sugar farms, then saved up to buy them."

Mel waited until she could speak properly, her mouth was so dry. "Revelations have been raining down on me like chunks of debris from out of space."

Dev's response was to nod slowly. "And her parents, your grandparents?"

Mel couldn't answer for a moment. "Dead in a car crash," she managed with stark finality. "Sarina doesn't mourn them." She found it too distressing to mention the accusation Sarina had brought against her father. She couldn't bear to think about it herself. Sarina could well be delusional.

Dev's face registered his scepticism. "Hasn't Sarina taken an age telling you all this?" He spoke with harsh condemnation.

"I don't think she would have told me at all, only I unnerved her saying the old witch doctor was after her. I'm convinced from her reaction she knew nothing of any conspiracy against Michael."

"If there *was* one." Dev cut her off. "We'll never know, Mel. We weren't the main players. We were kids. We have to strive to put it behind us."

"Easier said than done," Mel answered, finding recovery difficult. Why don't you turn the wicked old devil over to the police?"

"On what charge?"

Her mind raced. "You don't believe your grandmother

could have been a part of it? She said many terrible things to me. You know that. I told you everything that ever really mattered. Easy for her to enlist Tjungurra's help."

"No, I won't have it. She wasn't *that* bad. And she had a right to be jealous. Anyway, they're gone, Mel, my grandparents." He picked up a small round stone, then sent it skittering across the surface of the water. "Sarina was the catalyst. Condemn *her* along with the rest." Because of Sarina, he never did get the chance to say goodbye to his grandfather, a giant in his life. Sarina was a woman who had seduction in her very nature. A man's admiration was pure oxygen to her.

"So what are we left with?" Mel was demanding to know.

"Some answers never come, Mel. Bitterness is a sickness, a cancer. It eats its way through us. My grandfather wanted Sarina madly. Who knows if it was love or not? It was certainly lust. My grandmother lived with hatred. Mike Norton was caught in Sarina's web, too much in love with her to anger her with questions. Did he know he wasn't your father?"

Mel felt a wave of grief. "How would I know? My mother only feeds you slivers at a time. All I do know is he loved *me*."

"Of course he did!" Dev said, conviction in his voice. "I was only a boy but I still remember how Mike adored his astonishingly pretty little princess. Maybe your mother told him, maybe she didn't. Lies and the truth are as one with her. We've both seen her reinvent herself, literally overnight. It could *all* be fantasy."

"Which is why I'm going to check it out," Mel said with determination.

"Go to Silverton?"

Mel ran a finger over her aching forehead. "Yes."

Dev *didn't hesitate.* "I'll take you, *even if it is a wild goose* chase. But if Sarina lived there, someone will know. Her face alone is a standout. She might well have been using a false name. It wouldn't surprise me."

"Me, neither," Mel confessed, remembering the odd things her mother had said. "I think the trauma of having me so young, so unsupported by family, could have turned her mind. The experience made her incapable of feeling compassion for others. She didn't receive it. She didn't give it. Who am I to judge her?"

"Before you get too forgiving, Mel, you might remember, she went to work on my grandfather. She would have been sending out messages, the great dark eyes, the subtle nuances in the voice. She used her beauty. She knew he was a married man. But she thrust that aside as of little consequence. Most people would side with my grandmother, even if she didn't handle the situation at all well."

"That's why she enlisted the old *kurdaitcha* man's help," Mel insisted, causing Dev to groan.

"A *theory,* Mel, based on the fact the old man turned up again."

"To die?" She didn't doubt he was dying, but what else had he come for?

"That's what he said."

"And that's what you accepted." Mel looked out over the lagoon, where the water was so clear and pure one could drink it. "Why wouldn't you cover up for your grandmother? Too late to do anything about the old man. He'd perish within a day in jail."

"You know he would."

"So you're offering to fly me to Maru Downs?"

"Fly us to Maru. Anything to get you to move forward, Mel," he said tersely.

The expression in Mel's eyes turned cool. "I can only do that when I can separate the truth from the lies. Surely that makes sense?"

"Something has to." Dev's response was weary.

Mel stood up, then began to button up her cotton shirt.

As he looked at her, violent sensations rushed through him. He knew if he pulled her to him he wouldn't be able to stop. Mel belonged to him. And he to her. "It might take a day or two to organise it."

"Fine." Tears sprang into her eyes.

"Mel! Your tears can break my heart in an instant." He reached out then, cupping a hand around her nape, kissing her with his open mouth. He threw everything of himself into it, feeling, after a mere moment of resistance, her tongue mating with his in the eternal dance of love. The places a tongue could go! The places Mel had learned from him. He couldn't bear to think Mel could be right about Tjungurra. The charge was too serious to walk away from, but there was little choice. They both had to walk away from it.

Mel broke the kiss, resting her face against his neck.

"Everything is going to be different, Mel," he promised her. "Better."

"It would be too terrifying to think otherwise." She slowly pulled away. "Are you going back to the house?"

"I have to. Patrick O'Hare will be here for lunch. He has a business proposition he wants to put to me. He and my grandfather had quite a few things going together."

Mel knew that for a fact. She took a long breath, keeping her tone neutral. "I'd be surprised if he comes alone. Siobhan will tag along. Hope burns bright. It glitters like gold. Siobhan won't miss an opportunity to see you."

"Don't start, Mel." Dev jerked his blond head up impatiently. "Siobhan is easy enough company. I hope you're going to join us."

"Of course." Mel was seized with shame that she had felt such a violent pang of jealousy.

Dev's voice roused her. "O'Hare has been after Illuka for

quite a while." He named a Langdon outstation. "I'll sell for the right price." He knew Mel was spot on about pretty little Siobhan and her hopes. She did fancy herself in love with him, her hopes buoyed by her parents' wholehearted support for a union between the two families. Strangely, or perhaps not so strangely, Siobhan had never mentioned the bond everyone knew existed between him and Mel. Maybe Siobhan had allowed herself to believe that bond was platonic, not sexual. A cousinly sort of thing. He disliked the whole concept of matchmaking. He had never given Siobhan any reason for hope. It had been friendship all the way.

# CHAPTER EIGHT

SIOBHAN O'HARE made a special effort to look her best for her trip to Kooraki with her father. Her father, needless to say, was only too pleased to take her. Both parents, her mother especially, entertained hopes that she might, if she hung in there, land arguably the most eligible bachelor in the country—James Devereaux Langdon. She and Dev had always been friends, and at not that far off thirty it was high time Dev took a wife. Plenty of eligible young women were standing in line—she was the closest geographically, at least—Dev had only to make a decision. Now that he had stepped into Gregory Langdon's shoes, there was extra pressure on Dev to marry and have a family, hopefully sons to run the Langdon cattle empire.

She had a big advantage, being Outback born and bred and a member of the O'Hare pioneering family, with its proud history. She had hoped, prayed, finally convinced herself she had as good a chance as anyone. There *was* that persistent niggle at the back of her mind. Her mother felt it, too. That niggle was Amelia Norton. One had to be realistic. Amelia was a very beautiful young woman, exotic and astonishingly beautiful. That was her Italian blood. She even had an intensely attractive voice and a beguiling way with her hands, little turns of the wrists and upraised splayed fingers. Her Italian blood again. Not only that, she was clever. She held down a top job with a leading investment bank.

The big turn-off was the mother, the former housekeeper who overnight had become a rich woman. It was now apparent to everyone that Sarina Norton had been Gregory Langdon's mistress. No one seemed prepared to forgive or forget that. There could be a public scandal looming if anyone leaked information to the press. Her family never would. They were trusted friends. She knew there was a strong bond between Dev and Amelia, but surely it was almost like *family?* In no way did Dev and Amelia act like lovers. That gave her heart hope. Their behaviour was more like affectionate bantering, sparring cousins. Still, the strong connection was there. Given the chance, she would sound Amelia out.

Just as Mel had predicted, Siobhan arrived with her father. Both father and daughter greeted Mel warmly, though an indefinable light shone in Siobhan's bright blue eyes. She was looking extremely pretty. Her short copper curls glittered in the sunlight. Her soft fair skin was lightly peppered with freckles across her pert nose. She wore a very becoming white linen dress, sleeveless, round necked with circular medallions of cotton lace and crewel work adorning the skirt. When Dev bent to kiss her cheek she held up a rapt face like a flower to the sun, her hand involuntarily stroking his arm.

Siobhan in the sunlight! All light and white petunia skin. She was smiling at Dev in a way that made Mel's heart ache. Dev wasn't in love with Siobhan. But it was there for anyone to see—Siobhan was head over heels in love with Dev. Such a marvellous feeling to be in love, Mel thought with a twist of the heart. Hell to be in love with the wrong man. The O'Hares were good people, much respected in the vast Outback community. Siobhan was blessed. She enjoyed approval all round. She was much loved by her parents. That alone was a priceless gift, in Mel's view.

Lunch was served in the cool of the loggia that looked out over the rear landscaped gardens and the turquoise swimming pool with its beautiful mosaic tiles. A poolside pergola was a short distance away, with cushioned banquettes and a long, low timber table. Mel had often eaten a breakfast of tropical fruit there.

Her mother's former second in charge, now elevated to the position of housekeeper, Nula Morris, was proving her efficiency by serving and presenting a light, delicious meal of chilled avocado, lime and cilantro soup. It was followed by sweet-and-sour seafood salad that had its origin in Thailand. Her mother had often served Thai dishes, mainly because Gregory Langdon had loved them. A coconut and ginger ice cream garnished with mint sprigs had been made to end the meal if anyone wanted a scoop or two. Mel was the only one to decline. She had eaten with little enthusiasm. She didn't have much of an appetite these days.

Over lunch Siobhan came alive. Pretty face thrown up, riding high, she broke completely free of her usual shyness around Dev to sparkle. She launched into a stream of funny stories and gossip that made them all laugh. That clearly delighted her. Siobhan had a talent for mimicry that added to the comic effect. Her father smiled on her proudly. His little girl, wasn't she wonderful? Dev, too, was looking at her with easy affection, something that must have gladdened the heart of both daughter and father. Mel tried to capture some of the mood. She was fully aware of Dev's sharpening attention on her, the *watchfulness* behind the white smiles. Tension continued to burn slowly between them like a fuse.

Mel tormented herself with a visual image. Dev and a radiant Siobhan standing before an altar, Siobhan in the love-

liest of satin and lace wedding gowns, a short starburst of
tulle around her head, a posy of white and cream roses in
her hand. Every woman wished and prayed for happiness in
love. Oh, to find it in marriage to that one man, a soulmate!
That was the way things should be. The sad reality was that
many chose the wrong man and lived to regret it.

Afterwards the men withdrew to Dev's study to talk business,
leaving the two young women alone. Mel thought it might
be a good idea to retain a little distance between herself and
Siobhan, only Siobhan had other ideas.

They were strolling in the garden, heading in the direction of the bougainvillea-wreathed arcade. "So when are you
thinking of heading back to Sydney?" Siobhan asked, linking
her arm through Mel's in a gesture of friendship, but really
settling into an interrogation of sorts.

"I'm not exactly sure," Mel replied, well aware that Siobhan
was trying to pick up signals.

"It must be hard for you, Amelia, coping?"

Her approach angered Mel but she kept calm. Unhurriedly,
she withdrew her arm, pretending she wanted to study the
huge yellow and scarlet spikes of the Kahili Ginger Blossom.
It might have been a rare plant instead of one that thrived in
the garden. "Coping with what?" Mel asked, keeping moving.

Siobhan wasn't to be put off, her gentle voice gathering
strength. "This business about your mother," she said. "We
all feel for you, Amelia." She began to describe circles in the
air that apparently denoted "feeling."

"Why should you think I need your kind feelings,
Siobhan?"

Siobhan's petunia-petal skin coloured up. "I just wanted
you to know you have *friends*."

Mel considered that. "I do have friends, but that's nice of you, Siobhan."

"Oh, that's all right," Siobhan answered with a smile.

"I should tell you I have all the friends I need."

Siobhan made a funny little sound of distress. "There, I've upset you. But you don't need *enemies,* Amelia, because of your mother. All those noughts!" she exclaimed. "Twenty million dollars wasn't it?"

Mel came to a halt, her passionate face betraying her anger, her great dark eyes on fire. "Who told you?"

Siobhan's stomach gave a downward lunge. She took a hasty step back, replying in a voice of soft amazement. "Why Dev, of course."

"Not true!" Mel flatly contradicted. As petite Siobhan moved back she took a step closer.

Siobhan gave a nervous laugh. "Would I lie to you?"

Mel brushed that aside. "You just did. I think you're anxious to help me on my way, Siobhan. I know you feel deeply for Dev."

Siobhan blushed scarlet. "Is it that apparent?"

"It is to me. I don't blame you in the least. Dev is an extremely handsome and charismatic man. So what is it that's worrying you about *me?*"

Siobhan looked highly uncomfortable, shrugging her delicate shoulders. "I need to find out the lay of the land. You and Dev are close. Everyone knows that. You always have been."

"You have difficulty with it?'

"No, no!" Siobhan protested breathlessly. "I understand. You were a very lonely child. No friends of your own, your mother the housekeeper. Dev must have been your knight in shining armour."

"And you wish to know if he still is?" Mel asked bluntly.

Siobhan pulled her pert features into an expression of apology.

"Give it to me straight, Siobhan," Mel advised. "You want to know if Dev and I have a sexual relationship? Is that it? You want to know if there's any chance it might come to something?"

Siobhan pulled back contritely. "Please, Amelia, I have no wish to upset you."

"Then why bring up the subject?"

"Apologies, apologies! You're someone I really admire, Amelia. You're so beautiful." Privately, she and her mother were in agreement that Amelia could do something to tone down her sexuality. "And you're *clever*. Dev is forever singing your praises. I just wanted to know if I had a chance with him, that's all."

Mel waited while Siobhan had her say. "That's *all?* That's a *lot* to know, Siobhan. Why don't you ask *Dev,* not me?"

Siobhan's pretty face was shocked. "I'm not good at that sort of thing. Much too forward. I thought you might help me as a sort of favour. I've always liked you. So do my parents. We've always felt sorry for you."

"So you keep running past me," Mel said shortly. "I'm in no need of your pity, Siobhan. I do very well. You, on the other hand, might consider this. *Lies* are easy to tell but very difficult to make right. Dev *didn't* tell you how much Gregory Langdon left my mother."

Siobhan's pretty face wore a look of guilt. She waved her two hands in front of her face without answering.

"That doesn't tell me much," Mel said.

"He *might have* told Dad," Siobhan mumbled, digging herself further in. Put on the spot, she found she couldn't admit to anything bad about herself.

Mel relented. "I accept your family has high hopes for a union between your two families, Siobhan. I expect you're getting plenty of loving but constant pressure from your par-

ents to bring that about. It would be considered a tremendous coup."

Proudly, Siobhan threw up her copper head. "Is that so
dreadful? Should I be defending our family position? I've
had a huge crush on Dev since I was a girl," she proclaimed,
her voice rising. "I know he's very fond of me. If you're not
in the picture in that way, Amelia—I fully accept your long
friendship with Dev—I feel I have a chance with Dev. There's
no one else on the scene, as far as I know. Megan Kennedy
couldn't hold him and she sure tried hard enough. She told
me Dev was dynamite in bed."

Mel felt a dull roar in her ears. "How massively indiscreet
everyone has become these days. Personally, I don't believe
in kiss-and-tell. But you're in no position to second Megan's
opinion."

Siobhan coloured up violently. "No, no! But Dev has to
marry soon. It's expected of him. Especially now." Siobhan's
expression was contrite. "You must surely understand?"

Mel stared away across the garden to the calm, dark, green
waters of a man-made pond. It was so beautiful, densely
framed by pristine white arum lilies, with their lush green
foliage and a spectacular jostling of purple flowering water
plants deeper into the bog. "I do, Siobhan," she said quietly.

"Oh, that's great!" Siobhan spoke as if a huge weight had
been lifted from her shoulders. "You won't give me away, will
you? I mean, you won't tell Dev about our conversation?"

"Of course not," Mel said. "This is private and it will remain that way. Good thing I'm not Megan Kennedy. Don't
get *too* optimistic, Siobhan," she warned.

"I won't." Siobhan nodded, as though heeding good advice. "I mean, Dev's only just lost his grandfather. He would
have trouble thinking about marriage right at this point."

"Perhaps he's already made up his mind," said Mel.

Siobhan pinked up again. "Maybe he has," she said with a hopeful smile, her blue eyes full of twinkling lights.

All Mel felt was emotionally drained. Her mother's parting words resounded in her ears.

*In the end you'll find your dreams will dissolve. Just like mine.*

Patrick O'Hare had flown over to Kooraki in his yellow bumblebee of a helicopter. Business matters concluded to both men's satisfaction, father and daughter made their farewells. Siobhan hugged Mel, grasping the taller Mel close as if they were new best friends.

"We must stay in touch, Amelia." She smiled jauntily, as though at long last she had gained some sort of an ascendancy over Mel. "Mum and I often go to Sydney or Melbourne to do our shopping or take in a show. I'd like to give you a call when I'm in Sydney." She looked to Mel for confirmation.

"Please do." What else could she say? Please *don't?*

Dev was driving father and daughter down to the airstrip. They were seated in the Jeep and before Dev climbed on board he turned back for a word with Mel. "I'll be back," he advised in a voice that suggested she might take it into her head to hop in a Jeep and tear off to the Simpson Desert.

"What's the panic? I'm not going anywhere."

He gave her a taut version of his white smile. "Not yet."

"I have an investigation to attend to, Dev," Mel said.

"And I'm going to help you. I thought we'd agreed on that," Dev responded tersely, rubbing his cleft chin. "You don't have to go it alone. Whatever the true story is, Mel, there's bound to be fallout."

"I'm prepared for it," she said firmly. "For all we know, my mother's windfall might soon make the papers."

"A nine-day wonder," Dev pronounced. "Your mother's

latest version of her life story mightn't be the final one. There could be yet another draft," he warned. Sarina Norton was definitely damaged.

"That's what we have to find out. Did Michael have family?"

"It would have been checked out at the time. No one, as far as I know, turned up for the funeral."

"I wish I'd been much older," said Mel, a thousand regrets rising to her mind. "I'd have known so much *more,* instead of being kept in the dark. You'd better go," she said sweetly. "Siobhan is looking anxious."

"Funning, are you?" Dev clipped off. "Just be here when I get back."

It was a good fifteen minutes before Dev returned. He found Mel in the library. "The good news is O'Hare is willing to meet my price for Illuka," he said, slumping, albeit elegantly, into a wing-backed chair.

"And the bad news?"

"Well, I don't know if it's *bad,* exactly," he teased, "but Siobhan gave me an epic hug and a kiss goodbye."

"Lucky you." Mel closed the book she had taken down from a shelf, a signed copy of Patrick White's *The Tree of Man,* set in the Australian wilderness. It had contributed to his winning the Nobel Prize back in 1973. The Nobel committee commented that White had "introduced a new continent into literature." Australia, the oldest continent on earth. Mel had read and re-read the book. She never tired of it. "A sea change appears to have come over our Siobhan lately," she observed.

"Yes, indeed. I've never heard her so chatty."

"Put her out of her misery, Dev," she advised. With his iridescent eyes on her, her heart was starting to beat high in her chest.

Dev continued on his way. "It's the Celt in her. Makes her unpredictable."

"And she's upping her game."

"Then she's peaked way too fast," Dev said sardonically, eyeing Mel as she sat at the circular library table. She was wearing a simple white ribbed singlet that set off her golden skin, paired with black linen chinos, a tan leather belt slung around her narrow waist. Mel always did look great in whatever she wore. Definitely not your girl next door.

"I have to fly to Sydney Monday next," he told her.

"Business?" Mel looked across at him. Dev would be expecting far more of it.

He gave a faint sigh. "Always business. I need to call in on one of Granddad's stockbrokers. Want to come?"

"Not if it delays my trip to Silverton," she answered. "I can find the town by myself."

"Sure you can, but I can make your journey easy and safe. I don't like the idea of your haring around the bush by yourself. It's still frontier country, Mel. Sydney first, then Silverton right after. How's that?"

She took her time to reply. "I guess I'm happy enough with that."

He gave a satirical whoop. "*You're* happy, *I'm* happy. Hallelujah!" He stood up purposefully, as though he had wasted enough time. "Why don't you come on down with me to the Five Mile? We're shifting a big mob into a holding hard. We could do with some help. Some of the boys are still out in the desert rounding up strays and any cleanskins they can find. We'll divide the cleanskins with Patrick O'Hare. The trouble is, cattle split up as they graze and a lot go missing each year. Just roaming wild. They love it."

"Freedom," Mel said. "We *all* love it. I'll need to change. Give me half an hour. I'll join you."

"Great! Thank God I can trust you not to lose yourself."

Dev rested a hand on her shoulder as he passed her chair. "I've lost count of the number of warnings I've had to issue to visitors over the years. Remember the guy who told me he *utilized the eeny, meeney, miny, moe set of coordinates*?"

Mel had to laugh. "That was the polo player, wasn't it, Chris Quentin?" A search party had been organized to find him. She had been part of it.

Dev sighed. "Not much good in the bush, old Chris. He was probably just riding along thinking of *you*. It was getting to the stage where I thought he was going to ask for permission to marry you."

"How do you know I wasn't tempted to say yes?"

Dev gave a spluttering laugh. "Ah, come on, Mel," he mocked. "You're addicted to *me*. I'm the same with you." The mockery in his voice deepened. "You're my favourite woman in the whole wide world, no matter how many Stop signs you've erected along the way. I bet you wouldn't swear to obey me until death—or divorce—us do part."

The thought shook her. "Langdons didn't believe in divorce," she retorted.

"Not so far. Looks like Ava is set to make history." His expression sobered. "Of all the guys she could have chosen, why *him*?"

"We both know Ava saw her marriage as an escape."

"Who could blame her?" Dev sighed. "God, you were the most gorgeous bridesmaid. Extravagantly beautiful." Ava had four very good-looking bridesmaids in attendance for her wedding, two blondes, two brunettes. Mel had been maid of honour. The bold colours of their dresses had been a talking point. Ava had borrowed them from her favourite flower, the tulip—a fabulous deep purple, an intense pink, a dark crimson and a richly glowing amber. With such strong blocks of colour, one might have thought they would clash but they had looked luscious. "Whatever happened to that amber dress?" he asked.

"I've still got it. I did look good in it, didn't I? But no way did I trump Ava. No bride could have looked lovelier."

"Perfect foils," said Dev, the best memories of that day still clear in his mind. "Now, I'm outta here. You might take Gunner. He could do with a ride."

"Right!" Gunner, with studbook blood, was a chestnut gelding who she had found to her delight could do tricks. She was happy to be put to work. That way she wouldn't have time to *think*. Maybe when she was out on the vast empty plains she might see the ghost of the gentle man she had called *"Daddy."* Michael Norton had been a good man. She would remember him with great affection mixed with sadness all the days of her life.

By the time Mel rode into the Five Mile the afternoon tea of scones with butter and jam, fruit cake and billy tea was just finishing, the ring of a bell announcing the break was over. She could see Dev already standing outside Number One yard, talking to a few Aboriginal stockmen, all experts at their job. The atmosphere was light and good-humoured. Morale was high at Kooraki. During the ride over she'd experienced a few hairy moments she would have to tell Dev about. A dingo as big as a large dog, its yellow-brown coat merging with the ripening spinifex, had materialized out of nowhere and started following her.

Immediately she'd pulled out her whip, cracking it and swinging Gunner's head in the slouching wild dog's direction. She'd urged the bay to speed as she'd yelled at the top of her voice to the dingo, "Buzz off!" As she'd closed the gap, whip cracking, the dingo took off, running for all it was worth, its long, dark straw-coloured body flattened out like a dachshund. Mel had suddenly realized the wild dog wasn't so much shadowing her, as she had supposed, but a couple of wallabies she had spotted. The dog had obviously picked up their scent. Usually it was the dingo that struck terror into the wildlife, the cattle, especially the young calves. It was appalling, the death and destruction dingoes could wield. She had seen it all. Calves, lambs, not the Big Reds, the kangaroos well able to defend themselves, but the smaller wallabies and possums. She wasn't on the side of animal lovers on this one. Dingoes were killers. Now it was the dingo's turn. It tore off across the perfectly level plain while the wallabies got to live another day.

She was greeted with smiles, waves and doffed battered hats. She was known to all of the men, many from early childhood. Tethering Gunner, she looked up at a spectacular display overhead—a flight of a hundred and more galahs. They screeched and called to one another, flashing their lovely pink undersides as they flew overhead, swerving above and through the trees. Although she had witnessed these spectacles for most of her life, they still held her spellbound. The numbers and varieties of Outback birds were amazing: the great flocks of budgerigar, finches, parrots, black cockatoos, the sulphur-crested white cockatoos, the kookaburras and kingfishers, and that didn't include the waterfowl that turned the swamps, waterholes and lagoons into moving, jostling masses of waterbirds. The Outback was in such extraordinary good condition, so *green,* it was almost surreal—a result of Queensland's unprecedented Great Flood of early 2011. There were literally millions of wild flowers still hectically blossoming with multicoloured butterflies, bees and dragonflies floating over the vast carpets that continued on to the horizon.

As soon as Dev saw her, he came over. "Everything okay? You look a bit flushed."

"Tiny scare, not on the Tjungurra scale. I had to chase off

a fair-size dingo," she told him, as she had to. "It was going after a couple of wallabies."

"Where was this?" Dev shot back.

"Near Tarana Waterhole."

"Okay…I'll get one of the men to pick it off. I know the animal you mean. It's a cross with a runaway station dog. They're even more dangerous than the pure breed."

He turned his head for a moment, looking towards the five holding yards, then he turned his attention back to Mel. "The men have been working since dawn. They've done a great job. As you can see, they're channelling cattle from the largest yard into smaller ones, and eventually to the stock race, of course." The stock race was a narrow V-shaped alley. "We've got most of the cows and calves yarded. Halfway through the heifers and steers. No one likes mixing cows and calves with bullocks. The bulls will go into Yard Three but you won't be going near them, needless to say."

Mel nodded. She had no need of the warning. Herding the bulls was dirty, dusty, dangerous work. The alley was only the width of a beast. If it became spooked or panic-stricken, for whatever reason, it would try to charge back the way it had come, causing mayhem. The toughest hands were the ones that handled the bulls. They were the ones who wielded the stout canes, whacking any recalcitrant beast back into line. That afternoon the bulls seemed calm enough but everyone was aware of their potential danger. Many a station hand over the years had been gored, hooked or grazed in the ribs by bull rogues.

"I'd like you to partner Bluey," Dev said. "He's coming along okay. A bit erratic, over-eager, but he'll learn." Bluey was a young jackeroo, needless to say, with the nickname of Bluey, a carrot-head with an engaging face covered in big orange freckles, for all the sunblock he slapped on. She and

Bluey would be doing the lightest job. The one with least chance of injury. Mel wasn't about to argue.

"Right, Boss." She tipped a hand smartly to the brim of her akubra, thinking she probably had more expertise than Bluey, real name Daniel.

Everyone got down to business. She and Bluey worked as a team, though Mel found herself doing quite a bit of shepherding the over-eager young jackeroo. Together they were half coaxing, half pushing the remaining heifers and steers into line. Mel could see out of the corner of her eyes forty or so bulls remained to go through the alley into Holding Yard Three.

It was shortly afterwards, to Mel's instant alarm, Bluey decided to expand his horizons. For no good reason, he broke away from his job to assist a man on horseback who was wielding a whip above the head of the bad-tempered beast entering the alley. She yelled a warning to the stockman. He took immediate heed, but the tip of his whip caught the charging Bluey painfully on the left shoulder. Bluey let out a great yelp that brought forth an answering cacophony of sound from the penned cattle. However, that wasn't the problem. Bluey's yell had set off the bull next in line. With a diabolical bellow, head down, it made a butting charge at the hapless young man, hooking one of its horns through Bluey's belt.

Mel recognised, but didn't pay heed to her own danger. She felt a hot flare of fright, but she acted instinctively. Adrenalin pumping, she seized the first fallen branch that was to hand and began belting the bull's swaying rump, not slackening for an instant. The bull didn't appreciate being attacked. It gave up momentarily on Bluey. Strained horns raised to the sky, it began snorting its rage. Mel stood utterly still, none too sure she was doing the right thing, but reasoned correctly that if she made a run for it the bull would instinctively charge and overtake her before anyone could intervene.

Only someone did—someone who had the courage and
expertise to handle a critical situation. Dev materialized as if
by magic, moving in silence and at speed, his tall lean body
moving with catlike grace. He launched himself first at Mel,
flinging her out of harm's way, though the impetus sent her
sprawling on the rust-red earth. Next he tackled the maddened
bull, who now had Dev as his quarry. Half a dozen men were
moving with stealth but alacrity to assist him. The foreman
stood, rifle in hand, prepared to open fire on the valuable
beast.

Only there was no need. Under different circumstances,
a top-class rodeo, it would have been quite a performance
that Mel would have been thrilled by, only this was present
danger. She watched in a frozen panic as Dev managed to
gain the enraged bull's attention. He had to be hypnotising
*the beast because it didn't move as he got a powerful grip on
it*, twisting its head and throwing it expertly to the ground.

The crisis was all but over but it left a nasty taste in everyone's mouth.

The bull safely corralled, Bluey, to everyone's amazement,
walked up to Dev with a big grin on his face, his hand outstretched. "That was terrific, Boss!" he exclaimed in wholehearted admiration. "Reckon you'd win the top prize at any
rodeo."

Dev ignored his hand so Bluey dropped it limply to his
side.

The head stockman, with a shock of pepper-and-salt hair
and a fulsome black beard, lifted his head long enough to
roar an enraged, "You bloody fool, Bluey!"

Several other men added to the words of condemnation,
signalling their collective disgust.

Bluey was initially stunned by this reaction, then his freckled skin abruptly emptied of admiration. He flushed beet-red, looking young and vulnerable.

"Look at me, Daniel," Dev ordered in a steely rasp.

It was enough to cause Bluey to flinch. "Yes, sir." His red head came up.

Dev was only just barely suppressing his anger. "How long have you been on the planet?" he asked in a tightly controlled voice.

Bluey cleared his throat. He looked tremendously upset and embarrassed. It wasn't any performance to gain sympathy. Everyone could see his mortification was real. "I'm twenty-two, Boss," he said, visibly shaken.

"Twenty-two!" Dev pondered aloud. "Well, let me tell you, you mightn't live much longer if you try stunts like that again. You heard what Lew said, didn't you?" Dev's expression was grim. "What you did, your rash judgement, your inexperience could have caused Mel and you possible serious injury. Do you understand that now? I know you thought you were helping but your help wasn't needed. Mungo is well able to handle himself. *You* aren't. He really should take his stock whip to you. It might teach you a lesson."

Bluey by this time was spluttering and choking up with shame. But he was ready to take his punishment like a man. "So I'm okay with that," he mumbled, real tears standing in his blue eyes.

Dev relented. "Okay…" he snapped. "This time we'll let you off with a caution. Do the job that's allotted to you, Dan. You can support a mate, sure, but the men are far more experienced than you. You have a great deal to learn." Having delivered his verdict in a halfway forgiving tone, abruptly Dev lashed out, clipping the hapless Daniel over the ear. "Go and apologize to Mel," he ordered, "though what she did was pretty foolhardy." And brave. But he made no comment on that.

"I heard that," called Mel, accepting the foreman's helping

hand to her feet. "I had to do something, Dev," she sharply defended herself. "It could have been a disaster. Over in seconds."

"Take it easy now, lass," the foreman warned out of the side of his mouth. One look at the boss's seriously taut face had prompted the warning. It was easy to label the boss's expression. Anger. Shock. Fear. All of them combined. The foreman had been there on the terrible day when Mel's dad had been killed. The boss's fear was clearly for Mike Norton's beautiful fiery daughter. Everyone on the station knew how close they had been since they were kids. All of them had been unnerved by the young jackeroo's mindless action. None more so than the boss.

Mel was the first one to notice the blood seeping through Dev's denim shirt. She stared at the spot, then up at his face. He looked calmer now. Langdon in control.

"You're hurt?" Without waiting for an answer or his usual shrug-it-off reaction, she surged forward, unbuttoning his shirt. Nothing was going to happen to Dev on her watch. There was a nasty graze of several inches, stretching from close to the armpit across his rib cage. "Oh, that doesn't look good."

"Don't worry, Mel," he urged, a note of impatience in his voice. "I'm up to date with all my inoculations."

"I don't care," she retorted briskly. "This needs clearing up and some antiseptic applied. And don't tell me not to fuss."

"Mel, I'm not about to bleed to death," he assured her.

She clicked her tongue. "I really hate the way men are so careless with their health. And that's a sad fact."

"Not careless at all," Dev protested. "I told you all my shots are up to date."

"Then humour me," she begged. "Come back to the house.

Set my mind at rest. It's a wound and it needs washing and disinfecting, Dev. You know that."

"What about you?" His brilliant eyes moved over all he could see of her.

"A bit of a sprawl in the dust. Nothing." In fact she had skinned her right elbow.

Dev looked around at his foreman said, "Can you finish up here, Lew?"

"No problem." Lew nodded briskly. "Mel's right. You should get that cleaned up to be on the safe side, Boss."

"So you're ganging up on me." Dev gave a half smile. "Dan is off the job for today, Lew. Number Four bore is playing up. Send him out to give Sutton a hand." Not until he had given young Bluey a good talking-to, Lew thought.

He tipped his dusty wide-brimmed hat. "Will do, Boss."

"You're not going to sack him, are you, Dev?" Mel asked anxiously as they moved off.

He glanced down at her. "Hang on." He paused to remove a few dry leaves and a twig or two from her hair. "He can have a second chance. He won't get a third. That was remarkably foolish, what he did."

"Don't worry, Dev. He'll take it to heart."

"He'd better," Dev said shortly. "Don't expect me or the men to keep tabs on him, Mel. You could have been seriously injured, savaged, even mutilated. You realize that?"

"Hell, I'd say so!" she half joked, half shuddered. "But *you* were the one who put my heart in my mouth."

"So you do love me after all?" His iridescent eyes glittered with self-deprecation. "Isn't that great?"

"Let's press on," Mel said briskly. "I need to attend to that gash."

"Florence Nightingale."

"Florence Nightingale, nothing! More men died in her

hospital than on the front line. Infection, poor hygiene—life-and-death matters they weren't properly aware of at the *time, sad to say. You know when she returned* home she went to bed for the rest of her life?"

Dev held open the passenger door of the Jeep for her. One of the men would return Gunner to the stables. "I dare say she got around to bedside chats with family, friends and neighbours," he suggested. "I'm really impressed with the things you know, Mel."

"More like what I *don't* know," said Mel tartly.

# CHAPTER NINE

THEY were back at the homestead, in the well-stocked first-aid room. "All right, you first," Dev said briskly.

"What?" Mel turned away from the large cabinet that held all sorts of dressings.

"You heard. You hurt your elbow and you're holding your arm a bit oddly."

"It's stinging, that's all," she said dismissively. It was quite tender, but then the elbow always was a sore spot.

"Let me see."

No point in arguing with him. Mel proffered her arm. Dev turned it gently so he could see her elbow. It exhibited a sore-looking red patch, a result of skinning it in her fall.

Dev manoeuvred her to the nearest sink. "I'm sorry I had to be so brutal," he said. "But there was no time to lose."

"God, Dev, you saved me from injury." She uttered a small sound of gratitude and admiration.

"So I did. I believe that puts you in debt to me for the rest of your life. Just goes to show how much I love you, Mel. I'd die for you."

Although he spoke lightly, something in his tone drew her lovely dark eyes irresistibly up to his. "I think I know that."

He gave a sceptical grunt. "You *think?*"

"All right. Expect me to die for you," she answered.

Dev watched her face. Always the magic with Mel. "That settled, I beg you to stand still while I clean this up."

"You said that like you expect me to argue," she retorted.

"Well, don't you always?" He slanted her a devastating smile.

She gave a lilting girlish laugh. Just like the old days. "I'm not going to allow you all your own way, James Devereaux Langdon. Say, would you like me to call you James from now on?"

"Don't try it." He set his chiselled jaw.

"Maybe I'd like to hear it. James…Jamie…Jimmy…Jim…" She tried variations of his given name on her tongue, only he caught her unawares.

His hand moved under her chin and his mouth came down to stop her little taunts with a hard kiss. It deepened and deepened, enough to take her breath away. Their mouths locked. Their bodies locked. Their hands locked. Eternity wouldn't be long enough.

*Long minutes later,* Dev hauled himself up by his strong arms to sit on the wide bench than ran the length of the room. His blood-stained shirt Mel had soaking in cold water in one of the stainless-steel sinks. The sight of his body stirred her blood—his wide shoulders, the bare bronze chest that showed off his fine physique, the hard muscle, the tapering waist, his stomach as flat as a board. Mel thought he probably had the best workout routine in the world just being what he was, the cattle baron.

"This is deeper than I first thought," she said, swabbing the long gash very gently. "But it's stopped bleeding."

Dev pretended a nonchalant yawn. "Mel, I'm not a bleeder." He wanted her to finish so he could carry her up to bed, make love to her in broad daylight. He remembered the times they had made love under a million blossoming desert stars, the constellation of the Southern Cross overhead, the galaxy of the Milky Way luminous and glittering like a river of diamonds spanning the black velvet sky.

Mel was his other half.

Mel didn't answer. She was absorbing his want. Only she had an agenda that badly needed addressing and she wouldn't be deflected. She kept busy swabbing little coagulated beads of blood from the wound. When she was done, Dev drew her body in between his long legs while Mel, from long familiarity, let her head slump against his uninjured shoulder.

"Let's go upstairs," Dev muttered into her herb and citrus-scented hair. "I want to make love to you. Love in the afternoon. How does that sound?"

Ferociously exciting. "As much pain as pleasure," she said. Despite her resolution to keep her cool, sexual hunger was blotting all else out. She touched her mouth to his bare collarbone, inhaling the scent of his skin. Emotion was flooding her. She wanted certainty, an end to all the lies. She wanted a perfect world where sordid scandals of the past couldn't intrude. Could she get it?

"Don't think I'm going to wait forever for you, Mel. I'm not a saint."

"I know that." Little shivers of excitement were racking her whole body.

"Neither are you," he whispered in her ear. Whatever he said, he knew he would wait. His intention was to make her feel unsure of him. God knew she had caused him enough pain and frustration. Frustration was a dangerous emotion. "Your room or mine?" he asked, staring into her large lustrous eyes.

Mel's husky murmur came from under her breath. "It's all the same to me."

Dev moved off the bench, slinging his arm around her. He wanted Mel all to himself. He wanted her above everything. He had taken her virginity, the two of them so young and mad with longing, struggling to hold off consummation. He would never forget their first time. He had done a lot of time-travelling over the years, reliving the whole ecstatic experience that was still, after all these years, crystal-clear in his mind. Mel was and always would be the *one* in his life. That *one* person who meant more to him than all the rest.

Dev punched in the number of Sarina Norton's luxury hotel while Mel was taking a shower. They had arrived at her apartment only twenty minutes before, after a long tiring flight. A mellifluous male voice—really should be a newsreader—told him with regret that there was no guest of that name staying at the hotel.

Dev feigned a short laugh. "*Scusi,* I should have said Signora Cavallaro." Sarina had reverted to her maiden name, it seemed.

Immediately he was put through to her room. Sarina answered after the third ring. *"Buongiorno."*

How *was* that? Sarina had invented yet another persona. *"Quanto bello!"* Dev responded in kind to Sarina's sexy opener. *"Bene in meglio,* Sarina." It did, indeed, get better and better.

Instantly Sarina switched to cool, clipped English. "Who *is* this?" she asked in the imperious tone of a dispossessed contessa. "I am expecting a call from the concierge."

"Cancel it, Sarina." Dev spoke in his normal commanding tones. "Dev Langdon here. Surely you remember me?" he asked with deep cynicism. "It happens I'm here on business, but it's imperative I have a few final words with you. This morning, if you wouldn't mind," he said with exaggerated cordiality.

Sarina took a moment to catch her breath, then her voice rose on a melodramatic note. "I thought I had answered all your questions."

"How could you have done that?" Dev challenged.

"Aaargh, Amelia has gone to you," Sarina said in a deeply wounded voice.

"You make that sound like a betrayal. Mel always comes to me, Sarina. You know that better than anyone. I've heard this riveting *new* episode in your life story. I need to establish if it's God's truth."

"So what are you going to do, sue me if it isn't?" Sarina tried the challenging approach.

"No," Dev answered coolly. "The Langdons as a family will contest the will."

No sound from the other end, then Sarina's quiet moan. *"Jesu!"*

"As a good Catholic, surely you shouldn't be taking the Lord's name in vain?"

"I *knew* you'd try it." Sarina saw herself as forever the victim.

"Not if there are no more fabrications. Mel and I intend on going to Silverton, by the way. If that's a lie, you'd better stop me now. I have precious little time to waste, Sarina, so it won't do to cross me."

"Cross *you?*" said Sarina. "I wouldn't dare."

"The only way to go."

Dev had only just put down the phone when Mel, wrapped in a pink towelling robe, walked into the living room. "Who was that?" she asked, staring across the room at him. "And don't say wrong number." Her antennae were up and working.

"You're going to insist on a name?" Dev leaned back in the leather armchair.

"You're up to something, aren't you?" she persisted, fixing him with her great dark eyes. "I know you, Dev. Just like you know me."

Dev's laugh was off-key. "Sometimes this *knowing* gets out of hand."

"You can't laugh it off, Dev. It was my mother, wasn't it?"

"*Is* your mother Signora Cavallaro?" he queried.

Mel slumped onto the couch. "Is that what she's calling herself now?"

Dev nodded. "She's a true chameleon, able to blend into whatever surroundings she finds herself in. She has a full-blown Italian accent, too. Very sexy." Dev took note of her troubled expression. "Don't let her drag your mood down. I'm here, Mel. We're together. I'm not prepared to travel to Silverton on a wild goose chase."

"You're going to see her? *Again?* You don't need to see your stockbroker?"

"I most certainly do," he clipped off. "This trip is in the nature of killing two birds with the one stone. Sarina always claimed her family settled in Sydney. We're here now. For all we know, this could be in the nature of a homecoming for her," he said acidly. "I don't trust Sarina at all. Neither do you. She's like a scriptwriter, making it up as she goes along. You can come with me if you like. Or I can see your mother alone."

Mel fired up. "She could try to seduce you."

Dev held up his hands, palms turned out. "Hey, hey, Mel, take it easy."

She fixed her pink bath robe modestly across her knees. "Sorry, but I've reached the stage where I feel my mother is capable of anything."

"Perish the thought she's capable of seducing me." Dev spoke with more than a hint of contempt in his tone.

"What's the betting, as we thought, she finds herself a rich husband?" Mel asked, thinking she would never solve the enigma that was her mother.

"One would have to feel sorry for the poor guy," Dev offered dryly. He rose to his splendid height. "I'm seeing her this afternoon. I've told her we want the final draft of the soap."

"Or you'll send some of Tjungurra's mob after her."

"*Better. I'll say I brought him with me. It's all down to* Sarina. I'd do anything for you, Mel."

"Anything but propose marriage again."

"That, Amelia *bella,* is the *last* thing I'm going to do," Dev confirmed. "For your sins, you're going to have to propose to me. A novel twist, but absolutely necessary."

"The miracle is you still care about me at all." She gave him a small sad smile. "Do you despise all my hangups, Dev? All the barricades I've erected?"

His expression hardened. "I despise your mother for what she did to you. Our biggest folly was ever believing her. Now, I'm going to take a quick shower. We'll dress, then go out for a leisurely lunch. After that, we'll call in on Signora Cavallaro."

Sarina greeted them at the door. She was dressed for the occasion, the very picture of European elegance. Her thick glossy hair had been recently styled in an updated, side-swept curving pageboy to just below her ears. Her deep natural wave had been straightened. She was wearing a sapphire-blue silk dress with strappy leather heels in a contrasting bright green with a matching green leather belt around her waist. To set it all off, she was wearing dazzlingly beautiful diamond and emerald earrings. They looked extremely valuable. A present— probably one of many—from Gregory Langdon, Mel thought, and stashed it away for the right moment.

Apparently Sarina had judged the time had arrived.

"Come in," she invited with cool poise, studying with approval Dev's tall, lean body and wide shoulders, the perfect clothes hanger. He was wearing a dark charcoal Armani suit with a beautiful pale blue shirt and a blue, silver and red-striped silk tie. He looked extremely handsome, reminding her of how impressive Gregory Langdon had once been.

Mel felt unnerved by her mother's pronounced Italian accent, the educated accent she had learned from the cradle and had toned down for years on end. Now it had come to the fore. "Just one question, Dev." Sarina smiled at him as though they communicated on a different level. "Why is Amelia here?"

Dev took a firm hold of Mel's hand, moving past Sarina into the deluxe hotel room. "*I'm* the one asking the questions, Sarina," he said in a clipped voice. "Let's all take a seat, shall we?"

Mel realized this was crunch time. Her mother was making a show of confidence but Mel knew better. Under the polished veneer, she was afraid of Dev. She knew he wasn't a man to mess with. Sarina, at bottom, was no fool.

"So, we're all here together *again,*" Dev said suavely. "All your fault, Sarina, because you simply won't come clean. Maybe you're incapable of it. I've heard the latest story. I need it confirmed. We're done with wading through lies. More of them and I'll commence legal action against you. You were a young, beautiful, *married* woman. My grandfather was a man with an unhappy home life. He was old enough to be your father. Seduction. Manipulation. Fortune-hunting. My grandfather's declining physical and mental health, the fact you nursed him in his last days. Telling things like that."

Mel winced. That was a powerful battery of charges.

Sarina didn't deign to look at her daughter, as though she were but a minor player. "No need to go there, Dev," she said, playing the woman of the world to the hilt.

"Give it up, Mum," Mel begged, sympathy rising irresistibly.

Sarina turned on her. "Why don't you keep out of this, Amelia? I told you the truth."

"Maybe, but it's absolutely amazing how well you can lie.

I don't know the name of my biological father, *yet*. Look on the bright side, Mum. You might be able to hold on to your fortune."

Dev broke in. "We need that all important *name,* Sarina. No problem, surely? You're big on names. Think carefully before you answer. You may have exerted influence over my grandfather, but not *me*. You have a duty to Mel to put things right."

Sarina blinked at the forcefulness of his tone. "I have your word you won't take any action against me?"

Dev gave a sardonic laugh. "I won't repeat myself, Sarina."

Sarina, the born actress, the fantasist, inventing scenario after scenario, began to speak...

As they were leaving, Dev held out his hand. "The earrings, Sarina," he said, startling Mel. "I'd like them back. They look brilliant on you, but they happen to be the Devereaux emeralds, the possession of my grandmother. They were to come to Ava. She has the necklace and the bracelet, all part of the set, but we were wondering where the earrings had got to. Now we know. My grandfather had no right to give them to you, if indeed he did."

Mel reacted with dread. Her mother couldn't possibly have stolen them. Her whole being shied away from theft.

"Of course he did!" Sarina cried, scarlet flags in her smooth olive cheeks. "I am not a common thief. Would I have worn them had I stolen them?"

"Wouldn't put it past you," said Dev, still with his hand out.

"Give them back, Mum. You'll be able to buy plenty of expensive jewellery when your money comes through."

Sarina lifted a hand to her ear. She removed the magnificent earrings with their large Colombian emeralds, then handed them over to Dev, who slid them into his inner breast pocket. "Gregory tricked me in so many ways," she said with extreme bitterness. "He swore he would marry me as soon as he was able."

Dev's tone was curt with disbelief. "I think it was more a question of self-deception. He wasn't going to marry you, Sarina. Ever."

"Like you won't marry Amelia here." Sarina threw back her head in such a way that Mel had the awful image of a taipan about to strike.

"It's eating you up, isn't it, Sarina?" Dev said smoothly. "You just can't suppress your jealousy. Even of your own daughter. Let's go, Mel," he said. "If you've held up your end of our deal, Sarina, I'll have your money released quickly. That's all you were ever going to get. *Money*."

Back at the apartment, Mel was trying to cope with the layer upon layer of deceit and betrayal that had been allowed to accumulate over the years.

Dev, too, was very quiet. He took off his tailored jacket, then loosened his silk tie and the top button of his shirt before pulling the tie down. "I feel like a drink," he said. "What about you?"

Mel huffed. "I don't think I should go there."

"Maybe a G&T?" Dev said, walking into the galley kitchen and opening the refrigerator. He knew there were a couple of bottles of tonic inside. The gin, vodka, et cetera were in the drinks cabinet.

"The thought of any of this getting out is appalling."

"It won't come from *my* family," Dev reassured her. "They all know better. Whatever else Sarina is, she's not a complete fool. She won't talk."

"You don't think it will get into the newspapers?" Mel asked with a flare of hope.

"Is it so *terrible*?" Dev responded.

"*I* think it is. My mother manipulated everyone who got in her way. Your high-and-mighty grandfather included, it seems."

"Beautiful women have been doing that since the beginning of time," Dev said. "The great courtesans. Your mother is rarin' to go."

"*La dolce vita!*"

"Big time." Dev found crystal tumblers and fixed their drinks, aware of the swirling tensions between them. One wrong word from either of them and they would be in over their heads. So many fiery clashes in their time. Sometimes it was her fault. Sometimes it was his. His *mind* understood all the humiliations Mel had suffered as she'd progressed from childhood into adolescence, then adulthood. He had done everything he could to ease her pain. Only now he had to cope with a powerful opposing force. Frustration. Frustration and a lack of patience that became more and more driving as the years had passed. Mel had lacked a father and in essence a good mother to guide her. She could even be defined as an orphan, with no real sense of identity.

Well, now they knew who her biological father was. One Karl Kellerman. Kellermans were listed in the Silverton Shire's phone book. Dev had already checked it out. A list of six, including a K & R Kellerman.

Mel accepted her drink and took a long sip. "So my maternal grandparents didn't get killed in a car crash after all," she said in an emotionless voice. "And my mother's maiden name is really Antonelli, not Cavallaro. Where did she get Cavallaro from?"

"God knows!" Dev sighed, then sat down beside her. "You have living family on both sides, Mel."

"Who won't want anything to do with me."

"You don't know that. Their side of the story is probably completely different from Sarina's."

"Maybe." Mel had already considered that, given her mother's entrenched deceits. "But this Karl Kellerman—German name—didn't have much going for him in the way of honour, even common decency. No wonder my mother was all messed up. He betrayed her."

"That's for us to find out."

"At least I wasn't aborted," Mel said wretchedly.

"Don't say such a thing!" Dev reacted strongly. "Drink up, Mel."

"Drown my sorrows, you mean. I'm illegitimate," she announced as she placed the crystal glass carefully on the coffee table.

"Honestly, Mel, who cares?"

Mel turned her angry, mortified face to him. "*I* do!" she said fiercely.

Dev stood up. "Okay, you're illegitimate," he said. "Do they actually use that term these days? You were a love child. I was a love child. So was Ava and most kids."

"You're both Langdons, Dev," Mel said, straining to rein in her emotions.

Dev shook his handsome blond head. "Is this going to turn into another big angstfest, Mel?" he asked.

*Don't let it be,* the voice inside her head screamed in warning.

"I'm trying to deal with it, Dev, as best I can," she said in a quieter voice.

Dev grabbed hold of his jacket, shouldering into it. He was moving like a man abandoning her to her fate. "I'll leave you to the process of sorting yourself out, Mel. I don't want to say anything that might make things worse. I'm going out for a while."

"Where?" asked Mel, her back to him.

"Out," he said.

* * *

Dev didn't come back for hours. But he *did* come back. She didn't ask him where he had been. He didn't say for a good ten minutes. Then he spoke as if he had reached some juncture in his mind. *"I ran into Scott Davenport."*

"Oh?" Scott Davenport was one of Dev's oldest university friends. "How is he?" Mel asked. "And Frances?"

"They're both well," Dev said. "They're having a dinner party tonight. As we're in town, Scott insisted we join them. I made him ring Frances first. She said she was delighted."

Mel thought carefully. She could decline. Or she could accept the invitation. She knew this was a testing time. Maybe a make or break time for her. She was aware of the enormity of the risk she was taking with Dev. She couldn't live her life forever on the defensive. She had to make a leap of faith.

"That would be lovely," she said, trying to inject warmth into her voice. She knew that arriving on Dev's arm would be quite a talking point later for the other guests. She wondered briefly who they might be. The chic crowd, the high-flyers. Come to that, she was one herself, wasn't she? "What sort of thing should I wear?"

"Dress up," Dev said. "Not black tie, but Frances likes her dinner parties on the formal side. I have a hunch the two of them have an important announcement to make. They've been married...what?" he asked.

"Two years." Mel rose with feigned composure to her feet. A marriage wasn't fulfilled until there were children. Now, more than ever, she heard her own biological clock ticking.

# CHAPTER TEN

FRANCES DAVENPORT, a real charmer, greeted them at the door, kissing them both in turn. Her golden-brown eyes shone with pleasure.

"This is a lovely surprise," she cried. "Come in. Come in. Everyone's here," she told them cheerfully. "You look *gorgeous,* Mel," she said sincerely, thinking she had never seen any other woman project such beauty and sensuality as Amelia Norton. "I was hoping to see you again. Someone here you both know—Siobhan O'Hare."

Dev didn't turn a hair. "Scott didn't say," he responded smoothly, not missing a beat.

Had Siobhan heard about Dev's trip? Mel wondered. So what could she be shopping for—a trousseau? In the world of money, power and influence, dynastic families cemented their fortunes with suitable marriages. These weren't high Victorian times and a rigid class system, but family background and money would always count.

"Siobhan? A snap decision, I gather," Frances was saying. "She has a shopping excursion in mind. I've promised to go along with her. I think you've met all the others. Annabel Corbett. Remember her, Dev?" She gave him a teasing side-long glance.

"I do, indeed," said Dev rather dryly.

"It's okay." Frances started to laugh. "She's about to get

engaged. Now, come along." She linked arms with them. "Oh, this is going to be such a lovely evening. I know it."

The entry of Dev Langdon and Amelia Norton struck two people in the Davenports' luxurious living room with considerable force. One was Siobhan O'Hare, in her lovely hyacinth-blue chiffon dress that she had chosen with such care. The other was Annabel Corbett, who had been feeling at home and relaxed up until that very moment. Annabel was twenty-nine now, in a bit of a rush to get married. She wasn't madly in love with her soon-to-be fiancé, Bart Cameron, but Bart and his family, like hers, were old friends, well established in society. Bart would do. That was until she laid eyes on Dev Langdon again.

Annabel didn't know it, but her mouth fell open. She felt she was about to cry. Dev looked absolutely stunning—the physical attributes, that smooth, confident aura, even the walk. He was so sexy, so masculine, so golden...so...so... darn *everything.* She wanted to jump up and grab him. She knew who he was with, of course. Amelia Norton, a go-getter with Greshams, so she'd heard. It had to be said she looked drop-dead terrific in a sleekly draped cocktail dress in a rich ruby-red. Had Amelia better connections, she could have been the toast of the town. She had heard a murmur about Cattle King Gregory Langdon's will. Everyone knew Amelia Norton's mother was the Langdon *housekeeper.* She had near overheard something to do with the mother. It had been at the intermission of the opera *Carmen.* Two old ladies had been whispering behind their hands. One was Cassie Stewart. The other Valerie Devereaux. Obviously what they were discussing was hush-hush. But secrets couldn't be protected for long.

On seeing them together, Siobhan felt her every last hope had been wrecked like a yacht dashed up against perilous rocks.

Although Amelia wasn't projecting a woman-in-possession aura, Dev, on the other hand, was projecting a clear message. The exquisitely sophisticated woman on his arm was *his* woman. As far as Siobhan was concerned, there was no mistaking the signal. His grandfather dead, Dev was getting his life into swift order. Amelia had always been in his life. Now Dev was showing for the first time his adult *passion* for his childhood friend. Siobhan felt not jealous but hopelessly outclassed. Amelia was the classic Italian beauty. She couldn't compete with Amelia, no matter what she did. Neither could any other woman in the room, for that matter. She realized now that she and her mother hadn't been particularly realistic. People fell in love or they didn't. Some love affairs ended badly, others flourished. Siobhan suddenly saw things the way they really were. Life could be a messy affair.

Time now for her to move on.

Scott had chosen fine wines to go with the various delicious courses. Succulent Sydney rock oysters for starters, pâté de foie gras made in the French tradition, a choice of superb steak with either peppercorn or mushroom sauce or a classic chicken dish. A sweets trolley was to follow.

Mel sat beside Alistair Milbank, the stockbroker, feeling an easy sense of friendship and familiarity. She had come to know Alistair well. He was a close friend of her boss at Greshams, a kind, courtly man in his early sixties. He was considered absolutely loyal to his friends and very trustworthy, as he had to be in his line of work. Because he admired Mel's brain among other things, Alistair wanted to talk a little business until their host called him to order.

"Now, now, Alistair!" he warned.

"A wonderful shiraz, Scott," said Alistair, breaking off to lift his glass. Still, Alistair couldn't help asking Mel in an undertone, "Is it right what I hear?"

"What *do* you hear?" Mel whispered back, holding on to her composure.

"Your mother was left a positive fortune by Langdon?"

Mel lifted a hand of caution. "Not here, Alistair."

"I can take that as a yes, then?" Alistair asked, bushy brows raised.

"Could I ask you to keep quiet about it, Alistair?" Mel fixed him with her great dark, lustrous eyes.

A man could drown in them, Alistair thought. "Of course, love," he said, gently patting her hand. "It's really nobody's business, anyway, is it? Have I told you how absolutely breathtaking you look?"

Mel managed a smile. "Several times, Alistair. Do you mind if I ask how you came by your information?"

"If you must know, dear girl, my old Aunt Cassie. Cassie trusts me. She tells me everything. I look after her affairs now that Ed has gone. I'm just wondering how *you* would feel, if it got out into the wider domain?" Alistair looked questioningly at her.

Mel was surprised to hear herself answer with confidence. She couldn't dissociate herself from her past; it had blocked her emotional development in its way, but she could begin the process of unifying herself. She had an identity now. It wasn't the one she would have wished for, but she had a far better sense of who she was. "I can deal with it, Alistair," she said calmly.

Alistair gave a quiet chortle. "I've no doubt you can. Always thought you'd go a long way, my dear. Besides, as I say, it's nobody's business, really."

Mel nodded her agreement.

"Now, what shall we have?" Alistair was already eyeing the sumptuous sweets trolley. He took the decision making very seriously. "I do have a sweet tooth."

"Like most men." Mel smiled. She was unaware that the

tall, good-looking blonde across the table, Annabel Corbett, had never taken her eyes off them during their murmured conversation.

Had Annabel been a good lip-reader, she would have been able to make out what Alistair was saying. As it was, she had been able to catch some of Amelia Norton's murmured responses.

*Keep quiet about it?*

Quiet about what? There was a story there. Annabel knew she would never get it out of Alistair, but maybe Siobhan O'Hare? Siobhan was yet another one who'd had her sights set on Dev Langdon. The O'Hare cattle-and-sheep station bordered Langdon's Kooraki. If there were any juicy secrets to be told, Siobhan might know them. She had seen her stricken face when Dev and the Norton woman had walked in. Siobhan might well be in the mood to talk. She hadn't been feeling so bad of late, but tonight she couldn't take the idea of Amelia Norton landing the biggest catch in the country. When the moment presented itself she would take wee Siobhan aside.

Scott and Frances made their all-important announcement as the long, leisurely dinner drew to a close. The very slim Frances, who was not showing, was expecting their first child in six months' time. All the women gathered around to kiss and congratulate her. Dev undercut some of the overflow of sentiment with a funny joke about his friend, Scott, but everyone could see Scott was as thrilled and happy as his wife.

Annabel availed herself of the opportunity to whisk Siobhan away. "Siobhan, poppet, love your dress!" she exclaimed, barely registering it.

"Thank you." Siobhan managed a smile but she was wary of Annabel Corbett, who had been some years ahead of her at school.

"Listen, don't hold back on me," Annabel said, "but there

seems to be a lot of gossip circulating about Dev Langdon and the family."

"Like what?" Siobhan's stomach flipped but her face stayed composed.

"You tell *me*," Annabel whispered urgently. "What's with Amelia Norton, for a start? What's she doing here with Dev? She's not his sort."

"Maybe you need glasses," Siobhan suggested, thinking she could have done with a pair herself. "Amelia is very much Dev's kind of woman. Joe the goose could see that."

"Joe the goose! Who's Joe the goose?" Annabel asked in amazement.

"Just a saying." Siobhan shrugged Annabel's hand off her arm.

"Oh! I don't know much bush jargon. Have I made a big mistake, but has it got something to do with Norton's mother, the housekeeper?"

"Why are you asking *me,* Annabel?" Siobhan looked directly into the other woman's avid eyes.

Annabel appeared taken aback. "Who better? I could see how shocked you were when they walked in. *Everyone* was gawking."

"As they ought to." Siobhan gave a short laugh. "You'd have to say they make a stunning couple." Siobhan had become aware that Dev was looking keenly in their direction. His six-foot-three frame alone made him stand out from the rest.

"Couple?" Annabel sucked air back through her teeth.

"Wouldn't you say? What's it got to do with you, anyway, Annabel?" Siobhan asked. "Aren't you getting engaged?"

Realization hit Annabel that she had backed the wrong horse. "So I am," she said, affecting a one-up-on-you tone. "But how can you *not* hate the woman who must have set out to destroy any hope you had with Dev? It's not as though she's one of us."

*"One of us?"* Siobhan reluctantly admitted to herself that she had felt a bit like that. "You always were a terrible snob, Annabel."

"You can't be *serious?*" Annabel near shrieked.

"And hey," said Siobhan, "Dev is my friend. So is Amelia. I'd like to keep it that way. Dev was no more romantically interested in me than he was in *you.* Incidentally, if I were you I wouldn't attempt to upset him or his family with any gossip-mongering. I'd say there was probably a price to pay."

That had belatedly occurred to Annabel. "God, you're really jumping to conclusions," she hastily back-pedalled. "I only wanted a quick word."

"Well, you got it," said Siobhan. "You must excuse me, Annabel. I want to see Amelia. She looks ravishing tonight, *don't you think?*"

"A bit too flamboyant for my taste," snapped Annabel. She turned, rushing away. She felt furious now she'd had to *squeeze* into her figure-hugging black-and-gold sheath. So much for the cabbage diet!

Because of the strict ban on drunk driving, the dinner guests had organized Silver Service limousines to take them home. Dev and Mel were dropped off at Mel's apartment.

*Everyone knows. Everyone must know,* Mel's inner voice told her. She thought briefly of the morning papers and shoved the thought right out of her mind.

*Que sera, sera.*

Neither of them spoke in the lift beyond Dev's saying casually, "That went well. Scott has asked me to be one of the godparents."

"Lovely! I'm very happy for them both."

"Jealous?" His eyes sparkled like gems in his handsome dark golden face.

"Good grief, no."

"I know how you feel about kids, Mel," he said. "Time's slipping away."

The lift arrived at Mel's floor. "For you, too," she said tartly, stepping out. "However did you get mixed up with Annabel Corbett?"

He simply laughed. "Now that's just insane, Mel."

"I think she'd be prepared to ditch her soon-to-be fiancé if she thought she was still in with a chance."

"Then she really is nuts. Women can fancy themselves in love without giving a thought to reality," Dev said dryly. "Siobhan looked extremely pretty."

"She certainly did. You didn't know she would be in town?"

"I said so, didn't I?" Dev answered coolly, taking the key out of her hand and opening the door. "She and Annabel seemed to be having a few words at one point."

"Well, you *were* trying to give them reason," Mel said, giving him a sidelong dark glance.

"I—beg—your—pardon?"

"Their hopes must have crashed, the way you were shepherding me. I thought we'd vowed not to show how we felt in public."

"And what feeling would that be, Mel?" he said suavely, taking off his jacket and placing it over the back of a chair.

"Perhaps you wanted to give people a shock?" she suggested. "That Annabel is just so uncool."

"So she is! But think about it, Mel. Did anyone look or act shocked, outside of Siobhan and Annabel?"

The truth of that gave Mel a much needed jolt.

"Your mother taught you not to trust anyone. But you're a woman now. A woman well able to shape her own destiny. I just don't believe how you can keep putting yourself down. Alistair Milbank, among others, thinks the world of you, and I mean professionally, as well as everything else."

"Maybe going back to Kooraki, mixing with your people, has my undoing," Mel suggested wryly. "Look, I'm going to take this dress off." She started to remove the crystal-studded barrette that held one side of her lush fall of hair behind her ear.

He could never walk away from Mel. "You look so *good* in it you should never take it off," he said. "Feel like a night-cap?"

She shook her head. "You have a big day tomorrow, don't you?"

"True," he said smoothly, loosening his tie. "What are *you* doing?"

"I'm going to start the ball rolling."

"Just as well you can't run off without me," said Dev, sighing quietly. "There won't be any big scandal, Mel," he promised. "I have people working on it. They can keep the whole thing contained."

"Can anyone ever bury scandal properly?" Mel asked.

"The best I can do is a mop up. It's already in progress," Dev assured her.

"It's not as if *I* have done anything wrong," Mel said with a rush of self-belief.

"Mel, go to bed," he said. "You're all eyes."

"I don't get a kiss good-night?" She wasn't being provocative. Dev's kisses fed body and soul.

"Well, I know I'd strive to be good, but there's a weak side to me." He smiled, getting to his feet and joining her.

"You're always there for me, aren't you, Dev?" She stared up into his jewelled eyes.

"As you might say, *l'unione fa la forza.*"

"It's true. There *is* strength in unity. I'm far luckier than I deserve, Dev," Mel said humbly.

His beautiful mouth twisted slightly as he considered what she had said. "Just remember, actions speak louder than words, Mel. We need to find our way out of this. And very soon." He bent his head to find her mouth while she leaned into him, thinking he had always put her needs before his.

Dev broke the kiss as he knew he had to. "Sleep well, *principessa.*"

The savannah lands of the north were an endless sea of emerald-green in the wake of Queensland's Great Flood. The turquoise Coral Sea, aquamarine in the shallows, lay to the east. It stretched far, far away to the horizon, its waters a maze of reefs, islands, coral banks, sandy cays and the eighth wonder of the world, the Great Barrier Reef, a continuous rampart of coral as solid as sandstone stretching north and south for nearly thirteen hundred miles. Parts of it were still uncharted, to be approached with great caution, which made Mel reflect that Captain James Cook had to be one of the greatest seamen of all time and even he had nearly met with disaster. The great French navigator Bougainville had turned back. He had written in his logbook of the sighting of a "tumultuous surf" rising out of the ocean. That could only mean a huge reef.

They landed on Maru Downs mid-morning. Dev had taken the station's long-range chopper so they could reach Silverton without recourse to a four-wheel drive. They spent an hour there, Dev talking to the outstation manager, whose wife offered tea and an assortment of cupcakes, baked ahead of their arrival. She and Mel made light conversation, but Mel could only think of two things. This was where Michael had worked as a stockman—he'd probably still be alive if, fatally, he hadn't met her mother—and next, the journey of discovery ahead of them. Mel was glad neither the manager nor his wife knew anything of Michael's story. It had all happened *before their time.*

Silverton, as it turned out, was one of the old gold-rush towns. Dev had sought and gained permission to land on the town's show grounds. He had no difficulty with that request. The Langdon name was enough.

At this time of year the town couldn't have looked prettier. The broad stretch of lawn in the park was densely green, the great mango trees were in blossom, crimson poincianas formed magnificent giant umbrellas against the brilliant sunlight, cascara trees laced their hanging pods with bright yellow blooms, while the ubiquitous bougainvillea climbed over every standing thing in sight.

Outside the town, a distance of a few miles, one came to the sea, with its beautiful white beaches. The beaches were lined with stands of coconut palms bent at odd angles by the prevailing trade winds, with clumps of spiky pandanus bearing their pineapple-like fruit. Mel had already discovered on that amazing resource the internet that the Kellerman Group was a family owned business established a few years before she was born. Over the twenty-plus years the business had succeeded in becoming one of the largest producers and suppliers of processed dried fruits, fruit pulps, purées and pastes to the industry.

The Kellermans must be doing well. A few years back they had built a state-of-the-art processing plant. There was even a picture of three of the company directors—Marcus Kellerman, a handsome middle-age man, with his sister, Zelma, and her husband, Bruno Campigli. Marcus and Zelma—her half-brother and -sister? They were many years older. She would soon find out if the man who had fathered her was still alive.

As for her maternal grandparents, she couldn't think they would want to see her. The horrifying charge Sarina had brought against her father remained in Mel's head like a taint, although it could be a long way from the truth. There were so many dark places in Sarina's soul.

"Sure you want to go through with this?" Dev slowed the hire car as they came into range of several very expensive-looking properties with magnificent uninterrupted views of the sea and offshore islands.

"They can only throw us out."

"I don't think so," said Dev with his built-in self-assurance. "Ah, here it is. Moongate." He brought the car to a halt outside a graceful colonial-style residence set well back in beautiful landscaped tropical grounds. "Not short of a bob of two. This property must be worth millions."

"I'm nervous, Dev."

He reached out for her trembling hand. "What did Franklin D Roosevelt say in his inaugural address? 'The only thing we have to fear is fear itself.' We're not coming out with accusations. We're on a courtesy visit. Karl Kellerman was one of your mother's teachers. Well, that's the rumour, anyway," he said with black humour. "Come along, Mel. Let's get this over with."

Mel could feel the adrenalin kick into action.

A pretty maid with a sweet smile on her face greeted them at the door.

"Who is that, Rose?" a woman's voice called.

Dev took over. "James Langdon and my fiancée, Amelia Norton," he responded by way of introduction. "Mrs Campigli?" he asked as a good-looking blonde woman, hair shot with silver, came into view. She was well dressed, a tad on the conservative side, but her whole demeanour was pleasant and full of self-confidence.

"That's right," she agreed. "You may go, Rose." She dismissed the maid smilingly. "Langdon, now, there's a famous name in our part of the world."

"Gregory Langdon was my grandfather, ma'am." Dev gave her his wonderfully attractive smile.

"Well, come in, come in," Zelma Campigli invited, pink in the cheeks. "You caught me at home, for once. How may I help you? But, please, let us sit down first. Would you like coffee?" Eclipsed by Dev at his most charming, Zelma Campigli now transferred her smiling gaze to Mel. Now her beringed hands suddenly gripped together. "Why, I know you! You have to be an Antonelli."

Again Dev stepped in when Mel floundered. "You would remember Sarina, Mel's mother," Dev said smoothly. "She spoke of Silverton and the families she knew. We're in the region for a day or two, so we took the chance we might find you at home. I hope you don't mind. You have a very beautiful home. This is a beautiful part of the world."

"It is," Zelma Campigli agreed carefully, but her eyes never left Mel's face. "Just let me order coffee," she said, showing them into a large welcoming living room with a palette of coral, yellow and lime-green that took the colours from the floral print on the two large matching sofas. "Won't be a moment," she said, then all but scurried away.

"We've thrown her," Mel whispered. "Or, rather, *I've* thrown her. My resemblance to my mother."

"I guess, but now we know we've come to the right town. Let's take things calmly, Mel," Dev advised. "I'm sure our talk will prove instructive."

When Zelma Campigli returned, something had altered about her face. "Obviously you'll be calling in on Sarina's mother?" she said, taking a seat on the opposite sofa. "You must have passed the Antonellis on your way here. The pinkish terracotta house with the pillars and a suggestion of Tuscany. It's only a few minutes' drive."

Dev nodded as though he knew just the house. "It didn't look like anyone was at home."

Zelma shook her head. "Adriana is bound to be there," she said quietly. "She doesn't leave the house often since she lost Frank. It was a great blow. They were inseparable, like my late mother and father. Absolutely devoted couple. You will know my father was the principal of the local High School for many years. He taught Sarina. May I ask, Amelia, how is your mother? None of us knew what happened to her. She simply went missing, like many other troubled young persons."

"You had *no* idea of her whereabouts?" Mel asked.

"As I said, my dear, no one did." Her tone was slipping a bit towards becoming condemnatory. "Frank and Adriana were devastated. You, no doubt, know the boy's death had a lot to do with it?"

Mel's heart jumped. "My mother has never talked about her past until very recently, Mrs Campigli. What boy are we talking about?"

"Oh, my dear, I'm so sorry." Zelma looked back at Mel oddly. "The Cavallaro boy. He and Sarina, fellow students, were very *close*," she stressed. "We all remember how it was. My father called on both families to discuss the situation. They were both way too *young* to become so involved."

"How do you mean?" Mel couldn't bear to get snowed under again.

Zelma Campigli shook her handsome head. "My dear, it was all so wretchedly sad. Dino Cavallaro crashed the car that belonged to his father. He didn't even have his licence at the time. It was a miracle, my father always said, Sarina hadn't been in the car with him." Zelma's voice dropped almost to a whisper. "She was such a beautiful girl, but very headstrong. We all knew her parents were having a difficult time. They treasured her, their only child. Dino's parents were just as worried. And you knew none of this?"

Mel fell silent. Dev reached out to take her hand, keeping it in his. "Thank you for helping us get to the truth, Mrs Campigli. Mel's mother has never spoken about so many things. Obviously she couldn't come to terms with the boy's accident. He *was* her boyfriend?"

"They were violently in love," Zelma near exploded. "That was the great worry, you see. So young!" She took a deep breath, pressing back against the sofa. "May I ask where Sarina is?"

"No reason why you shouldn't know," Dev said. "She's in Sydney at the moment. She married a man called Michael Norton. He worked for us, first on Maru Downs, then on Kooraki, which you probably know is in the Channel Country in the far south-west. Mel is their child."

Zelma appeared much surprised. She blinked, then, after a moment, nodded. "You're the image of your mother, my dear. Sarina could not have wished for a more beautiful daughter." The maid hovered and Zelma beckoned to her to wheel in the trolley. Clearly Zelma wanted this extraordinary meeting to come to an end.

So many years had passed. So much sadness. Zelma couldn't imagine how any young person could have been as callous as Sarina Antonelli. But her behaviour had always been a bit on the strange side. Better not to raise the question of who was the father of her child. Her parents had been convinced that young Sarina Antonelli had been pregnant at the time of her disappearance. It now appeared that both Sarina and her child had survived.

"She didn't believe I was Michael's daughter," Mel said as they drove away.

"It makes sense, in its way," Dev mused. "The Cavallaro boy was your biological father, Mel."

"I feel sick. It makes me feel sick," Mel said. "Mum probably started lying in her childhood. It's possible she can't help it, like faulty wiring in the brain. Or she *believed* her lies. I told her once she was delusional. Her parents didn't throw her out. She did a deliberate runner. Met up somehow with Michael, manipulated him into taking her with him. Karl Kellerman was just a red herring. She named him as an act of revenge, with no regard to the morality of it. She must have blamed everyone who tried to break her and her Dino up."

Dev glanced at her with concern in his eyes. "Your grandparents were victims along with you, Mel. Your grandfather is dead, but your grandmother is still alive. We could stop off and meet her. We now know the house she lives in. Your decision, Mel. I'm with you, whatever you decide. Consign the past to the past. Or find your grandmother. Which is it to be?"

Mel's heart contracted. She smiled through a shimmering haze of tears. "We call in on my grandmother. Who knows, she might even love me."

Decades might have passed, but when Adriana Antonelli's still brilliant dark gaze fell on the young woman standing on her doorstep she reached out and gathered her into her arms.

"My granddaughter, my granddaughter!" she cried in the most wonderful, stirringly fierce voice. "Blood of my blood! Flesh of my flesh! You're here. You're really here, at last. I knew one day I would meet you. It is God's will."

Watching on, Dev knew Mel had at last found her rightful place. And at the ordained moment. He felt privileged just to be there. Mel turned from her grandmother's embrace to put her arm around him, drawing him proudly forward. Her expression was radiant...dazzling to his eyes. "This is the man

I love, *Nonna,*" she said, her voice shaky with high emotion. "His name is James Devereaux Langdon." Her voice grew stronger. "We're going to be married. Very *soon!*"

"And we want more than anything for you to be at our wedding, Adriana," Dev added in princely fashion.

Adriana Antonelli expressed her great joy with a shout of laughter. "Come in! Come in!" she invited excitedly. "Do not stand at my front door. We have much to talk about."

"Amen to that," Mel murmured very softly, lifting her head to give Dev a glorious smile. "Love you."

He leaned down to her, kissed her very softly on her cushiony mouth. "Can't fight destiny," he whispered. *"We are such stuff as dreams are made on."*

There is a pattern, a meaning, a *truth* to life. One never gets to find it without going on a voyage of self-discovery—pushing every possibility for development, recognising, then containing the losses, the wounds, the fears and anxieties, the conflicts that no one can avoid in life, until, by our own striving, we reach a safe harbour.

\* \* \* \* \*

# His hat shadowed his eyes in the dim light of the foyer,

So when he nodded briefly Angela couldn't read his expression. Something seemed to keep him from opening the door, made it feel like there was more to her question than she'd voiced—and more to his answer.

When she finally thought he must be able to hear her heart beating through her chest, he opened the door. Angela let out a deep sigh of relief, until he turned and tipped his finger to his hat in farewell.

A gentleman.

She shut the door behind him. Perhaps. But not like any gentleman she'd ever known. And perhaps *that* was *the* problem.

Dear Reader,

*Welcome to Cadence Creek—home of the sprawling* Diamondback Ranch and two very sexy men: Sam Diamond, rancher, and his cousin Ty—a real down-to-his-boots cowboy. These two bachelors need two good women to make them settle down, and I've got just the pair. These girls may come with baggage, but they're made of strong, resilient stuff. Angela Beck is a social worker on a mission, and Clara Ferguson's a sweet, nurturing soul looking for a place to call home.

It all starts with the launch of Butterfly House, a special women's shelter for victims of abuse. Angela won't let anyone stand in the way of her plans—not even Sam Diamond, who saunters into a board meeting with a devilish smile. She and Sam don't exactly see eye to eye. But as we all know, things are rarely as simple as they seem. Turns out Sam is exactly the kind of man Angela needs—and Angela is the woman he's been waiting for his whole life.

I loved writing this story from start to finish, and I hope you enjoy it too. And don't forget to look for Ty and Clara's story, coming soon!

I love hearing from readers—you can find me at my site at www.donnaalward.com!

Until then—happy reading!

*Donna*

# THE LAST REAL COWBOY

BY
DONNA ALWARD

First published in Great Britain 2012
by Mills & Boon, an imprint of Harlequin (UK) Limited,
Eton House, 18-24 Paradise Road, Richmond, Surrey TW9 1SR

© Donna Alward 2012

ISBN: 978 0 263 89431 8
ebook ISBN: 978 1 408 97107 9

923-0512

Harlequin (UK) policy is to use papers that are natural, renewable and
recyclable products and made from wood grown in sustainable forests. The
logging and manufacturing processes conform to the legal environmental
regulations of the country of origin.

Printed and bound in Spain
by Blackprint CPI, Barcelona

A busy wife and mother of three (two daughters and the family dog), **Donna Alward** believes hers is the best job in the world: a combination of stay-at-home mum and romance novelist. An avid reader since childhood, Donna always made up her own stories. She completed her Arts Degree in English Literature in 1994, but it wasn't until 2001 that she penned her first full-length novel and found herself hooked on writing romance. In 2006 she sold her first manuscript, and now writes warm, emotional stories for Mills & Boon®'s Cherish™ line.

In her new home office in Nova Scotia, Donna loves being back on the east coast of Canada after nearly twelve years in Alberta, where her career began, writing about cowboys and the west. Donna's debut romance, *Hired by the Cowboy*, was awarded the Booksellers Best Award in 2008 for Best Traditional Romance.

With the Atlantic Ocean only minutes from her doorstep, Donna has found a fresh take on life and promises even more great romances in the near future!

Donna loves to hear from readers. You can contact her through her website at www.donnaalward.com, her page at www.myspace.com/dalward, or through her publisher.

To Jayne, who rescued a very special kitty.  And to
Chippie—truly one of a kind.

# CHAPTER ONE

ANGELA Beck tapped her fingers against the boardroom table and frowned. The seat across from her was noticeably empty and she grew more irritated by the moment. They'd held things up long enough, though why Molly Diamond was running so very late was a mystery. Molly was usually right on time.

"Angela, we really can't hold off any longer." Charles Spring, the President of the Butterfly Foundation board, folded his hands and looked down the table at her, his gray eyes stern over the rims of his glasses. "We need to get started."

Charles had graciously agreed to let the foundation meet in the boardroom of his oil and gas company's headquarters. It meant a drive into Edmonton, but Angela knew it was easier for her to commute than for the entire volunteer board to drive to Cadence Creek for a meeting. As a result she'd put together a list of things she needed for the renovations, determined to make the most of the trip. She didn't have any time to waste if she wanted to make her projected opening date.

"I know." Angela forced a smile and made herself remember that every person in the room was volunteering their time. She was the only one drawing a salary from the foundation. The reminder was enough to ensure her patience. The shelter was her dream, but success relied on a lot of people—people who didn't have this project as their top priority the way she did. She couldn't afford to alienate any of them—she'd come too far and invested too much.

"I'll call the meeting to order, then, at 2:18."

For an hour the board members discussed the latest fundraising campaign; Angela outlined the latest PR push and upcoming open house, adding her input to the proposed operating budget and counseling services she'd organized for residents of Butterfly House. She'd thought she'd worked long hours before as a social worker for the province, but that was nothing compared to her days lately, especially as she was a staff of exactly one.

"And now," she said, "I wanted to bring up the suggestion that we hire some short-term help for the minor renovations still needed to the house."

Charles tapped his lip and looked over at the board treasurer, a graying woman with glasses and a stern demeanor. "Iris?"

"Leave it with me," she suggested. "But don't get your hopes up. The budget is already stretched. What's allocated is barely going to cover the cost of materials. Start adding in labor costs and I start seeing red ink."

"Perhaps if we can get more donations…" Soliciting sponsors was definitely not Angela's favorite part of the job; she hated feeling like the center of attention and preferred to be behind the scenes. But it had to be done and so she did it—with a smile and an eye on the big picture.

The talk then turned to drafting up letters requesting sponsorship. Angela pinched the bridge of her nose. The place needed paint and window coverings and the floor in the living room was in dire need of replacement. Who would come good for all of that?

She straightened her back. She would do it, somehow. She was thrilled that her vision was becoming a reality and it was worth the long hours, the elbow grease and the worry. It would be better when the house was actually ready for residents. In its present state it looked the way she felt—tired and droopy. She'd make it right if she had to do it all herself.

They were down to the last item on the meeting agenda when the door opened and *he* sauntered in. Sam Diamond needed no introduction, Angela thought with disdain. *Everyone* knew who he was. She resolved to keep her expression bland as she looked up, wondering why on earth Sam had shown up instead of his mother, Molly, the Diamond family representative to the board.

Sam turned a slow smile on the group and Angela clenched her teeth. He was going to be trouble—with a capital *T.* She'd known it from the first moment he'd sidled up to her at the Butterfly House fundraiser and had asked in his smooth, deep voice, "Have we met?" Her tongue had tangled in her throat and she'd hesitated, feeling stupid and predictable as a purely feminine reaction warred with her usual timidity when it came to dealing with members of the opposite sex— especially in social situations. Well, maybe he'd had her at a disadvantage during their first meeting, but she'd kept the upper hand in the end and she would today, too. She was far more comfortable in a meeting room than at a cocktail party.

But she'd have to do it delicately. His family had made Butterfly House possible, and it wouldn't do to bite the hand that was feeding her project.

"Mr. Diamond." Charles lifted his head and offered a wide smile. "I'm afraid we started without you."

Started without him? Angela silently fumed. He was over an hour late and had just walked in as though he had all the time in the world! And Charles Spring…she felt her muscles tense. Old boys' club, indeed. Spring might frown at her over his glasses, but to Diamond he was as sweet as her mother's chocolate silk pie!

"I got held up." Sam gave the board a wide, charming smile and removed his hat. "I hope I didn't inconvenience anyone."

"Not at all! There's always time for the foundation's biggest supporter." Heads around the table nodded. Sam shook Charles's hand and then put his thumbs in his pockets.

"I didn't realize I'd be in the company of such lovely ladies," he drawled, popping just the hint of a dimple. Angela swore that she could hear the sighs from three of the board members old enough to be Sam's mother. "I would have made a better effort to be here earlier."

Angela thought she might be sick from all the flattery stuffing up the room. Where was Molly? Why had Sam come in her stead?

"I do hope your mother's okay," Angela said clearly. She took off her reading glasses and put them down on the table. Sam pulled out his chair and met her gaze as he took a seat. Recognition flared in his eyes for a moment, then cleared as if they were perfectly polite strangers.

"She's fine, why do you ask?"

There was an edge to his voice and Angela didn't like it. Maybe he was still nursing a bit of hurt pride where she was concerned. She blinked. Men like Sam Diamond weren't used to being refused. Especially when they bought a lady a drink and told her she was a pretty little thing.

She'd simply said, "No, thank you." It was only afterward that she'd realized that she'd given a Diamond—a pillar of the community—his walking papers. It put her in an awkward position. She needed his family's support.

She ignored the uneasy glances from the board members and pasted on a cool smile. "Molly hasn't missed a meeting yet. She's been so supportive of the foundation. So I'm a bit surprised to see you here today, Mr. Diamond."

Dark eyes met hers, challenging. "And you are?"

Oh, the nerve! He knew exactly who she was. She could see

by the gleam in his eye that it was a deliberate cut, intended to throw her off her stride. She lifted her chin and rose to the challenge. "Executive Director of Butterfly House, Angela Beck."

"You obviously didn't receive my message. I called this morning."

And this morning she'd been outside chasing Morris around, trying to get the infernal creature indoors before she had to race into Edmonton. She hadn't stopped to check messages. She resisted the urge to bite down on her lip. She wasn't feeling quite as in charge as she'd like. She was well aware that the Diamond family had a place on the board; after all, they'd donated the building and land for Butterfly House and promised an annual donation toward maintaining the facility. Which was all down to Molly's generosity, she knew. The younger Diamond had a reputation that preceded him and it wasn't all favorable. The fact that he'd tried his charms on her only made it more awkward. Maybe the deed was already signed, but without the continuing support the program would die a quick death unless she could find another sponsor with deep pockets.

"I'm so sorry, I didn't receive it. I've been in the city for several hours already."

Angela was aware that every pair of eyes were on the two of them and that everyone seemed to be holding their breath. Everyone knew Sam. He was a big man, with big money and a big ego. Most of the residents spoke of him as if he were a god. Men respected him and women wanted him—until he trampled on their affections. She'd had her ears filled about that already.

But Angela could see the appeal. He was over six feet in his boots, sexy as sin and looking scrumptious in jeans and a shirt with a sport jacket thrown over top as a concession to business attire. Paired with his unassailable confidence, he made quite the package.

Just because she could understand the attraction did not mean she was interested, though. He was too... Well, he was too everything. She'd known it from the moment he'd tipped his hat and looked down at her with his bedroom eyes. And after she'd refused his overtures, he'd gotten this little half smile. "Do you know who I am?" he'd asked. Clearly she hadn't. But she did now. They both knew exactly who had the upper hand—and he was enjoying it.

How kind, gentle Molly Diamond had spawned such an egomaniac was beyond her. Did he really think his transparent charm would work on her now when it hadn't the first time?

"My mother won't be attending any board meetings for the foreseeable future. My father suffered a stroke last week and she'll be looking after him for the time being. She requested I sit on the board in her place."

Oh, brother. Sympathy for the lovely Molly and her husband Virgil warred with annoyance at the turn of events. Angela and Molly had hit it off from the start, and she'd so looked forward to talking things over with the older, friendly woman. Molly had insisted that she'd love to be involved with turning the house into a real home and had even helped plan the upcoming open house. Angela couldn't imagine Sam helping with those sorts of things. Undoubtedly his impression of "service to the community" was throwing money at it, then smiling and shaking a few hands and feeling proud of himself.

"I hadn't heard." Angela forced herself to meet his gaze. "I'm very sorry about your dad, Mr. Diamond. Please tell Molly that if she needs anything to give me a shout."

"Thank you."

But the words came out coolly, without the warm flirtatious charm he'd used on the other board members. Great. It seemed his pride was still smarting from her response that night. His question—*Do you know who I am?*—had struck a nerve and made her so defensive that goose bumps had popped up over her arms. "Should I?" she'd answered, looking over her shoulder as she walked away. Her insides had been trembling, but she'd covered it well. She was done letting domineering men run roughshod over her.

She'd utterly alienated Sam and she'd done it in front of the board. He turned his head away now, effectively ending the conversation. And why wouldn't he? She'd been prickly as a cactus. Both times they'd met.

Charles wrapped up the meeting, but before he adjourned he smiled at Sam.

"I'm sure Angela would be happy to fill in the gaps, Sam. She knows more about the project than anyone."

Angela felt the blood rush to her face as Sam's gaze settled on her again. "Of course," she murmured. She would just have to suck it up. What was important was getting Butterfly House off the ground no matter how often she had to smile. Maybe Sam wouldn't even be interested in the details and this would be short and relatively painless.

She could afford a few minutes as long as she could make it to the hardware store in time to pick up her supplies. By the time she finished running her errands, it would be evening before she returned to Cadence Creek. Her whole day would be gone with little accomplished.

The meeting adjourned and the board members filtered out of the room. Sam pushed back his chair just far enough that he could cross an ankle over his knee. Angela organized her papers, avoiding Sam's penetrating gaze as long as possible. Finally she put her pen atop the stack and folded her hands. She looked up and into his stupidly handsome face. "Shall I bring you up to speed, then? Or will you be on your way?"

\* \* \*

Sam forced himself to stay relaxed. Lordy, this Ms. Beck was a piece of work. She looked as though she had a perennial stick up her posterior and she clearly didn't approve of him any more now than she had two weeks ago when he'd offered to buy her a drink and she'd flatly refused, looking at him like he was dirt beneath her heel. Which was of no great importance. He didn't need her to like him. In fact, he didn't need anything from her. She needed him, especially now that his mother was otherwise occupied.

He ignored the shaft of fear and concern that weighed him down when he thought of his father and focused instead on the budget in front of him. He was only here because his mother had asked and he couldn't say no to her. Especially not now. In his mind, today's meeting was supposed to be a token appearance and then he could be on his way attending to more important matters.

Instead he found himself sticking around. Aggravating Miss Prim and Proper was a side benefit he hadn't anticipated, and it took his mind off the troubles at home.

"By all means," he said slowly, letting a grin crawl up his cheek purely to irritate her. "Educate me."

Damned if she didn't blush, he thought with some satisfaction. He tilted his head, studying her. Pretty, he decided, or she could be if she let her hair down a little. Now, as it had been at the fundraiser, it was pulled back into a somewhat severe twist, with only a few nearly black strands rebelling by her ears. Her eyes were a stunning color, too, a sort of greeny-aqua that he'd never seen before and he wondered if she wore tinted contacts. As he watched, she put her glasses back on—armor. He recognized the gesture. He was the same way with his hat.

"Is your father going to be all right?" she asked quietly, surprising him. He'd expected facts and figures from Miss Neat and Tidy.

"I think so," he replied honestly. "He's home from the hospital and Mom insists on nursing him herself. Since he requires round-the-clock care, something had to give in her schedule. Your foundation was it."

"Of course. Please give her my best and tell her not to worry about a thing."

Sam uncrossed his legs and leaned forward, resting his elbows on the table. "Let me be honest, Ms. Beck. I don't want to be here. With my dad sick, the running of Diamondback Ranch falls solely to me. I don't have time to sit on charity boards and shake hands, okay? All I'm concerned about is the responsible management of the foundation so my mother's donation is held to a...certain standard."

She looked like she'd just sucked on a lemon. "The Diamonds won't be associated with anything substandard," she replied sharply. "I get it, Mr. Diamond."

She made it sound as though it was a bad thing. Four generations had gone into making Diamondback what it was—the biggest and best ranch in the county. The standards set by his ancestors were a lot to live up to. And it wasn't just the responsibility of taking the ranch into the future that he carried on his back. Lord knew he loved his mother, but at age thirty-seven he was getting tired of the question of when he was going to provide a fifth generation. When the hell did he have time? His father was seventy-two, his mother in her late sixties. The ranch was bigger than ever and facing new challenges every day. His latest idea—making Diamondback more environmentally friendly—was taking up the rest of his waking hours. And now, with his father being so ill, it made him think about what would happen to Diamondback. To the family. He rubbed a hand over his mouth. Good Lord. Now he was starting to think like his mother. Men weren't supposed to have biological clocks, were they? So why did he suddenly hear ticking?

Now his mother had lassoed him into sitting on this silly board because the Diamonds had donated some land and a house for Miss Goody Two-Shoes to turn into a women's shelter. And he had said yes because Molly had looked very tired and worried and family was important. He didn't plan on being actively involved. He'd write a damned check and keep his hands off.

"Look, we provided the location. What more do you want?"

He hadn't thought it was possible that she would sit up any straighter but she did—her spine ramrod-stiff as her nostrils flared. "The spot on the board was your mother's condition, not mine."

"I know that," he answered, his annoyance growing. What had he done that had made her so hostile? Surely offering a smile and a glass of wine wasn't a crime? And he hadn't meant to be late today. "What I mean is, what in particular do you want from *me*?"

He heard the sharp intake of breath and could nearly hear the words spinning in her head: *not a thing*. Instead she put down her pen, looked him dead in the eye and said, "Your assurance that you won't withdraw funding and that you'll stay out of the way."

"That's blunt."

"Would you rather I was less direct?"

There was a glimmer of respect taking hold in the midst of his irritation. "Not at all. Please. Be honest."

But his invitation was met with silence. He wondered what she wanted to say, what she was holding back.

"Perhaps I should mention the elephant in the room," he suggested. "The fundraiser."

"What about it?"

But now he heard it—a tiny wobble, the smallest bit of uncertainty. "You really didn't know who I was?"

"And that surprises you, doesn't it? Because *everyone* knows Sam Diamond."

He raised an eyebrow at her sarcastic tone. "Frankly, in this area? Yes."

"You really do have an inflated ego."

Sam chuckled. "Are you trying to hurt my feelings, Ms. Beck? Look, you passed up the opportunity for a free drink. I'm not going to cry in my beer over it." But the truth was he had felt snubbed. Not because he thought he was God's gift but because she'd been standing alone and he'd taken pity on her. She was too beautiful to be hidden in a corner all night. And all he'd got for his trouble was a cold *no, thank you* and a chilly breeze as she left his presence in record time.

"Well, that's settled then." She ran a hand over the side of her hair, even though he couldn't see a strand out of place. It probably wouldn't dare be so impertinent. "Now if you'll excuse me, I have more important things to do."

"More important than impressing your main benefactor? Tsk, tsk."

He didn't know what made him say that. Sam didn't usually resort to throwing his weight around. Something about Angela Beck rubbed him the wrong way. It was as though she'd sized him up at first glance and found him wanting. And that grated, especially since he was already in a foul mood. He'd been late when he prided himself on punctuality. His last meeting with the engineers for the biogas facility had gone well over the time expected and had had less than satisfactory results. Sam was used to being ahead of the curve, not behind it.

He was set to apologize when she stood, placing her palms flat on the table. "This is about helping abused women, not stroking your ego. Your mother understands that. Perhaps you can suggest an alternative proxy for the board position as clearly you do not care about the cause."

Well, well. She had fire, he'd give her that. And it was all wrapped in a package that momentarily took his breath now that he could see her from head to...well, mid thigh, anyway. She had curves under the neat and tidy librarian clothes—straight black skirt and plain buttoned-down blouse. But she had him to rights and he knew it. And they both knew that Molly had stipulated a Diamond family member sit on the board and not the other way around. He was the only other Diamond in Cadence Creek. There *was* no one else.

He stood slowly, reached for his hat and put it back on his head. "Ma'am."

He was nearly to the door when he heard her sigh. "Mr. Diamond?"

He paused, his hand on the door handle. He turned his head to look at her and realized she'd taken off her glasses again. Her eyes really were stunning. And he shouldn't be noticing.

"Your mother didn't believe in simply throwing money at a problem," Angela said quietly. "She believed in being part of the solution. I find it strange she'd ask you to take her place if she didn't think you'd hold up that end of the bargain."

It wasn't that he didn't care, or that Butterfly House wasn't a good cause. He just had too much on his plate. Angela Beck was being far too smart. She'd worded her last statement in just the right way to flatter and to issue a finely veiled challenge at the same time.

A challenge he wasn't up to accepting. The foundation had its land, had its house free and clear. That would have to be enough.

"Good day, Ms. Beck," he replied, and walked out, shutting the door behind him.

# CHAPTER TWO

Sam pulled into the yard and killed the engine, resting his hands on the steering wheel. He hadn't been going to come. He had planned simply to leave well enough alone, go home to Diamondback, grab something to eat and collapse in bed so he'd be on his game for his daybreak wake-up call. Instead he'd found himself turning off the main road and driving through Cadence Creek, putting on his signal light and turning into the Butterfly House driveway. Angela Beck's last words bothered him more than he cared to admit, and he couldn't escape the need to make things right. He didn't necessarily want to apologize. He just wanted to explain why he'd acted the way he had today.

Angela was right. His mother *was* counting on him to step in now that she couldn't. He was a Diamond, and family was everything. He'd learned that at a young age, and it had been reinforced daily as he grew up alongside his cousin, Ty. Blood stuck together—no matter what Ty insisted these days. The ranch wasn't the same with him gone, and Sam wished both Ty and Virgil would mend fences.

Sam was only doing this for Molly—Lord knew she'd sacrificed enough over the years for the Diamond men. It didn't sit well that he was probably going to let her down, too. So when Angela had accused him of just that, it had smarted more than he wanted to admit. He hadn't exactly acted like a gentleman by walking away. So now he'd just smooth things over and ease his conscience.

Resolved, he hopped out of the truck and shut the door. The rambling yellow Victorian house was full of add-on rooms, giving it a boxy, unsymmetrical appearance. It had once been in its glory but now the gingerbread trim beneath the eaves was dull and the paint was chipping. The front porch sagged as he took the first step. This was what the Diamond money had paid for? This falling-down monstrosity was going to be a progressive women's shelter? He frowned, then jumped as a train whistle sounded to the west, followed by the faint rumble of the cars on tracks. What a dump! And on the fringes of town. What had his mother been thinking, endorsing such a place?

He knocked on the door. It would be better if he just explained and left. He'd find the right time to deal with his mother. If he bided his time, she might even be back on the board within a month or two.

The door opened a crack. "Mr. Diamond?"

Ms. Beck's voice came through the crack, clearly surprised at seeing him standing on the ramshackle verandah. "Sam," he corrected, angling his neck to peer through the thin gap between door and frame.

"Sorry. If I open it further, Morris will get out. Again."

Morris? Sam sighed. Who on earth was Morris? *Give me strength*, he thought. He was starting to think that growing a conscience had been a big mistake. But he was here now. Might as well press on and then put it behind him. He had far bigger things to worry about when he got home. Like how to save the family that was falling apart.

"May I come in, then? I'll shut the door behind me."

Indecision twisted her face. She didn't want him inside Butterfly House. He knew it as sure as he knew he was breathing. What he didn't know was why. Maybe he'd been a little heavy-handed this afternoon, but nothing that should keep the door barred against him.

"I only want five minutes of your time," he said. "I don't like how we left things this afternoon."

She opened the door and he stepped inside, only to find it quickly shut again.

There was barely room to move around in the foyer. Plastic bags were scattered everywhere, along with cans of paint in various shades, the colors announced by dots on the silver lids. He sidestepped around them and pressed against the wall to allow Angela to move past and ahead of him. When she did, the panels of his sport coat brushed against her blouse. Something slid through him, something dark and familiar that came as a surprise. Angela sucked in a breath, clearly wanting to keep from touching him in any way, her eyes wide with alarm.

Just as well. She was pretty tightly wound and he preferred his women to be a little more easygoing. Angela Beck was the kind of woman who was work, and he had enough of that to last him a lifetime.

"I just got home a while ago," she said, leading the way into the kitchen. "Excuse the mess."

"I dropped in uninvited. No need to apologize." He walked around boxes stacked with linens and came to stand in the middle of the room.

"I was just having something to eat. Can I get you anything?"

He looked down at the concoction in cardboard she held in her hand. It appeared to be some sort of chicken and rice in a brownish sauce. "Not if it looks like that," he replied.

She performed a perfect shoulder shrug and said, "Suit yourself." She took another bite, but then got a strange look on her face and put the meal down on the counter. He wondered if she was going to ask him to sit down as the silence wound out awkwardly.

"So this is the house," he said casually, trying to put things on an even keel. He looked around the kitchen and then ignored his customary good manners and took a seat at the table, hoping she'd follow his lead and they could stop standing in the middle of the room. Small talk. He could manage a few minutes of that, couldn't he?

"It is."

"And how many residents will you have?"

"We split up the master bedroom and added a bathroom. At full capacity, we'll have five women and myself." She remained stubbornly standing, which made him feel even more like an unwanted guest she'd rather be rid of.

He nodded, wondering where to go next. Five tenants weren't many, but the shelter was only meant to be temporary—for as little as two months with a maximum of a year's occupancy. It would mean that a lot of abused women could find help in the run of a year. She was doing a good thing. He just didn't fit into the picture.

"Begging your pardon," she asked, "but why are you here…Sam?"

"Are you always this abrasive?"

Her mouth dropped open and she stared at him. "Are you always this blunt?"

"Yes," he replied without missing a beat. "What's the point in dancing around anything? I tell it like it is. Makes it much easier to deal with issues."

Her mouth twisted. "In answer to your question, no," she admitted. "I'm usually not."

"Should I be flattered?" He couldn't resist asking. Flapping the seemingly unflappable Ms. Beck was an intriguing pastime.

"Hardly. You seem to bring out my worst."

Sam couldn't help it, he laughed. A low, dry chuckle built in his chest and the sound changed the air in the room, made it warmer. He looked up at her, watched as her gaze softened and her lips turned up the slightest bit in a reluctant smile. Desire, the same feeling he'd had as they'd brushed by each other in the foyer, gave a sharp kick. Angela Beck was an attractive woman. But when she became approachable, she was dangerous. The last thing he needed was to be tangled up in something messy and complicated. He'd been there and done that and it wasn't fun.

"Careful," he warned her. "You might smile."

"It's been known to happen. Once or twice. I'll try to restrain myself."

He was starting to appreciate her acid tongue, too. It spoke of a quick mind.

"Look," he said a little more easily, "I didn't feel right about how I spoke to you this afternoon. I have nothing against you personally, or your project. It's simply a case of hours in a day and only so much of me to go around, and I was in a bad mood when I arrived at the meeting. I meant what I said," he continued, "but I didn't put it in a very nice way."

"You're stepping back from the board then?"

She didn't have to sound so hopeful about it. He frowned. "I didn't say that. I just mean that the Diamond family assistance will be more of a behind-the-scenes kind of thing."

He didn't like the way her lips pursed. She should be glad he was still amenable to signing the checks.

"Your mother…"

"I know," he replied, cutting her off and growing impatient with the constant reminder of his mother's wishes. He stood up and faced Angela, wondering how it was possible that she could be getting under his skin so easily—again. "But I'm not my mother. My mother is in her sixties, her family is grown and she was looking for a cause to champion, something to fill her day with purpose. I don't need such a thing. Surely you can see how our time demands are completely different? My being here is entirely because it means something to her. But don't ask for more than that. I don't have it to give."

"That's what most people say," she responded. "I thank you for wanting to mend fences, but you're really just repeating yourself, Mr. Diamond. Butterfly House is low on your list of priorities."

Why did she have to make it sound like a character flaw? Sam bit his tongue, but she was making it hard with her holier-than-thou stance.

"What if I asked you to come out to the ranch tomorrow? Spend the day, take a tour?"

"I can't afford to take a day away from here!" Her lips dropped open in dismay. "There's too much to be done!"

He sat back, pleased that she'd taken the bait. "Exactly my point."

"It's hardly the same," she argued, wrapping her arms around her middle, the movement closing herself off from him even further. "You can hardly compare the Diamondback Ranch with this place. The differences are laughable."

She thought the Diamondback ranch was a joke? His blood heated. "Why do you disapprove of me so much?"

"Please," she said, contempt clear in her tone. "I've worked with people a long time. I know your type."

He bristled. His *type*? What exactly was his type? He didn't profess to be perfect but all he tried to do was put in an honest day's work. He knew he had a bit of a reputation for being single-minded, but what was so wrong with that? He knew what he wanted, and he went after it. There was something else in her tone, the same negative inflection she'd used the night of the benefit. It grated that she made that sort of snap judgment without even getting to know him at all. She had no idea of the pressure he was under these days.

"Really. And you came to this judgment somewhere between me offering you a drink at the fundraiser and walking through the door at the meeting today?"

She looked slightly uncomfortable and he noticed her fingers picked at the fabric in her skirt. "Among other sources."

"Ah, I see. And these other sources would be?"

She lifted her gaze and something sparked in her eyes. "You are not going to turn this on me, Mr. Diamond."

"Oh, don't worry, Ms. Beck." He put particular emphasis on the *Ms.*, hoping to get a rise out of her. Snap judgments that she wouldn't even qualify annoyed him. He was gratified to see her nostrils flare the slightest bit. "Because I know your type, too, but I'm too much of a gentleman to elaborate."

"A gentleman!" she exclaimed. Sparks flashed in her eyes. "From what I hear, you're far from a gentleman."

Sam wasn't in the mood to defend his character as well as today's actions. He had never, not once, been dishonest with a woman. He wondered where she'd gotten her information from and if it had anything to do with Amy Wilson? Dating her had been a mistake and he'd done her a favor by setting her free. But Amy hadn't seen it that way and had felt compelled to complain all over town. Most people knew to take it for what it was—sour grapes and hurt feelings. But Angela was new here and Amy could be very persuasive.

He had come here to apologize only to have his good intentions thrown back in his face and his character maligned. His temper flared. "Before you say anything more, think very carefully," he cautioned. "I'm sure you don't want to lose Diamond funding. If I recall, even with the house bought and paid for, there are operating expenses to consider. Not to mention your salary."

He saw her face go pale and felt his insides shrivel. Dammit. They were right back where they'd started despite all his resolve to smooth out the wrinkles. It was beneath him to threaten funding and yet he couldn't bring himself to back down. He'd look even more foolish. He should have put a stop to Amy's gossip ages ago, but he'd felt bad after the breakup, knowing he'd hurt her without intending to.

Now he'd gone and acted like a bully. He sighed and wiped a hand over his face, uttering a low curse. "What is it about you that brings out the worst in me?"

"The truth?" she replied acidly.

Angela's stomach seemed to drop to her feet as the words slid from her lips. She couldn't take them back and they echoed through the kitchen. He had just confirmed her opinion. Everything Amy had said about him really was true. He was caught up in himself and no one else, wasn't he? She really should learn to shut her mouth. More than anything else, the need to smooth the waters rather than make waves was the one thing she'd never quite eradicated from her own life.

Her head said to placate him because his funds were crucial to the project. But her pride—and her heart—wanted to tell him exactly what she thought. What sort of example would she set if she allowed him to threaten her job, the very existence of the project? The whole purpose of the shelter was to help women stand on their own two feet, to be strong. How could she allow herself to be weak? She certainly couldn't give in to the urge to back down every time she faced a challenge.

While she was contemplating her response, Morris chose that moment to strut through the kitchen. Lord of the house, master and protector, the orange-and-cream-colored cat stopped and regarded Sam with a judgmental eye.

"The infamous Morris?" Sam asked.

"I should have called him Houdini," Angela responded.

"He's quite the escape artist." It was unusual for Morris to come out when strangers were around, and she watched as he made his way over to Sam. Maybe she'd judged Sam too harshly before. You could tell a lot about a man by watching him with animals.

Morris went directly to Sam, surprising her, and he sniffed at Sam's jeans suspiciously. Sam looked at Angela helplessly, shrugging his shoulders. Angela saw the fur on Morris's back stand up and his tail stiffen. She took a step forward, opening her mouth to warn Sam. But she was too late. Sam shouted and looked down at his leg, rubbing the denim just above the top of his boot.

Morris scooted away, but Angela knew exactly what had happened and wanted to sink through the floor. She hadn't thought this meeting could get any worse, but Morris had taken matters into his own…teeth.

"Your cat bit me!"

Heat rushed to her face as his words moved her to action. She scrambled after Morris and picked him up. Cursed animal, he snuggled into her arms sweet as honey. "He has a thing about strangers. Particularly men." She rushed to the half bath and locked Morris inside. "I think he was abused as a kitten," she continued, wondering if there was anything more she could do to make Sam Diamond more aggravated. "The vet said his tail was broken in three places, that's why it's crooked. But he really isn't a bad cat, he just has a protective streak. He…"

Her voice trailed off. Sam was staring at her as though she was crazy. "I'll shut up now," she murmured.

"Really," Sam said drily, as if she'd stated the impossible.

Morris meowed in protest, the howl only barely muffled through the door.

"You're a real bleeding heart, aren't you, Ms. Beck?" He

glowered at her. "Maybe I need to come up with a better sob story, eh? Maybe that'll get you off my back."

That did it. "Since when did helping others become a flaw, Diamond?" She took a step forward, feeling her temper get the better of her. "Maybe if you took your head out of your charmed, privileged life for two seconds you'd see someone other than yourself. And as far as Morris goes, maybe I am a bleeding heart because I can't stand to see another creature abused. And if he's a little leery of men, he has good reason. I consider him a fine judge of character!"

Sam's dark eyes flared. "A fine judge of..." He made a sound like air whistling out of a tube. Morris howled again. "You know nothing about me. Nothing."

"I know you're a big bully who thinks I'll dance to his tune because I need his money. But I won't pander to you like Charles Spring and the others on the board. You can threaten, you can take funding away. Go for it. Because I would rather that than me betray all Butterfly House stands for by letting myself be pushed around by the likes of you." She finished the speech out of breath.

"Without the funding, this place never opens."

"Don't be so sure." Several times today she'd allowed Sam Diamond to mess with her confidence. But she was done with that. She'd faced worse than Sam Diamond over the years and come through with flying colors. Besides, she had an ace in the hole. She knew Molly Diamond was dedicated to this project. Molly believed in it and in her.

"You think I haven't faced adversity before?" She pressed her hand to her collarbone, felt her heart pounding against her fingertips. "I'm stronger and more resourceful than you think. So go for it. Pull the funding."

She wasn't sure what made her dare him to do such a thing when they clearly pushed each other's buttons so completely and quickly. That had only happened to her once before when she'd been seventeen and so very vulnerable. She'd fallen for Steven in record time and found herself smack in the middle of a volatile relationship. Her mother had taken one look at Angela's face and said quietly, "Passion burns as hot as anger, dear." But that wasn't the kind of passion Angela ever wanted, and her parents certainly hadn't set a shining example for her to follow.

It took everything she had to stand toe-to-toe with Sam Diamond now without cowering. And yet, as she looked into his handsome face, she somehow knew that she wasn't being entirely fair. She was making connections, assumptions without basis. All through her career she'd worked very hard to be objective. She'd had to be.

So Sam Diamond shouldn't be any different. But he was. And she admitted to herself that he had been from the moment he'd sauntered over and spoken to her in his slow, sexy voice at the benefit. Nerve endings had shimmered just at his nearness. He posed a different threat than physical fear. And that threat came from inside herself and her own weaknesses.

He hooked his thumbs into his pockets. "I'm not going to pull the funding. The Diamond family made a commitment, and we honor our commitments despite what some may think."

The tension in the room seemed to settle slightly, no longer at a fever pitch amplified by sharp words.

"I appreciate that."

He took a step closer and her heart started a different sort of thrumming. Earlier she'd taken great care to make sure she didn't touch him as they passed in the crowded hallway. She stood her ground. She didn't want him to know she was afraid. Goodness, she was a strong, capable, resourceful woman. It was ridiculous that one person could make her forget all of that just by breathing. She tried to remember what it was that Amy had said. That Sam Diamond took what he wanted until he was done and then he tossed it away like yesterday's garbage. Amy's words were completely opposite from Sam's pledge, so which should she believe?

"You're tired," he noted, and to her shock he lifted his hand and ran his thumb along the top of her cheekbone. She knew there were dark circles beneath her eyes. Makeup had concealed it for most of the day, but it was growing late and as the makeup faded, her fatigue came to the surface.

But more than that—he was touching her. She flinched slightly at the presumptuous yet gentle touch, but he didn't seem to notice. His thumb was large, strong and just a little rough. She was tempted to lean in to the strength of his hand for just a minute, but she held her face perfectly still instead as her insides quivered with a blend of attraction and fear. "I've been putting in long days," she breathed. "There's a lot to do."

"I won't keep you, then," he replied, dropping his hand. She missed the warmth of his thumb and took a step backward, shocked at her response. No one ever touched her. Ever. And certainly not in such an intimate way.

"I'm sorry about Morris. He's a very naughty cat. Did he get you very badly?"

And then it happened. Angela saw the barest hint of a smile touch his lips. Not the smooth, charming grin from this afternoon. A conspiratorial upturning of his lips that Angela couldn't resist. It sneaked past all her misgivings and lit something inside her. She found herself smiling in return and chuckling. He joined in, the warm sound filling the kitchen.

Angela sighed as the laughter faded, looked over at Sam's face, now holding a spot of devilishness that made her understand why the women of this town all swooned in his presence.

"I'll live," he said, the earlier hostility gone. "It was more of a surprise, really." He lifted an eyebrow. "Just as well I have a tough skin. Maybe he smelled our dog or something. Buster has a way of putting cats on edge."

Was he teasing her now? The idea made an unfamiliar warmth curl through her. She had to admit, knowing he was a pet owner added to his appeal. She had a momentary image of Sam on a huge horse with a dog following at their heels....

Dangerous. And trouble. At the very least, Amy had that part right.

"Don't take it personally," she offered weakly. "It's not you…"

"If you say so."

"I couldn't just leave him," she continued, not knowing why it was important that Sam understand about her cat but feeling compelled just the same. Another meow sounded behind the door. "He was hurt, and just a baby."

Sam's face was inscrutable. "Do I strike you as the kind of man who kicks puppies, Ms. Beck?"

Did he? Lord, no. He might use charm as a weapon, and he might have a ruthless streak—that single-mindedness he'd mentioned—but she found it hard to believe he'd be deliberately cruel. There was something about the way he'd touched her face…

She shook her head, not quite trusting her judgment.

"Well, that's something, then."

He turned to walk down the hall, back toward the front door, around the bags of home-renovation supplies and paint and everything else that would take up all her waking moments for the next several days. Perhaps weeks.

Maybe she could sweet-talk someone local into donating their time. School would be out for summer soon. Maybe a couple of students at loose ends… There was so much to do before the open house. The logistics of organizing that alone were taking up so much time and energy, and she'd already drafted the press release and sent it out....

The press release. The media was going to expect to see Molly at that, too. New nerves tangled as she thought of dealing with the press alone. She looked up at Sam. Getting more from him would be like getting blood from a stone. She'd figure something out. She had a little bit of time.

"I'd better let you get back to your dinner," he said, putting his hand on the doorknob.

Her dinner. The tasteless glazed chicken that she'd popped in the microwave in lieu of a real meal.

"I trust that I'll see you next month at the board meeting, then?"

His hat shadowed his eyes in the dim light of the foyer, so when he nodded briefly Angela couldn't read his expression. Something between them hesitated, seemed to keep him from opening the door, made it feel that there was more to her question than she'd voiced—and more to his answer.

When she finally thought he must be able to hear her heart beating through her chest, he opened the door. Angela let out a deep sigh of relief, until he turned and tipped his finger to his hat in farewell.

A gentleman.

She shut the door behind him. Perhaps. But not like any gentleman she'd ever known. And maybe that was the problem.

# CHAPTER THREE

SHE'D been kidding herself.

Exhausted, Angela sank down on the lopsided front step and put her head in her hands. For ten days she'd worked her tail off, and there was still so much to do her head was spinning. Having to do the renovations herself meant no time for working on the embellishments, the little special touches she'd had in mind. The basement was littered with used paint cans and rollers, and she'd missed a stud trying to install a curtain rod and ended up having to do a substantial drywall repair in the yellow room. Yards of material gathered dust waiting to be sewn into curtains and duvet covers. Boxes of supplies were still taped up, needing to be unpacked. The carpet was torn up in the living room but the local flooring business had postponed installation of the new hardwood until tomorrow. The place was a mess.

The open house was only four days away. She needed Molly's help. Molly had been on board to look after feeding the crew from the youth center on Saturday. She was also supposed to be a spokesperson to the media so Angela could stay in the background, where she liked it. Angela had been so annoyed by Sam's attitude that she'd squared her shoulders and determined she'd show him and do it all herself.

But she'd been wrong. She needed help. And she needed *his* help if Molly wasn't able. It wasn't just about a pair of spare hands. The press release had gone out before that horrible board meeting and the local angle had been playing up Diamond involvement. To go ahead with the day and have the Diamonds conspicuously absent…to stand in front of a camera and have her picture taken, her words put into print…

Her stomach tied up in knots just thinking about it. This wasn't about her, it was about *them*—the women the foundation would help. The last thing she needed was anyone digging around in her past. She closed her eyes. It was truly a bad state if she was relying on the likes of Sam Diamond to be her ally!

She wiped her hands on her overalls, resigned. It came back to the same thing every time, no matter how much she didn't want to admit it.

She needed Sam Diamond's help.

She found him coming down a beaten track on horseback, sitting a trot effortlessly while a golden retriever loped along behind. Growing up in the city she hadn't really believed that cowboys and ranchers, like those in storybooks and movies, really existed. But they did. The Diamondback Ranch sprawled over the foothills, dotted with red-and-white cattle. The house was a huge log-type mansion that reeked of money and Western tradition at once. Just beyond a gigantic barn was a paddock where half a dozen gleaming horses snoozed in the warmth of the summer sun. And Sam Diamond was getting closer by the second, all six foot plus of him in his own über-masculine element.

She'd never felt so out of place in her life, and she'd been in some pretty uncomfortable spots over the years.

"Well, well. Must be important to tear yourself away from Butterfly House on such a gorgeous day."

She had to squint against the sun to look up at him. "You manage to compliment the weather and antagonize me all in the same sentence," she said. She forced a small smile. "And I might get mad, except for the fact that you're right. It is important."

He'd slowed to a walk but she still had to hustle to keep up with him.

"And it has to do with me…why?"

With a slight shift of the reins, horse and rider came to a stop. The dog, sensing home, bounded off in the direction of the house. Angela held her breath as Sam turned in the saddle and looked directly at her. On horseback he was an imposing figure, and he had a direct way of looking at a person that was intimidating. She wasn't comfortable being one hundred percent of his focus, but she made herself meet his gaze. He *looked far too good for comfort in his jeans, boots and dark Stetson,* and she took her sunglasses out of her hair and put them on, shading her eyes.

The horse Sam rode was big and black, and the way he tossed his head made his bridle hardware jingle. He was exactly the kind of mount she'd expect Sam Diamond to ride— big and bossy and used to having his way. But Angela refused to be intimidated.

When she didn't answer, he grinned. "Let's try that again, shall we? Good mornin', Ms. Beck. To what do I owe the pleasure?"

There was a mocking note to his words and Angela felt his gaze drop over her clothing and back up again. She'd considered changing out of her paint-streaked overalls and sneakers but decided not to. She felt safer in the shapeless garment rather than her work clothes that skimmed her figure more closely. Besides, the scale of work that had to be done was enormous. Fixing herself up would have taken valuable time she couldn't afford to lose.

"I need your help."

There, she'd said it, and it only hurt a little. Mostly in her pride.

"My help? My, my. That must have been hard to say."

"Yes. I mean no. You see…I had counted on your mother's help and without it I've fallen behind. I know it couldn't be helped," she rushed to add. "I don't blame Molly. She belongs with your father, of course. I've tried for the last week and a half to keep pace on my own, but we've got a press opportunity happening this Saturday and I'm not ready."

"As you can see, I've got my hands full here."

"Surely you can spare some time? I've been doing the renovations myself but there are some things I'm just not equipped to do. The front step is a hazard and the furniture needs to be moved into the living room before Saturday and somehow I have to have refreshments on hand for a dozen teenagers who will be at the house. Not to mention the press."

She was quite breathless at the end and felt a blush infuse her cheeks as Sam merely raised one eyebrow until it disappeared from view beneath his hat.

"Come to the house. I'll write you a check and you can hire some help for a few days."

Her blood began to simmer. For most people she would have said *put your money where your mouth is*. But for Sam, writing a check was an easy way to rid himself of the inconvenience of her and of Butterfly House. Her annoyance temporarily overrode her personal discomfort.

"You don't understand. This isn't just about slapping on some paint. It's about perception."

"Perception?"

"Yes, perception." She sighed. "It's not even so much the renovations. When you replaced Molly on the board, the press releases had already been sent and the arrangements made. You're the foundation's biggest sponsor, Sam. And everyone expects to see a Diamond presence this weekend. If there's no one there…"

"If it's perception you're worried about, I'm not sure I'm the image you want to present to the public. You'll do fine without me."

He laughed, but Angela wasn't amused. This project was about more than helping women reclaim their lives. It was about changing attitudes. And Sam Diamond, with his money and swagger, was the perfect test case. If she could bring him around, she figured she could accomplish just about anything.

"I won't say no to the check because the foundation needs it. But we need more than that, too. We need a showing of support. We need the backing of the community. I don't like it any more than you do. I wish I didn't need your help. But I sat on the step this morning trying to figure out how I was going to manage it all and I kept coming up blank."

"Maybe I can spare a man for a day or two, but that's all. Now, if you'll excuse me."

But that wasn't all. How easy was it for Sam to solve a problem by scrawling a dollar amount and washing his hands of it? "All I'm asking for is one day. One day for you to show up, be charming, give a visible show of support. As much as it pains me to admit it, the people of Cadence Creek follow your lead."

He rolled his eyes. "Here we go again. You don't give up, do you? Do you ever take no for an answer?"

She gritted her teeth. If he only knew how much she hated confrontation! She lifted her chin. "Do *you*?"

A magpie chattered, breaking the angry silence. "From the look of the house, it needs more than a slap of paint. It needs a demolition order. You'll never get it fixed by Saturday." Sam adjusted the reins as his horse danced, impatient at being forced to stand.

Angela got close enough that she had to tilt her head to look up at Sam. She wanted him to see what was at stake. It wasn't enough for him to sit atop his ivory tower of privilege—or his trusty steed—and bestow his beneficence. It was too easy. And the women she wanted to help hadn't had it easy. Their lives couldn't be fixed by a blank check.

"I have to. The house has been neglected, that's all. It just needs some TLC."

"Ms. Beck." He sighed, looking down at her from beneath his hat. "Do you want me to do everything for you?"

She felt her cheeks heat. "Of course not. But, for example, I was going to look after the painting and minor renovations while your mother lent a hand with some of the aesthetic needs—like window fashions, linens. On Saturday she was not only going to represent your family to the community and press, but she was in charge of all the refreshments. That's all fallen to me now. I do need to sleep sometime, Sam. And then there's the issue of what to say to people on Saturday when they ask about our biggest sponsor and their conspicuous absence."

"You tell them we're busy running a ranch. You tell them we're occupied with adding a new green facility to our operation. Or that we're busy employing a number of the town residents. All true, by the way."

"Have you heard of volunteering, Mr. Diamond?"

His dark eyes widened as his brows went up. "I beg your pardon?"

"Volunteering—offering one's time with no expectation of reimbursement."

"I know what volunteering is," he replied, impatience saturating each word.

"Millions of people volunteer every day and still manage to work their day jobs. Most of them also have families of their own—and you don't have a wife or children that I can see.

You can spare Butterfly House the cash, but can you spare it the time?"

Angela swallowed, took a breath, and stepped forward, grabbing the reins of his horse with far more confidence than she felt. She stood in front of the stallion's withers, her body only inches away from Sam's denim-clad leg as it lengthened into the stirrup. "What are you so afraid of, Sam?"

He slid out of the saddle and snatched the reins from her hands, his movements impatient. "You can save the holier-than-thou routine. I've made up my mind."

She could sense success slipping away from her and frustration bubbled. "You go to great lengths to avoid personal involvement. Why is that? Maybe it's true what they say about you."

"And what's that?" He stood before her, all long legs and broad chest. She felt incredibly small and awkward next to his physicality, dumpy in her overalls next to his worn jeans and cotton shirt that seemed to hug his shoulders and chest. She felt a little bit awed, too, and it irritated her that she should be so susceptible to that because, despite the fact he was a pain in the behind, Sam Diamond was also drop-dead sexy. The sad thing was she was nearly thirty years old and had no idea what to do with these feelings. She'd gotten very good at presenting a certain image, but inside she knew the truth. She had no idea how to be close to anyone.

"Never mind." She turned away, hating that he was able to provoke her without even trying.

He reached out and grabbed her wrist. "Not so fast. I think you'd better tell me."

Her heart seemed to freeze as her breath caught for one horrible, chilling moment. Then, very carefully and deliberately, she reached down and removed his fingers from her wrist and stepped back. She wasn't sure which emotion was taking over at the moment—anger or fear. But either one was enough to make the words that had been sitting on her tongue come out in a rush.

"That you're a cold-hearted..." She couldn't bring herself to say the word. She kept her gaze glued to his face for several seconds.

Finally the hard angle of his jaw bone softened a touch and he said quietly, "Where'd you hear that? Let me guess, Amy Wilson?"

She had, and her lack of response confirmed it.

"You shouldn't judge someone by what you hear."

"I don't." At his skeptical expression, she sniffed. "I don't," she insisted. "I form my own opinions. I deal with people all the time, you know. And I judge people by what I see them do." And right now he wasn't scoring many points. Her wrist still smarted from the strength of his fingers circling the soft flesh. She touched the spot with her fingers.

His gaze caught the movement and then lifted to meet hers. There was contrition there, she realized. He hadn't really hurt her; he'd merely reached out to keep her from running away. It was her reaction that was out of proportion and she suspected they both knew it. Awkward silence stretched out as heat rose once again in her cheeks.

"And so you've judged me." The horse got tired of standing and jerked his head, pulling on the reins. Sam tightened his grip, uttered a few soothing words as he gave the glistening neck a pat. "I suppose you won't believe me if I say I'm sorry about that." He nodded at her clasped hands.

It was a backward apology, and did nothing to change the situation. That was what she had to remember. "Sam, you give from your pocketbook if it means you don't have to get involved. I just haven't figured out why. Is the ugliness of real life too much for you?" She kissed her last hope of success goodbye, knowing she was crossing a line but needing to say it anyway. How many times over the years had people turned a blind eye to someone in trouble? How many people had avoided the nasty side of life because it made them uncomfortable? How many people had known what was happening in front of their faces and hadn't had the courage to make the call? Angela's life might have been very different. It was the only thing that kept her moving forward in spite of her own fears.

"That's ridiculous." He turned his back and started leading his horse across the barnyard.

"Then prove it. Try giving of yourself." She went after him, desperately wanting to get through. "These women have been through it all, Sam. They've been beaten, degraded, raped…" She swallowed. "By the men who professed to love them. Despite it all, they got out. They sought help, often leaving everything they owned behind. This house will help bridge the gap between overcoming an old life and building a new, shiny one. What in your life is more important than that?"

He didn't answer. But she sensed he was weakening, and she softened her voice. "All I'm asking for is a few hours here and there. You have a gorgeous house, food on the table, a purpose. I just want to give these women the same chance. If you show the people of Cadence Creek that you support these women, doors will open. They'll have a chance to be a part of something. People look to you to lead. Lead now, Sam. For something really important."

She took a step back, uncomfortable with how impassioned her voice had become. For a few seconds there was nothing but the sounds of the wind in the grass and the songbirds in the bushes.

"You realize how busy this ranch is, right? And that I'm going it alone now that Dad's sick?"

"But you have a foreman, and hands. Surely they can spare you for a few hours?"

"You're forgetting one important detail."

"I am?"

"If I help you, we're going to be seeing more of each other." He made it sound like a prison sentence. "And I don't mean to be rude, but we're kind of like oil and water."

She felt her vanity take a hit before locking it away. Her personal feelings weren't important here. It shouldn't matter if Sam liked her or not. She only needed his support.

"Don't worry. There's lots of house to go around. We hardly have to see each other. I can stand it if you can." Besides, there were lines she didn't cross, ever, and it was a big leap from noticing the fit of a man's jeans to personal involvement. They rubbed each other the wrong way. Then she remembered how he'd brushed by her the other night and how her body had suddenly become attuned to his. The real trouble was in the few moments where they had rubbed each other exactly the right way. At least on Saturday there would be tons of other people around and she'd be too busy keeping the kids busy and the food on the go to worry about Sam.

They were at the fence gate now and there wasn't much left to say. He threw the reins up over the saddle horn and mounted, settling into the saddle with a creak of leather. "I'm not afraid," he said. "Two hours. I'll give you two hours Saturday afternoon to talk to whatever press you've lined up. Just keep your social-worker analysis to yourself, okay? I'm not interested. Save it for your clients."

"Scouts' honor," she replied, lifting two fingers to her brow. She couldn't help the smile that curved her lips. It wasn't all she'd asked for, but more than she'd dare hoped and she counted it as a significant victory. Perhaps she'd be spared the public face after all.

He shook his head and gave the horse a nudge. As they were walking away he twisted in the saddle, looking back at her. "I'll send over a check. I'd advise you to cash it before

I change my mind and stop payment on it. Maybe you can cater your food for Saturday with it."

He showed her his back again and they took off at a trot, stirring up dust.

Sam looked up from his desk and realized it was nearly dark outside. That meant... He checked his watch. It was going on ten o'clock. He'd been at it longer than he realized. But he wanted to start the construction on the new project before the end of summer, marking a new era for Diamondback. As he got older the more he realized he was caretaker not only of the Diamondback name but the land. The environmentally friendly initiatives were exciting, and he loved the idea of reducing Diamondback's footprint. But his father's stubborn refusal to sign off on the contracts was stressing him out.

He sighed, rubbed a hand over his face. It grated on his nerves, having the responsibility of the ranch without also having the authority to make the changes he wanted. And with Virgil's health so precarious, he was doing some fancy footwork these days trying to get his way without upsetting the proverbial apple cart. Between his father and the everyday running of the ranch, he hadn't been lying when he'd told Angela that he didn't have a moment to spare.

But then she'd had to go and challenge him and he'd been suckered in. It rankled that she knew how to push his buttons without really knowing him at all. He didn't think he was usually so transparent.

She'd looked exhausted. There was the annoying realization that she'd been right in just about everything. A Diamond family member *had* promised to appear and her assertion that Butterfly House would need community support was valid.

But for Sam it had been more than that. It had been the look in her eyes, the way all the color had leached from her cheeks in the split second he'd grasped her wrist within his fingers. The expression had been enough to give even his jaded heart a wrench. There was more to Angela than the prim and proper businesswoman he'd met at the board meeting. This was personal for her and he wanted to know why.

He scowled. It was none of his business. The last thing he needed was to get sucked into someone else's problems. If only his mother would agree to a hired nurse, she could go back to being Angela's right hand and cheerleader. He worried about Molly, taking on all of his father's care herself and refusing any help. With a sigh he closed his eyes. He was trying to hold everything together and not doing a great job of it.

A light knock sounded at the door and he turned in his chair. "Mom. You're still up?"

Molly Diamond came in, and Sam thought she looked older than she had a few short weeks ago. There were new lines around her eyes and mouth, and she'd lost weight. The light sweater she wore seemed to hang from her shoulders.

"I just got your father settled. You're up late."

"Just going over the latest information on the biogas facility. I'm close to finally having the details nailed down. The sooner the better, we've had enough delays. I'm excited about it."

"Sam…" Molly's brow furrowed. "Right now those plans are more like building castles in the sand."

"Then help me convince him," he replied easily. "He won't listen to me. This will take Diamondback into the future."

"What sort of future? Who for, Sam?"

There it was again. The constant tone that said *when are you going to start a family?* Surely she realized it wasn't a simple snap of the fingers to find the right woman. There had to be love. Whoever he married was taking on not only him but Diamondback as well. He gritted his teeth. "Two different subjects, Mom. And right now this facility is the right thing."

Molly sighed. "It's a big undertaking. And your father sacrificed a lot to make Diamondback what it is. He's just... cautious. Please don't trouble him about it. Not now."

"It's the way of the future. And I've spent a lot of hours putting this together." Disappointment was clear in his voice.

"And it's taking its toll," she said, coming to the desk and pulling up a chair. The desk lamp cast a circle of cozy light and despite the recent troubles, Sam thought how lucky he was to have grown up here. It hadn't always been easy, and there'd been a good many arguments and slammed doors, especially in younger years.

But he'd never once questioned their love, never once felt insecure. He thought of Angela, standing in the farmyard in paint-smeared, shapeless overalls and dark glasses. He wondered what her upbringing had been like, thought about the women who would benefit from Butterfly House. Not everyone had had the advantages that he'd had.

"What's really on your mind, Sam?"

"Nothing, really. Just trying to keep up."

"You met Angela Beck," Molly said, leaning back against the cushion of the chair and crossing her legs. "She's a worker."

"A dog with a bone, more like it," he muttered. Molly laughed and it was good to hear the sound. Ever since she'd found his father on the floor of their bedroom after his stroke, there hadn't been much to laugh about.

"She's doing a good thing, Sam."

"I know. But you're much better at this kind of thing than I am. I belong out there." He lifted his chin, looking out the window. In the darkness, only the reflection from the lamp looked back at him. "We totally rub each other the wrong way. We can't occupy the same space without arguing. I have intentions of being nice, and I end up being an idiot."

To his surprise Molly laughed. "At least you acknowledge when you're an idiot," she answered, "which puts you a step ahead of most of the population."

"Mom, why don't you let me hire some help for you?" He leaned forward, resting his elbows on the desk. "Then you can still work on this project. It'll be good for you." Plus it would mean he wouldn't be pulled away from the farm, and he wouldn't have to come face-to-face with Angela's acute observations—never mind her smoky eyes and delicious curves. She'd tried to hide them in the overalls, but they were still there. He didn't like that he kept noticing. Didn't like that she seemed to be on his mind more often than not.

"Because I want to be with your father." Molly looked tired, but Sam noticed how her eyes warmed. "You'll understand someday, when you're married and you've been in love with that person for most of your life."

Sam sighed. "Mom, I'm thirty-seven. Don't count on it, okay? At this rate, Ty's your best chance for a grandkid."

Ty. Sam's cousin by blood but also his adoptive brother. Any child of his would be considered a grandchild. But Ty was barely on speaking terms with the family. Neither said it but they knew it was true. He hadn't even come home for Virgil's seventieth birthday.

"I'm not saying that, don't panic. I'm just saying that I need to do this for Virgil. And that leaves Butterfly House up to you. It's not a long commitment. Once it's fixed up, the management of it will be in Angela's fine hands. A board meeting here and there is not too much to ask."

"You failed to mention the open house this weekend. She was here today, demanding I show up."

Molly put a hand to her head. "Oh, my word, I'd forgotten

about that. I promised to help. We wrote the press releases together, before your dad…"

Her voice broke and Sam's heart gave a lurch. "It's okay. I told her I'd show up and do all the official handshaking. But, Mom, I can't go on doing this forever. I'm too busy. Maybe Dad will improve enough that you can step back in after a month or so," Sam suggested, shutting his folder.

"Maybe. But, Sam…"

He looked into Molly's dark eyes, eyes that reminded him of who he saw in the mirror. She was the strongest woman he knew, and he liked to think he'd inherited some of that strength.

"You've been brought up to believe that Diamondback is everything, but it's not, not really. Sometimes I think your Dad and I sheltered you too much, made it too easy on you. We wanted things to be better for you than they were for us starting out, but you've never really seen what it's like to be hurting, and struggling, and wondering if life will ever be good again."

"So this is for my own good?"

She chuckled. "You'll thank me one day, you'll see."

"Don't count on it." But he couldn't help the smile that curved his lips.

"I know you didn't sign up for this, Sam. But it would mean a lot to me if you could help out." Molly put her hands on the arms of the chair and boosted herself up. She gave a small stretch. "Well, I'm off to make a cup of tea before bed. Tomorrow's another day."

"I think I'll look in on Dad before I turn in."

"He was awake when I left. He lives for your updates, Sam. I know you're butting heads right now, but keep talking. He needs you. He needs to feel a part of this place."

Sam nodded, clicked off the light and followed his mother to the office door. They parted ways in the hall—Molly to the kitchen, Sam to the main level spare room, where his parents had slept ever since Virgil's stroke.

When he looked in, his father was asleep. Sam's heart gave a hitch. His larger-than-life father was reduced to a bed and a wheelchair. His words were muffled and unclear and he seemed so different from the giant who had slain boyhood dragons, from the man who had built this ranch, living for—and off—the land.

Now it was all up to Sam.

He could understand his father going crazy. He could even understand why Virgil was fighting so hard to remain in control. Because Sam couldn't imagine a day where he didn't wake up under a Diamondback sky and smell the Diamondback air. Why couldn't Virgil see they were fighting for the same thing?

# CHAPTER FOUR

THE smell of paint hung in the air as Angela took another pin out of the curtain hem and carefully kept her foot on the pedal of the sewing machine. She'd planned simple curtains, tab-style that would thread through the pretty café rods she'd bought. Maybe it was the fabric that was causing the trouble, or maybe it was the fact that she'd been up and working for nearly twelve hours. Either way, she'd ripped out two seams already, and then indulged in an uncharacteristic spate of cursing when the bobbin thread tangled on the bottom.

She reversed, finished the seam, cut the threads and closed her eyes. There was still so much to do before Saturday. She was never going to make it this way.

"Is it safe to come in?"

She started in her chair as the deep voice echoed down the hall. "Sam?"

"None other." The screen door thumped into the frame and she pressed a hand to her pounding chest. She shouldn't be so jumpy, but it was an automatic reaction she'd been conditioned to years ago.

She hastily folded the fabric and put it on the kitchen table with the rest of the sewing bits. What on earth was he doing here? She hadn't expected to see him until Saturday afternoon.

His boots thumped on the wood floor and suddenly there

he was, larger than life, in his customary jeans and boots but he'd traded his button-down shirt for a black T-shirt. The way the cotton stretched across his chest made her want to rest her hands against the surface to see if it was indeed as hard as it looked.

"What in the world?" His eyes widened as he took in the sight of the table.

She followed the path of his gaze. Not a glimpse of wood table was visible beneath the strewn-out cloth, pins and thread. More fabric hung over the back of one of the chairs and Morris batted a scrap along the floor, too entranced with the way it slithered over the tile to worry about Sam's presence.

"I'm not a neat seamstress," she remarked.

"I hope you have something else for me to do," he said, folding his arms. "Though I've been known to pick up a needle and thread before."

Angela swallowed. She tried to picture him in a chair, a tiny needle in his strong, wide hands, and it wouldn't gel. Sam was more untamed than that. She looked up at his glittering eyes and decided *untamed* was a good word indeed. There was a restless energy about him that made her uneasy. Especially when what she needed from him was reliability.

He shrugged. "Of course, I'm usually stitching together hide and not dainties."

She would hardly call the blue damask *dainties*, but she didn't bother correcting him as now her mind was full of the image of him doctoring horses and cows. He was stubborn as a mule—she could see that plain as day. But she couldn't shake the idea that he'd treat his animals with capable and gentle hands.

Oh, dear. It wasn't a good idea to think of Sam Diamond in those terms. He was already looking a little too attractive.

"Do?"

"Yes, do. You didn't finish everything on your list, did you?"

Gracious, no. There was still lots to be done, but his sudden presence threw her utterly off balance. "I wasn't expecting you," she stammered.

"I thought you could use some help before the big day."

She kept her mouth shut for once, biting down on her lip and feeling a bit bad for all the nasty thoughts she'd had about him. She scrambled to come up with something he could do on the spur of the moment.

"Of course I can use the help. Um…I'm not exactly sure where to start."

"I brought some tools and supplies in the truck," he suggested, resting his weight on one hip. "You mentioned the other day that the porch steps and floor needed some work. Maybe I could tighten them up, replace a few boards. I don't think anything's rotted, but I won't know until I have a good look. In any case, you can't paint until it's repaired."

"That'd be fine," she replied, relieved he'd thought ahead and she wouldn't have to show him anything. It also meant he'd paid attention and given it some thought. It was what she'd wanted, right? For him to notice that Butterfly House needed help? So why was getting what she wanted making her so flustered?

"It'll give me a chance to clean up in here. I finished painting the blue room today. Your mother helped me pick out the fabric. That's what I'm sewing…"

"My mother and I have different skill sets."

She smiled, trying to imagine Sam debating the benefits of certain colors and fabrics or chatting about recipes. The image didn't fit. But visualizing him using his hands was something entirely different. For all his untamed energy and irritating ways, Angela was beginning to see that Sam was the kind of man who formed foundations. He shored up the weak spots and made them strong—at Diamondback and now here. She didn't want to be relieved at passing off even just a little of the responsibility, but she was, just the same.

"I'm happy to have your skills, since I'm not adept at construction. Some light carpentry work would be wonderful, Sam, thank you."

The words were friendly and for a moment neither of them said anything. Friendliness was a new vibe between them and Angela didn't quite know what to do with it. But wasn't it better than being at each other's throats all the time? If they could make peace, maybe this tight feeling in her chest that happened every time he was around would disappear.

"If I need anything I'll give a shout."

"I'll be here."

He treated her to one long, last look before turning on his heel. He was out of sight when he called out.

"Oh, and Angela? Be careful. You smiled just now. You might want to get that checked."

She balled her fingers into fists as the door shut behind him. Oh, he was impossible! Just when she thought they were coming to some common ground, he had to provoke her again. And yet there'd been a teasing note in his voice that made warmth seep into her. It was foreign, but it wasn't an unwelcome feeling.

She folded the finished panel and yanked out the second, all pinned and ready for stitching. At least he was out there and she was in here and she didn't have to look into his sexy, teasing face!

But the sound of the hammer could be heard over the hum of the machine, and Angela's brows knit together. Sam Diamond was not going to be an easy man to ignore.

He was still working on the porch when she finished pressing the last completed panel. Carefully she laid the curtains over the ironing board so they wouldn't wrinkle and tidied up her sewing mess. Twilight was starting to fall and he'd soon have to quit as he lost the light. Angela took a breath, considered, and then went to the fridge for the jug of lemonade she'd mixed up earlier. She poured two glasses and started for the front door. Whatever her misgivings where Sam was concerned, it would be nice if at Saturday's event they appeared as a team rather than on opposing sides. In hindsight, the incident earlier in the week had been pure overreaction on her part. Sam had made the first step coming here today. Now it was her turn.

She opened the screen door with a flick of her finger and a nudge of her hip. Sam looked up and for a moment Angela's heart seemed to hesitate as their gazes locked. There was a gleam of sweat on his forehead and as he stood, he hooked his hammer into his tool belt, a thoroughly masculine move that sent her heart rate fluttering.

*Oh, my.*

She'd never been particularly susceptible to the rugged workingman type before, but Sam was in a class of his own. And when he smiled and asked, "Is that for me?" the only thing she could do was extend her hand and give him the glass, careful not to let their fingers touch.

She held her own lemonade in her hand, forgotten, as he took two big swallows, tipping his head back so that she could see the movement in his throat. Her tongue snuck out to wet her lips. She'd bet any money the skin on his neck was salty and warm from his hard work.

He lowered the glass and Angela snapped out of her stupor, hiding her face behind her own drink as she took a sip. She was no better than the other women in town, was she? There was no denying that Sam had a certain appeal, but she'd always prided herself on being immune to such things. She'd always been a "keep your eye on the prize" kind of girl—that philosophy had held her in good stead through many, many difficult years.

And so it would now, too. Besides, Sam wasn't interested in her. He'd made enough disparaging comments during their first few meetings for her to know that she was not his type.

"Thanks, that hits the spot," he said, leaning against the porch post.

"I finished my sewing and thought you might be thirsty," she replied. She'd just go inside now before she embarrassed herself. She consoled her pride with the fact that she was human, after all, and her eyes were in perfect working order. It was nothing more than that. She turned on her heel but his voice stopped her.

"Stay. The boards are sound now and I dusted the cobwebs off the chairs."

The invitation was tempting. Sitting in the warm purple twilight with Sam Diamond and sipping tart lemonade sounded like a good way to end the day. Too good. "That's okay. I still have things to finish up inside."

She dared look up at him, and she was surprised to see concern softening his hard features.

"You've been burning the candle at both ends." He moved his hand, gesturing at the chair. "Let it wait until tomorrow."

She raised an eyebrow. Did he want to spend time with her? Had he cleaned off the chairs for this specific reason? Her heart sped up thinking about it. Besides, Sam was a bit of pot calling kettle. "Would you leave it 'til tomorrow if you had things left to do?"

Delicious crinkles formed at the corners of his eyes as he gave a small smile of acquiescence. "Touché."

But he was right, she admitted to herself. She had been working hard and she knew part of her sewing trouble had come from being tired and inattentive. "Well, maybe just for a minute."

She took her glass and sat in one of the Adirondack chairs, letting out a sigh as she sank into the curved wooden back. They needed scraping and repainting like everything else, but for right now it was perfect. Sam likewise sat, took off his hat, and stretched out his impossibly long legs. He took a sip of what was left of his lemonade and turned his head to look at her.

"Can I ask you a question?"

A mourning dove set up a lonely call and Angela rested her head against the chair. "It depends."

"Is this project personal for you?"

She turned her head and studied his face. When his gaze met hers, she knew. He'd guessed. The invitation to sit had been deliberate, she knew that now. And she was scrambling to come up with an appropriate answer that would appease him and yet tell him nothing. Her hesitation spun out, weaving a web around them consisting of what she didn't say rather than what she did.

Finally she sighed. "Of course it is. I've put a lot of energy into it. I couldn't have done that if I weren't committed to its success."

Sam put his glass on the arm of the chair. "That's not what I meant."

"I know," she admitted, meeting his gaze.

"The other day, when I grabbed your arm…"

She saw his Adam's apple bob as he swallowed. A sinking feeling weighed down her chest. Was that why he was here tonight? Guilt?

"Don't worry about it," she murmured, lowering her eyes.

"I can't stop thinking about it." His voice was husky now in the semi-darkness and it sneaked past her defenses, making her vulnerable. She didn't want him to care. Didn't need him to. And yet it felt nice to have someone see beyond the image she showed the world every day.

"All the color drained from your face, and your eyes..." He cleared his throat. "You recovered quickly, but not before I saw. And it suddenly made sense. I'm sorry, Angela. I never meant to frighten you."

He met her gaze fully now, and she was surprised at the honesty in his eyes. He looked different without his hat—more approachable, more casual. Probably too casual to be sitting here alone with her. And now they were sharing something. It created an intimacy that felt a little too good. It would be so much easier if she could simply treat Sam like a client! She never lost her objectivity with clients.

"Is that why you came back? Because you feel guilty? Because it was nothing, Sam, really."

He hesitated. "It made me think about what you said about the foundation, that's all. Put it... Well, put it into context, I suppose."

It was a good answer and Angela leaned her head back against the chair. It felt odd to be talking and not butting heads, but good. It was progress. His voice was quiet and hopeful and it touched Angela's heart. She'd accused him of not wanting to face the ugliness of life, but here he was anyway. On some level he cared.

But could he handle her personal "context"? She doubted it. Nor did she care to tell it, so she tailored her response to satisfy his curiosity while only truly skimming the surface. She didn't want to go all the way back. Not ever.

"Before I became a social worker, I found myself in a bad situation, yes. But I left. So you see I'm not so bad off after all. You just took me by surprise the other day.

"Did he...you know. Hit you?" He struggled over the words.

How to answer? Her story was not simple or easy. She could see where his assumptions were leading him and it was probably the easiest, cleanest way out. "Once," she admitted, hearing the crack in her voice. She cleared her throat. "It had been bad for a while, but after he hit me I left."

It barely scratched the surface of her tangled history but it did the trick. "So when I grabbed your wrist...it was thoughtless, Angela. I'm sorry."

"It was the reaction of a moment. And already forgotten. Don't worry about it." She tried a smile that didn't quite feel genuine.

"I'm glad," he replied. "The last thing I'd want to do is..."

He let the thought trail off, but it didn't matter. She understood. This was a different Sam and Angela wasn't sure what to do with the change. Being aware of his physical attributes was one thing. But starting to *like* him? Bad news. All the same, she needed him as an ally. She wanted to trust him—especially this Sam, who was currently without the self-important edge she'd sensed from him at the beginning. A man who was thoughtful and caring.

But she didn't want to be the foundation's poster child. Rather she wanted him to make the connection to the women who would call this place home. She felt a moment of sadness, wishing her mother could be one of those women. She knew it would never happen, but she couldn't extinguish the tiny spark of hope that still flared from time to time.

"The women coming here have gone through the hardest part—leaving their particular situation. Now they're ready to rebuild their lives and need a nudge and helping hand to get started. Our first resident is already lined up. Once she's settled our first task will be to help her find a job. When our residents are on their way to a new life, then they'll go out on their own."

"Like a butterfly out of a cocoon."

"Yes, exactly like that." She smiled, glad he'd connected the dots. "We hope they'll leave with a little cash in their pockets, as well as some confidence and hope for the future."

Silence fell for a few minutes as the shadows deepened. Angela sipped her drink while they watched a pair of squirrels race through the yard and up a poplar tree. She was ever aware of Sam sitting next to her, the length of his long, strong legs, the way his T-shirt sleeves revealed tanned, strong forearms. He'd reached out tonight. Nothing could have surprised—or pleased—her more. Even if it had cost her a corner of her privacy.

"It's a good program," he admitted.

Sam was saying all the right things, but there was a little voice in the back of her head saying that she shouldn't be too quick to believe. All her training, all her life experience had taught her that she had to be clear-headed and objective. To feel compassion and a need to help, but not to insert her personal feelings into a situation.

"This situation," Sam said carefully, "was he your husband?"

"No," she replied, making the word deliberately definite so as to close the subject. She kept her private life private. She'd learned to be skeptical years ago, somewhere between the fear and the anger. Home life had been frightening and fraught with anxiety. Sam's question made her feel that he could somehow see right past her barriers and it made her uneasy. No one needed to know how personal this cause truly was to her heart. How close she'd come to history repeating itself before she got out.

She couldn't meet his eyes now. She'd always made a point of judging what she saw, but she hadn't with Sam. She'd formed an opinion because of things she'd heard and then read that into her impression of him rather than giving him the benefit of the doubt. She didn't very much like what that said about her.

* * *

Sam watched Angela lower her eyes. He knew very well he hadn't made a good impression the first few times they'd met, but he was trying to make up for it. His reasons for being abrasive in the beginning had been his own stress talking. But his sincere questions tonight had taken the snap and sparkle out of her eyes. He found he missed it.

"You're doing a good thing here, Angela."

"I'm pleased you think so." She looked up briefly.

"I'm not a liar, and I wasn't trying to be mean before. I do have my hands full—we're trying to finalize details on a biogas facility at the ranch. Let's just say it hasn't gone as smoothly as I'd like. I haven't had many moments to spare. I probably could have been more tactful." He offered a smile, hoping to change the subject. He didn't like seeing her look so sad.

"Biogas?"

Gratified she'd taken the bait, he continued. "We can turn our organic waste into energy. Specifically, enough energy to run our entire operation and then some without touching the power grid. But it's newer technology and it doesn't come cheap." Even talking about it made him excited. The initial capital was what his father kept harping on, but Sam knew their coffers could take it. The reason for his dad's worry he suspected was not as black and white and had to be handled more delicately. And Sam wasn't used to dealing that way. There'd been a lot of adjustments since his father's sudden illness.

"You? A 'green' farmer? I never would have guessed it."

"I get the feeling that you formed a lot of opinions about me that may turn out to be wrong."

She blushed a little and he watched the way the breeze ruffled her hair in the increasing darkness. The last of the June bugs were starting to hit the porch door as the light from within glowed through the rectangular window.

"Our ranch has been in the family for generations. Each new generation bears a responsibility—to the family, to the land. I'm nothing but a steward, until..."

"Until the next generation? But aren't you an only child?"

He rested his elbows on his knees. "Yep."

It was the one way he knew he'd disappointed the family, but he refused to enter into a marriage that wasn't real, that wasn't based on love and respect. He was probably foolish and an idealist, but that was where he drew the line. He imagined admitting such a thing to Angela. He suspected she'd laugh in his face. It was rather sentimental, he supposed. He wanted the kind of marriage his parents had.

The only reason he hadn't pushed harder about the development was that Virgil's stroke had made Sam suddenly aware of the fact that his dad—who'd always seemed invincible—wouldn't always be there with him. Coming to terms with that was a hard pill to swallow.

"You've gone quiet all of a sudden."

He smacked his hands on his knees and pushed himself to standing. "Just tired. I should get a move on." *Before I say too much*, he thought. He was finding her far too easy to talk to.

"I appreciate the help tonight, Sam. I know you're busy."

He chuckled. "That must have been hard for you to say."

"Maybe a little." Her lips twitched. "I probably haven't been entirely fair. If we hadn't sent out press releases and set up media..."

"It's okay. I handed off a few things to my foreman. It's a few days, nothing more. I'll manage."

Angela drained what was left of the lemonade from her glass and stood up. "Well, thanks for coming. At least I won't have to worry about anyone falling through the porch on Saturday."

"No problem." He picked up his glass and followed her

into the house. He put it in the sink as Angela draped the blue
curtains over her arm. "You don't have more to do?" he said,
hooking his thumbs in his pockets.

"Just hang these curtains. I have to put them up tonight
because I don't want to fold them and crease the fabric, and I
can't leave them out or Morris will be sure to have fun playing in the material hanging over the ironing board."

Ah, the devilish Morris. Sam figured he should consider
it an achievement that he'd gone from being bitten to simply
being ignored. The cat was nowhere to be seen. "I'll give you
a hand."

"No, really..."

"Which room?"

She met his gaze and he knew she was exhausted when
she gave in without too much of a fight.

"Upstairs, first door on the left."

# CHAPTER FIVE

ANGELA followed Sam up the stairs, staying a few steps behind and trying to avoid looking at the worn patches on his jeans. She failed utterly. They'd learned more about each other tonight and it had created some common ground—ground that Angela wasn't sure she was comfortable treading. He was far harder to dismiss when he was like this.

"Do you have the rods installed?" Sam's deep voice shimmered in the darkness of the stairway. How he could sound so good saying something so banal was impressive. She pushed the reaction to the side and told herself to remain focused on practicalities.

"They're not up yet. They're ready though, and my tool box is in the closet." They reached the landing and Angela let out a sigh of relief as they emerged from the confined space of the stairway. "Here we are. Hang on and I'll flip on a light. The last bracket I installed I made a mess of and had to fix the drywall."

They stepped inside the room and she hit the switch. Light from the overhead fixture lit up the room and she looked at Sam, standing there with soft blue fabric draped over his arms. It looked out of place against his tanned masculinity, and the effect of the contrast was appealing. She paused to enjoy the picture. She might be immune to his charms but she could still appreciate his finer points. And they were *very* fine.

"Let me take those from you," she murmured. "This will only take a minute or two."

She moved to take the panels from his arms and as he slipped them into her hands their fingers touched. His were warm and rough and it tripped her personal distance alarm big-time. The tips of his fingers grazed the inside of her wrist and butterflies winged their way through her stomach as she snatched her fingers away.

Okay. The last thing she expected to feel around Sam Diamond was this flicker of physical awareness. She slid the fabric the rest of the way out of his hands and stepped back. She wasn't sure if he had touched her deliberately or not. But she was positive of one thing. He couldn't ever know that he affected her in any way. She simply didn't *do* touching. It hit too many triggers.

Instead she inhaled, and counted to ten as she exhaled.

Sam didn't seem to notice her reaction; instead he looked around the room. Angela felt an expanding sense of pride. "It's pretty, isn't it?" she asked, seeking level emotional ground again.

"The color—it looks like something my mother would pick out. Like the old chinaware she's got."

Angela smiled. "She did pick out the color, and the material, too. I think it's kind of classic, don't you?"

"She's classic," he replied, smiling, and Angela tried to ignore the way his eyes warmed when he spoke about Molly. Sam was clearly devoted to his mama, and he always spoke of her with love and respect. But Angela had to wonder if there was a reason why someone as handsome and well-established as Sam hadn't been snapped up off the market? He was a good-looking, successful guy. Amy had said that he'd given her a line about not wanting to lead her on and give her false expectations and made it sound as if it was merely an excuse to be rid of her. Angela now wondered if he'd been sincere while ending the relationship, and if the wonderful example Molly set had created a standard that other women simply couldn't live up to.

Not that she was inclined to try to reach the mark herself. She'd never really bought into that idea of married bliss, two halves of one whole and the whole nine yards. So far she'd done just fine on her own.

"Well, the curtains are the finishing touch. Shall we?" She nodded toward the two large windows on the north wall, suddenly impatient to see the final effect. Looking around the room, she was struck once more with a sense of satisfaction. She'd done a good job here if she did say so herself. The hardwood only needed a good cleaning and polishing and then Angela was leaving the room be. The women would want to put their things there, make the space their own. She knew very well how important it felt to have a say. For years she'd been forced to keep her room just so. She'd longed to change the paper, the color, put things on the walls. None of it was allowed. She'd never been able to have anything that smacked of individuality. But the residents here deserved a room of their own for the duration of their stay, and she was determined that they would get it.

"The rods are in the closet. Just a sec." She laid the curtains over the bed and went to get the café rods and her toolbox. In a few short minutes Sam had measured, marked and screwed the brackets to the wall. Angela slid the tabs over the rod and stood on tiptoe, arms above her head, holding it steady while Sam threaded the rod through the hole and screwed the decorative finial on the end. As he reached to do the other side, his hands slid over hers. The electricity from the touch rocketed through Angela's body and she lowered her hands quickly, stepping away from the window. That wasn't supposed to happen again!

This reaction—this attraction—was just wrong on so many levels. She didn't even want to like him, let alone feel...what was it she was feeling, anyway? Desire? It couldn't be. Desire meant wanting, and she didn't want this. She didn't know what to do with it.

It was just some weird chemistry thing. It must be, because nothing like this had ever happened to her before. Touches, even simple ones, always made her want to shy away. But Sam's left her wanting more and that scared her to death.

And there was still another curtain to contend with.

There was no sound in the room now and it put Angela more on edge. Did he know what he was doing to her? Was he playing a game? The moments ticked by and she wished he'd say something. If he provoked her she could at least respond. As it was she was beginning to think that he'd felt it too. Heavens, one of them being jumpy was enough. It was easier to deal with him when he was teasing or baiting her. In the silence her body still hummed from the innocent contact.

It was akin to torture to lift her arms again, holding the rod while he threaded it through the first side. She inhaled a shaky breath, Sam looked down at her, and the finial dropped to the floor and rolled a few feet away.

"Hang on," he said, his voice soft and husky. She stood, frozen to the spot while he retrieved the curled knob, and when he came back to put the second end through the bracket he stood behind her, his hands raised above hers as he reached for the rod.

His chest pressed gently against her back and she shivered, aware that with her arms up her breasts were very accessible. All he'd have to do was slide his hands down over her shoulders and he could be touching her. There was a pause—just a breath—but she was as aware of a man's body as she'd ever been. She was trapped in the circle of his arms, blocked by his body, telling herself she had no reason to be afraid and yet trembling just the same. There was an intimacy here that she wasn't prepared for. And yet neither of them had spoken a word or made an overt move.

She couldn't breathe. She had to get out of here, get away from the hard warmth of his body and his scent…oh, for goodness' sake, when did the smell of fresh-cut lumber and lemon become so appealing? "Have you got it?" she asked, hoping her voice didn't sound as shaky as she felt.

"I've got it," he replied.

She let go of the curtain rod as though it was burning her hands and slid out from beneath his arm. The air around her cooled and she exhaled with relief. What surprised her most was the empty sense of disappointment that rushed in where moments ago desire and fear had battled.

He cleared his throat and resumed screwing the finials on the rod as if nothing had happened. When he was done, he smoothed out the panel so that it lay flat. "There you go," he said, turning around.

When she looked at him something seemed to snap in the air between them. All it would take was one step and she could feel the heat of his body again. One step and she could explore the sensations that rocketed through her body when he was near. She saw his eyes widen as the moment spun out and the air seemed to ripple between them. He was so powerful, so forceful without any effort, and Angela knew he could swallow up a little wallflower like her in the blink of an eye.

"That's unexpected," he acknowledged quietly, and Angela wished he'd never spoken at all.

"I don't know what you mean," she countered, picking up the screwdriver and dropping it in the toolbox, hoping it would put him off. Being close to him set off tons of personal boundary alarms, but the truly terrifying thing for Angela was her own betraying reaction to him. She was back to not trusting herself or her judgment, and it made her stomach twist sickeningly. She'd made too many mistakes to risk making another.

"I mean whatever it was that just happened." He pursued the subject, and she wished he'd just shut up and let the matter drop. "And it obviously scares you to death. I suppose, considering your past..."

She forced herself to face him, schooling her features into what she hoped was an unreadable mask. This was why she didn't talk about her own history. Suddenly it defined her and everything she did. "All that happened here is that you helped me install some curtain rods. And that's all that can happen, Mr. Diamond," she added significantly.

The corner of his mouth turned up. "So we're back to Mr. Diamond again. You're plenty rattled."

"Are there no bounds to your ego?" She snapped out the question, but it stung because he was one-hundred-percent right. Had he provoked her deliberately in those long moments when he'd let his chest ride so close to her back? She didn't want to think so. Whether it had been intentional or not, she'd fallen for it. She straightened her spine. Now she felt vulnerable *and* ridiculous, not to mention transparent. "I appreciate all of your help with the project, but if you're looking for more than that..."

"Ms. Beck." He took a step closer and her heart started beating strangely again. "I have just about all I can handle with Diamondback and my other commitments. I'm not 'looking for' anything."

"Then..."

The rest of the question was silently asked. What was going on between them? The pause deepened and so did his dimple. "What do *you* propose we do about it?"

"Do about it?" There was a definite squeak in her voice now and she wasn't sure if it was fear or anticipation. She cleared her throat. "We don't do anything. You're the one playing games, Sam."

"I don't play games," he replied, standing taller. "You don't strike me as someone into casual relationships, Angela." His smile faded. "And I'm not looking for anything serious. So that pretty much takes care of that, right? We'll just forget it ever happened."

"Right," she parroted, so completely off balance now she wasn't entirely sure what he was saying and what he wasn't. She didn't do casual relationships because she didn't do *any* relationships. She could never let anyone close enough. Not that he needed to know that.

"Now if you'll excuse me, it's getting late and I'm sure we both need our rest."

"Of course."

He brushed by her. Moments later she heard his truck door slam and the engine start. She sagged, resting her flaming cheek against the cool blue wall, watching through the window as he drove away.

He'd been utterly sincere in his last words. So why didn't Angela quite believe him? He'd certainly been in an all-fired hurry to leave.

He was right about one thing—she was dog-tired. But she suspected sleep would be a long time coming tonight. Sam Diamond had a way of challenging everything. And what freaked her out the most was realizing that even knowing her past, he hadn't run. She had.

Sam pushed his mount harder over the trail, enjoying the feel of the wide-open gallop and the wind on his face. Nothing had prepared him for the jolt he'd suffered the moment his body had touched Angela's. And then she'd had the nerve to accuse him of playing games.

It had bothered him ever since he'd left her standing in the bedroom, her face pale and her greeny-blue eyes huge as they stared at him. He couldn't get her off his mind. He could still see the spark in her eyes. He'd seen something else, too—fear. She was afraid of him and he'd had the strangest desire to pull her into his arms and tell her it was all right.

Knowing her past, though, made him question every action, wondering how it would appear to her. So instead of following his instincts, he'd got himself out of there. Angela wasn't a woman he could trifle with. And anything more than trifling scared him witless.

To top it off, his father had truly dug in his heels about the biogas facility, flat-out refusing to sign any papers so they could release the money and begin construction. Sam had been so angry he'd nearly yelled at Virgil—a man still recovering from a stroke. He'd managed to hold on to his temper, but it had only taken one small mention of Power of Attorney and Virgil's eyes had blazed at him. Despite his verbal difficulties he had very clearly made his point as he shouted, "Not crazy!"

Sam had slammed out the door instead, deciding that a good, old-fashioned hell-bent-for-leather ride was in order to work off the tension. Nothing was going right. Everything felt unsettled and off balance. Every attempt he made at holding the family together was a flop. He'd come terribly close to telling his father to start walking and get back where he belonged, but he'd reined in his emotions. It wasn't Virgil's fault. It wasn't anyone's fault. They were all just trying to *cope the best they knew how.*

His horse started to lather and Sam knew he couldn't push him any harder.

As he started over the crest of the hill, Sam stared at the

flat parcel of land marked with surveyor's stakes. Seeing it waiting, so empty and perfect, made his shoulders tense. He was a grown man, for God's sake. A man who could make his own decisions, not a boy beneath his father's thumb. The whole issue made him feel impotent and ineffectual. Was this how Ty had felt before he'd taken off for parts unknown? Once more Sam wished his cousin were here to talk things over with. It wasn't the same with him gone.

The more nagging problem was that he was still thinking about Angela. That wasn't a good sign.

He slowed and let the gelding walk, the restlessness unabated in himself. He remembered the guarded look on her face as she'd admitted she'd gotten out of a bad relationship. Something had happened in that moment. More than knowledge—he'd guessed as much when she'd blanched after he'd grabbed her wrist. It was something else.

It was trust. And the moment in the bedroom had taken that delicate trust and shattered it. Maybe she was right. Maybe he had played games because he'd indulged in the attraction even knowing their connection was fragile at best.

He dug his heels into the gelding's side. He needed to get away from here for a while, clear his head. The least he could do was make it up to her, right?

Angela counted down the hours. Less than twenty-four now and everyone would be here. A reporter and photographer from the local paper, someone from the town council, even the Member of the Legislature was slated to attend. The very idea of being front and center made her lightheaded with dread, but she reminded herself that it was part of her job. And with Sam here, she could stay under the radar.

The more important problem was that she didn't even have a chair for them to sit on beyond the somewhat scarred table and chairs in the kitchen. Somehow she had to get the sofa and chairs from the garage into the living room without scuffing the new floor.

She was struggling with the first armchair when she heard the steady growl of a truck engine. She peered over the top of the chair and saw Sam's face behind the wheel, cowboy hat and sunglasses shading his face. Her heart began pounding and she nearly dropped the chair. What was he doing here? After the curtain incident she'd been sure he wouldn't be back. And she'd considered that just as well.

He got out of the truck, shut the door, and took off the glasses, letting them dangle from one hand for a moment before folding them up and tucking them into the neck of his shirt. Oh, boy. He was Trouble with a capital *T*. Maybe he'd shown a softer side the other night, but it hadn't exactly ended well. So what was he doing back here?

He knocked on the screen door as Angela's arms started to scream in protest. She waddled the half-dozen steps it took to get into the living room and put the chair down as Sam called, "Angela?"

She brushed her hands off and walked to the door, trying to steady her pace and her pulse. "Sam. What on earth?"

"It occurred to me you might be a bit shorthanded trying to get ready for tomorrow."

Shorthanded. So he was only here to help? She paused, torn between needing his help and needing to be honest. "You left in an awful hurry the other night. I didn't expect to see you until tomorrow."

He looked at her through the screen door, watching her steadily and making her feel about two inches tall. How could she turn away a pair of willing, strong hands?

He held out the appendages in question. "And yet here I am."

"Aren't you too busy at Diamondback?"

"I needed to get away for a bit. Got in the truck and ended up here, thinking you might be able to put me to work."

"I...uh...see."

*Oh, brilliant response, Angela*, she thought, shifting her weight on her feet nervously. Having him show up while she was thinking about him didn't help matters at all.

One eyebrow raised. "Are you going to talk to me through this screen door all day?"

She sighed. Of course not. She was ashamed to admit that she was far more concerned with her own behavior than his. As the social worker, she was supposed to be the well-adjusted one, so Sam could never know about all the unresolved feelings he stirred up. "No funny business," she said, opening the door and inviting him in.

He burst out laughing. "Funny business?"

Her face heated. Despite her intentions to the contrary, she was making a fool of herself. "Oh, never mind. I do need help so don't say you weren't warned." He couldn't be that much trouble with six feet and a hundred pounds of sofa between them, could he? That little atmospheric moment was a one-off. "I was wondering how I was going to get the furniture moved in from the garage." A perfectly good, safe activity.

"The boys could have done it tomorrow."

"That's what I originally decided. But then I thought, what if it rains? And people are coming. I need somewhere for them to sit if we can't be outdoors, right?"

He looked into the empty living room and back to her again, his eyes disapproving. She knew it was silly to think of doing it all herself. And she hated that she somehow felt she needed his approval when she didn't.

"You should have called."

"*So you could have said you were too busy? No thanks.*"

His eyes widened with surprise at her quick response, and

then seemed to warm with a new respect. "You know, sometimes it beats me why I keep coming back here."

"Maybe you're a sucker for punishment." She tilted her chin. *Enough was enough. She kept letting him get the upper* hand and it was time that changed. At the same time, there was a new edge to the words now. Not the angry, spiteful edge that had been prevalent in their first meetings. But something else. It almost felt like teasing. Banter. Right now he was looking at her like he was up to something. The boyish expression made him look younger than she expected he was and very, very sexy.

"Maybe I am," he replied slowly, and punctuated it with a wink.

Angela burst out laughing. "Okay, you had me until the wink. Seriously?"

Sam shoved his hands in his pockets. "Over the top?"

"Yeah. A bit."

"Then I'd better stop making a fool of myself and get to work, huh?"

She led him to the garage while a new, unfamiliar warmth expanded inside her. It was a surprise to find that she was slowly growing to trust Sam. How could her first impression have been so wrong? She'd thought him all swagger and arrogance, but there was more to Sam Diamond than what she'd first thought was a huge sense of self-entitlement. He had a generous spirit and a sense of humor, the humble kind that meant he didn't mind poking fun at himself a little. She'd been wrong to accuse him of ego. What had happened was as much her fault as his.

As he lifted the other wing chair effortlessly, Angela swallowed, staring at the way the fabric of his shirt stretched across the muscles of his chest and arms. It was just as well that the project was getting closer to launch. Once things were underway their paths would rarely need to cross. Perhaps a chance encounter in town, or at a board meeting of the foundation.

Besides, after Butterfly House was well-established, she had plans. If she had her way, there'd be several houses like this one scattered around the country. It was going to take all her energy to make that a reality. There wasn't room for sexy distractions in those plans.

While Sam took the chair inside, she grabbed an end table and followed him. Together they positioned the chairs and put the table between, and Angela brought out a lamp to place upon it. It made the corner of the room cozy. Next they manhandled the sofa.

"We're not going to trip over your cat, are we?" he asked, puffing a little as they hefted it up.

"He's been hiding in the basement most of the day. I think you're safe."

"Okay, now tilt it a little," Sam suggested, "to fit the arms through the doorway."

It was heavy and Angela braced the weight against her knee as she fought for a better grip and turned it slightly for a better angle. "Easy for you to say."

"Shout if you have to put it down."

As if. Her competitive spirit rose up and made her determined to carry her weight. She gave the sofa a boost and said, "I'm fine. Go."

It wasn't done gracefully, but they managed to get the sofa into the living room and put into place without scratching the new finish on the floor. "It's starting to look like a room," she said, brushing off her hands.

"What's left?"

There were two footstools and a coffee table still in the garage, and within moments they had the room organized. A quick polish and vacuum and it would be fine.

Angela looked at Sam. He'd left his customary hat on

the coatrack by the door and his hair was slightly mussed and damp from lifting in the July heat. She looked down at herself—a smear of dust streaked across her left breast, light beige against the navy T-shirt. She dusted it off and rubbed her hands on her jeans. The room was done but she didn't want him to leave yet. She'd have too much time on her hands to fuss and flutter and worry about all the things that could go wrong tomorrow. Sam made her focus on other things.

"There's a mattress and box spring that just arrived yesterday," she piped up. "I don't suppose you'd care to help me get them up the stairs?"

"Sure. Might as well use me while I'm here."

"Use him" indeed. Angela ignored the rush of heat at his innocently spoken words. They took the mattress up first and leaned it against the wall of the sunny yellow room. The box spring was harder to manage. The rigid frame made it unwieldy to get around the corner of the stairs, and it took three tries to get the angle lined up correctly to get it through the door of the bedroom. Angela's face was flushed and her breath was labored as they finally got inside and shifted the box spring so that they could lay it on the bed frame she'd put together. She nearly had it when the corner slipped and it started to slide. A splinter from the wood dug into her finger and she let go as a reflex.

"Ow!"

Sam's face flattened in alarm as he tried to take as much weight of the box spring as possible, but it was too unbalanced. It tipped and dropped, landing squarely on her toes.

"Oh!" There was a sharp pain in her big toe that began radiating out in waves. Despite the splinter, she bent to lift the box spring off her foot as her eyes watered. She took a step toward the bed and gasped out a curse.

"Put it down," Sam instructed. "Just lay it down, Angela. I'll put it on the frame later."

They laid it across the frame and she exhaled fully as Sam rushed around the corner of the bed. "Did you break it? I thought you had it…"

"I did have it, until this." She held up her hand with the splinter still sticking out.

"Let me have a look."

She wasn't about to argue, and held up her hand for his examination.

"You should sit down," he suggested, looking into her face. She tried not to wince but wasn't entirely sure she was succeeding.

The pain in her toe was horrible and she wanted nothing more than to get off her feet. But there was nowhere to sit in the bedroom. "We'll have to go downstairs."

"Come on, then. Put your arm around my neck."

She looked at him, so shocked at his suggestion that she temporarily forgot about her toe and splinter. What would it be like to be picked up off her feet and held against his wide chest with his strong arms? It made something inside her lift up and go all fizzy. She couldn't quite make the leap between the idea and actual physical contact, though. Oh, how she wished she were one of those confident women who could slide their arms around a handsome man and be comfortable doing so. Instead Angela felt a cloying sense of claustrophobia, as if she were pinned—a butterfly under glass, vulnerable and unable to escape.

She shook her head. "That's okay. I can walk."

She hobbled to the stairs and used the banister for support as she made her way down the steps one by one. She refused to look at Sam, who stayed beside her on each step. She appreciated the solicitude but he was too close and she was too aware of his body blocking her against the stairway. At the bottom she grimaced but refused his arm when he offered it.

"Stubborn as a mule," he muttered, following her into the living room.

She sank into the chair. "You got that right. Did you forget?"

"I guess I must have." He was looking at her with concern and it made the parts of her that weren't throbbing with pain go all squishy. It was inconceivable that he might actually care about her, wasn't it? It was only a few weeks ago that he'd pointed a finger at her in the boardroom in Edmonton and told her not to expect a thing from him.

And now here he was. Doing a very good impression of being there for her and she was afraid she might be getting used to it.

The pain wasn't so bad now that she was off her feet and she sighed. This was just what she needed. How was she going to supervise a dozen energetic teens tomorrow if she could hardly hobble from one room to the next? Tears of frustration stung her eyes as she contemplated the to-do list. She hadn't even begun on the refreshments yet...

"Do you think it's broken?"

"I don't know. I hope not."

Sam's troubled gaze met hers, and then he reached in his pocket. He took out a Swiss army knife and plucked out a set of tweezers. "Let's see your hand first," he said, pulling over a foot stool and sitting on it. She held out her hand and winced as he gently squeezed the skin around the splinter. With a few quick plucks she felt the wood slide out of her skin. "It's a good one, but it's out."

"Thanks," she replied. And was going to say more but realized that Sam's hands were on her ankle, lifting her leg to rest across his knee.

"Let's have a look at that toe," he said quietly.

She held her breath as his warm hands circled her ankle and carefully removed her shoe and rolled her sock down over *her heel. Every nerve ending in her body was aware of his* gentle touch and she bit down on her lip. She could do this. She could handle being touched, even if it did feel far too intimate. The sock slid off into his fingers and he dropped it on the floor. His careful examination was intensely uncomfortable—a mix of shooting pain, uneasiness at the personal nature of his probing and delicious pleasure as he touched gently with his fingers. His thumb was along her instep and rubbed the arch as he turned her foot. It felt wonderful and she relaxed against the back of the chair.

"You've bruised it good," he said quietly. "I don't think it's broken. Even if it is, there's not much you can do for it but stay off it. We should try to get the swelling down, though. Got any ice?"

"There's an ice pack in the kitchen freezer," she said, and watched with her senses clamoring as he put her foot carefully on the footstool and disappeared, only to return a moment later with the pack wrapped in a dish towel.

"You need to keep it elevated and the ice on it. Take some ibuprofen. It's an anti-inflammatory."

"I don't have any. I have a policy about not keeping any drugs in the house, even over-the-counter ones." She had a first aid kit but no medication.

"Then I'll go get you some."

She leaned back against the chair, finally admitting defeat. Up until now she'd been sure she could have everything put together. She couldn't now.

She was going to look like an amateur.

Her bottom lip wobbled. Just a little, and she sucked it up, but not in time. Sam's brows pulled together.

"What is it?"

"There's no way I'll be ready now. I have reporters and politicians coming—" that very thought caused her heart to stutter "—and a dusty living room and no food. I have a dozen teens coming from the youth center to do yard work, and how am I going to supervise if I can't even walk around the property?"

She felt so very vulnerable, and it was truly a bad state of affairs if she was confiding in Sam Diamond. The last time she'd given him a personal glimpse it hadn't turned him away as she'd expected.

"It'll be ready, I promise."

"Please don't make promises you can't keep, Sam. I can't bear it."

She'd heard too many promises, had too many broken over the years, especially by people she was supposed to trust. She'd heard a lot of apologies, all of them sincerely meant. And then she'd felt the blistering rage when something didn't go her father's way. She'd heard it all from Steve, too, until one day he'd backhanded her across the face.

He'd done her a favor because that was the day she broke free of the pattern forever.

But she didn't believe in promises and assurances. Not even from someone like Sam.

"I do not make idle promises. I'll be honest and walk away before breaking my word."

Her heart surged at the sincerity in his voice. She *wanted* to believe him. So badly.

"Sam, I…" Her throat thickened. She didn't want to depend on him to make this right. She didn't want to depend on anyone.

"Hush," he said, bending over and putting his hands on the arm of the chair. "You'll have everything you need. It'll go off without a hitch. Can you trust me?"

His eyes searched hers and she noticed tiny gold flecks in the irises. He was asking her to trust him with Butterfly House, the one thing she cared about most. Could she? She wanted to. She wanted to so badly it hurt inside. But she was afraid—of everything he was making her feel. Her hesitation was slowly melting away—the armor that she'd used to protect herself for years. In its absence came a whole host of other problems. She had no idea how to handle a situation like this.

But in the end she had no choice. She lifted her eyes to his and took a breath. "Yes," she breathed. "I trust you."

There was a long moment where their eyes met, accepted. And then Sam leaned in and did the one thing she feared and longed for most: he kissed her.

# CHAPTER SIX

ANGELA'S heart skidded as his lips touched hers. She wasn't prepared for how they'd feel—gentle, warm and seductive. She remembered reading a book once where a character described kissing the hero as feeling like sliding down a rainbow. Angela had thought it a silly comparison at the time. Now she understood what it meant. It was *heavenly*.

She sighed a little as his mouth nibbled at hers, teasing and making her forget all about her throbbing toe. Hesitantly she responded, not quite comfortable with the intimacy of it all but wooed just the same. There were no demands made. There was only the whisper of his lips on hers. How long had it been since she'd been kissed this way? Had she ever been? It was as if he somehow knew she needed patience and tenderness.

But when his hand slipped from the arm of the chair to her shoulder, she pulled away, breaking the contact. This couldn't happen. She couldn't let him this close. For a tense second their mouths seemed to hover, only scant inches apart. Then, to her surprise, he leaned his forehead against hers. There was an openness in the gesture that surprised and touched her. Where was the irascible rancher she'd butted heads with at the beginning? The man who'd claimed he didn't have time for her or her cause? She knew he was still in there somewhere.

The most worrying thing was that she liked this new side of Sam. When was the last time she'd felt pretty, desirable, cared for? He made her feel all those things and more, without the crippling anxiety that usually accompanied any sort of romantic overture.

"I'm sorry, Angela. I wasn't going to do that today."

*Today.* Nerves bubbled up as she realized his words confirmed that he'd thought about it before. When? When they were hanging the curtains? Drinking lemonade on the porch? Arguing at Diamondback? She swallowed. It might have been easier to pass off if it had just been a spur-of-the-moment impulse. But knowing he'd considered doing it—that he'd ostensibly told himself he wasn't going to kiss her and now had—that changed things.

Something was going on between them, something bigger than she was comfortable with. Was he interested in a relationship? That was impossible. He'd made it very plain he didn't have time for romance.

"Then why did you?"

He squatted down beside the chair, leaving his hands on the arms. "Maybe because today you were human. Today you admitted defeat. I know how hard that was for you to do. I know what it cost you." He sighed. "Boy, do I know."

She swiped her tongue over her lips; now they held the tang of bitterness. Why did she have to fail in order to be attractive to him? She never wanted anyone to pity her ever again. She'd come too far for that. "You felt sorry for me."

"No!" He shook his head. "For the first time, the cold veneer you wear all the time slipped."

Was that how he saw her? Cold? She curled her arms around her middle. Is that how *everyone* saw her? She knew she was focused and she was guarded. She had been wary of letting anyone in, giving them any power over her at all. She refused to be beneath anyone's thumb the way she'd been under her father's. Every insult and slap had eroded her childish confidence bit by bit until she'd nearly believed she was nothing. She'd had to fight her way back. But this was the first time she'd really sat back and thought about how she must appear to others. Each time she saw a neglected child or a woman who'd lost her hope for the future, her heart broke a little more. If she appeared that way it was because she refused to let her compassion be a weakness for someone to exploit.

"I don't trust easily, that's all," she said quietly, wanting to explain in some small way. "When you trust someone and they betray that trust... I don't mean to be cold. Just careful."

She couldn't explain it any better than that. She didn't trust anyone with her secrets. She supposed being considered aloof was a small price to pay for her privacy.

"And you don't trust me, either, do you?" He frowned.

"I don't want to, no."

He got up and lifted her foot so he could sit on the footstool again, putting her feet on his thighs. "That implies that you do, on some level."

Angela closed her eyes briefly. She didn't want to have this conversation. She wished Molly had never stepped away from the board. As exciting as Sam could be, he complicated things. He managed to see her the way no one had seen her before and that was terrifying. The truth was ugly.

"You don't even want to be here. You said so," she defended. "And you keep coming back. You said you don't want anything romantic." She forced herself to say the word; they'd just kissed so it wasn't as if it was taboo now. "And now you're here and you're kissing me. What do you want, Sam? Because I can't keep up with your mixed signals."

"I want to help." His hand rested warmly on her ankle and she fought not to pull away from what he probably considered a casual touch but what meant so much more to her. "I know

I came on strong at first. I was overwhelmed at the ranch and feeling stretched to the max. Lately…" He seemed to consider for a moment, then forged ahead. "All the responsibility for Diamondback is on my shoulders, but Dad still pulls the strings and we're not seeing eye to eye. Today I had to go for a ride to blow off some steam."

"What happened between you?"

"He doesn't agree with putting in the biogas plant. I've showed him all the research. I've crunched the numbers. But he's dug in his heels and crossed his arms and said no."

Angela longed to reach out and touch his hand, but knew she didn't dare. "He's going through a difficult time. From what I gather, he was a vital workingman and now he's stuck inside and doing rehab."

"I know that. Seeing him this way is killing me, so arguing is making it all worse. My family's falling apart. Hell, I even called my cousin Ty to get his take on the whole thing."

"Ty?"

"Dad's nephew. Mom and Dad adopted him when he was a baby. He's a Diamond through and through. He reminded me that Dad is like a brick wall. There's just no easy way to break through."

"You'll figure it out," she assured him. "Diamondback means everything to both of you. It's natural that you're both very passionate about its direction."

"You're right. Diamondback—it's my life. I want to take it into the future, and Dad, he's just scared." He tilted his head and looked at her suspiciously. "Did you just go all social worker on me?"

She couldn't resist smiling just a little. "Of course not. You just needed to get it off your chest."

His hand rubbed absently over her foot, and he seemed completely unaware of the effect it was having on her. "Thanks for letting me vent. When I'm here, it's…"

"It's what?"

"Simpler. I can look at it with different eyes, and it makes sense. When I'm here I feel like even the smallest thing I do might make a difference to someone."

It did make a difference—to her. His words touched something inside her. She knew what it was like to need to act. She supposed that her feelings about her mother were similar to how Sam felt about his father. Beverly Beck would never leave her own personal hell and there was nothing Angela could say or do to change her mom's mind.

Sam had shared a part of himself with her today. She didn't want to care; she didn't want to rely on someone only to be disappointed. And she was in grave danger of relying on—and caring for—Sam.

"What you do matters," she finally replied. "To your family. Your mother worships you, Sam."

"I know that. And I love Diamondback. I love the open space and I take pride in what we do. It's in my blood."

Of course it was. It only took seeing him in the saddle to know he was a rancher through and through. "But?"

"I don't know. I'm not satisfied. Maybe I need a constant challenge to keep me from being bored."

Was that all she was, then? Angela took her recently budded feelings and buried them again. She wasn't anyone's challenge. She knew she wasn't exciting and adventurous. Certainly not dynamic enough for him. He was all strength and energy and restless ambition.

"I guess Butterfly House is the lucky beneficiary of your boredom, then," she said carefully.

"Perhaps it is," he admitted. "Now, what are we going to do about tomorrow? What's left?"

Angela swallowed thickly. Maybe Sam was right. Maybe *she did shut people out. Maybe there was a way to be friendly* without divulging deeper secrets. Her confession that she'd been in a bad relationship had seemed to appease him. Angela felt her own sting of shame. How could she profess to be brilliant at her job when her own mother refused to leave her abuser every day?

Instead of talking about it, Angela chose to do the only thing she could—help the hundreds of other women looking to start again. Now, just as things were coming to fruition, she was forced to rely on Sam to get the job done. She didn't like the pattern that was forming, but she had no choice at this point.

"I need to run the vacuum over the floors."

"Consider it done."

"And organize all the food. There are a dozen teenagers who will need lunch, not to mention others dropping by."

And she had to start on that now. She knew how much food hungry teens could eat. There would be sandwiches but she'd planned on making sweets as well as a pot of homemade soup. She took her leg off Sam's lap—instantly missing the warmth of his body touching hers—and put her arms on the chair, pushing herself up. She took two steps and caught her breath. Maybe she could hobble around, but she couldn't stand on her feet for long and carrying anything was out of the question. Frustration simmered. Why now? Why couldn't this have happened next week?

Because she'd let Sam distract her and had suggested moving that silly box spring and mattress. It was her own fault, plain and simple.

"You need to keep that foot up."

"I need to get things ready."

"Do you ever accept help without fighting it every step of the way?"

She turned around, bracing her hand against the wall. "I'm not used to having help, to be honest. And when I do have it, it usually comes with conditions. Heck, you're only here because your support came with a seat on the board."

His eyes darkened. "Ouch."

It wasn't fair, not after all he'd just told her. "Sorry. I guess I'm not a very good patient."

He shrugged. "Maybe it was true, at first anyway. But I'm here now and I'm offering, string-free."

They were not in this together and she didn't want to feel as if they were. Her insides quivered. How many times had she wanted to stand side by side with her mother? To fight together? And each time she'd thought they were close to escaping, Beverly had backed down. Angela had ended up disappointed and alone. Not just alone—but with wounds that cut a little bit deeper. Feeling more and more alone and losing all faith and hope.

Sam was standing beside her now, but once this project was over he'd be gone. And she'd be standing alone again. So it came down to which was more important: Saving face or saving her feelings?

She already knew the answer. She was strong and resilient. She could withstand the loss of Sam Diamond. She couldn't lose Butterfly House, though. It had to succeed no matter what.

"I'll make you a list."

She hobbled to the kitchen and grabbed a notepad. Sitting at the table she began to write out what she needed. "I have the makings for sandwiches here and I can make those sitting down," she said, "but I need sweets. Cookies, brownies, and I was planning on making butter tarts. A few dozen muffins. And I was going to make a pot of soup in the slow cooker."

"That's it?" His brows lifted, studying the list over her shoulder. "That shouldn't be too much trouble. I don't know what you were making such a big fuss over."

The fuss was less over the items and more about needing

his help once more. He was making himself indispensable and she didn't like it. Add into that the fact that she could still taste him on her lips and she needed to get him out of here as soon as possible.

She fought the urge to close her eyes. The warning bells pealed with a suffocating warning. Sam was taking over. Things with Steve had started the same way. He'd ingrained himself into her life until one day she woke up and realized he'd begun controlling it in a way she swore would never happen.

"I bought drinks but forgot cups." She wrote on the pad once more, trying to keep her hand from shaking. "And get paper ones, please, so we can recycle them."

"Leave it all to me. What about set up in the morning?"

"Clara, our first resident, is arriving first thing. She'll help me set up. But, Sam, really…"

"Sweets and soup. Consider it done." He ripped the list off the notepad and tucked it in his pocket.

She felt as though she was giving away control of the situation and it was killing her. This was her baby. If anything went wrong it was all on her. The trouble with it all was that she *wanted* to trust him. And that made her weak.

He put his hand on her shoulder and squeezed. "You don't believe me, do you?"

There was no accusation in the words. She turned her head and looked up at him. "It's not you, Sam. I don't really trust anyone."

"Maybe someday you'd care to share why that is." He said it quietly, a soft invitation. But she was already liking him too much. There could be no more kisses. No more shared intimacies. Definitely *no sharing of dirty secrets.*

"I doubt it," she answered truthfully. "But thank you. You're going above and beyond, and I do appreciate it." And after tomorrow she'd be able to breathe again.

"It's been known to happen once or twice. Once I commit to a thing, I give it one hundred percent. Don't worry about tomorrow. I promise."

He gave it one hundred percent, but, by his own admission, he got bored and moved on. That was what she had to remember.

"I'll be back in half an hour with the cups and some pain meds for that foot." He came back and took the pen from her hands, scribbling a number on the top. "If you need anything, that's my cell number."

"Got it."

"See you soon."

He left once more and Angela sat in the quiet. She touched her fingers to her lips.

She was usually so good at figuring people out from first impressions. She'd learned to read people. But the more she got to know Sam, the harder it was to reconcile him with the slick charmer who'd barged into their board meeting.

She closed her eyes. The worst of it all was that she had enjoyed being taken care of today. And that wasn't a good thing at all.

The rain Angela feared would ruin the day stayed well to the west, cushioned in the valleys of the Rockies. Instead, the summer day dawned clear and sunny with only a few cotton-ball clouds marring the perfect sky. She showered and hobbled to the kitchen to fix some tea and toast, waiting for Clara to arrive. She was due at nine, the teens at ten. For now there was little to do. True to his word, Sam had returned yesterday with a bottle of ibuprofen, paper cups and a willing hand as he gave the vacuum a turn around the downstairs. It was a leap of faith, but she was trusting him to deliver on the rest of his promises. So far he'd come good and it was either trust or blind panic. And she really didn't want to panic. She'd leave the hyperventilating for later when she had time for it.

At five to nine Clara arrived. Angela met her at the door. "Oh, you look wonderful," she exclaimed, standing back and examining Butterfly House's first official resident. It was really happening. After all this time, it was hard to believe. But seeing Clara on her doorstep with a suitcase made it real.

"I feel good," Clara admitted. Her brown hair fell in curls to her shoulders, and Angela noticed she'd put on some of the weight she'd lost during the first months she'd been in a shelter in Edmonton. She had lovely curves now, and dressed in denim capri pants and a loose blue shirt she looked casual and attractive. Angela wondered if the plain, slightly baggy style and understated color was intended to deflect attention. Trying to avoid being noticed—unconsciously or consciously—was common.

"Bring in your things, Clara. Three of the rooms are ready and you can have your pick. Then we can set to work."

Clara brought in a suitcase and carryall. Angela held open the door but Clara immediately noticed her limp. "What did you do to yourself?"

"Dropped a box spring on my toe yesterday."

"You should have called. I would have come early to help."

Heat rose in Angela's cheeks. "I had some help, but thanks. And I'm certainly going to put you to work today. I don't think I'll be very effective herding teens."

Morris popped into the kitchen through the basement cat door and Clara put down her bags. "Well, hello there," she cooed, and a delighted Morris rubbed his head against her hand. "Aren't you handsome?"

"Be careful. He can be a biter."

"Don't be silly. What's your name, kitty?"

"Morris," Angela replied, watching with fascination. After

the first incident with Sam, Morris had either hid out in the basement or simply stayed out of the way. He certainly didn't warm up to people as a rule. But here he was, snuggling up to Clara as if they were old friends. Perhaps her instinct about it being a man thing was dead-on.

"I'm glad you have a cat. Pets are so nonjudgmental. All they want is love."

Angela laughed. "Oh, I'm afraid Morris is typical cat. He judges on sight and has many demands. But it looks like you've passed the test. I'm glad. I rescued him and hoped he'd go over well here. I don't think I could bear to give him up now."

"He'll be great company. Now let's drop my things so we can get to work." Clara lifted her bags again and threw Angela a smile. Suddenly the day seemed full of possibilities.

They went upstairs and it was no surprise to Angela that Clara picked the sunny yellow room that matched her personality. Angela was glad that they'd finished it yesterday, and Clara could make the bed up with the new bedding later.

They'd just managed to set up the banquet table on the porch and put a tablecloth on it when Sam arrived. He lifted a hand from the steering wheel in greeting and Angela waved back, the now-familiar swirl of anticipation curling through her tummy. There was no doubt about it—she'd gone from dreading his appearance to looking forward to it. Something had changed yesterday and not just because of the kiss, but because they'd shared glimpses into their lives.

She resisted the urge to touch her hair, determined that any reaction she felt was kept inside and not broadcast for Sam or Clara to see.

He opened the back door of the truck cab and took out a plastic bin. "Someone call for food?"

"Morning," she said when he came closer. He smiled. It

was ridiculous that a smile should make her feel giddy, but it did. He'd come, just like he'd promised. She looked over to see if Clara was watching them, but she was busy putting drinks in a cooler on the porch. All in all, a sense of celebration and the feeling that everything was going to turn out all right was in the air.

"Good morning. How's the foot?"

"Sore," she admitted.

He lifted his hands a little. "Where do you want it?"

"Inside on the counter." She turned around and waved at Clara to come óver. With the way she was feeling, a little interference would be a good thing. "Sam, this is Clara Ferguson. She's moving in today. Clara, Sam Diamond."

"Miss Ferguson." Sam put down the bin and held out his hand.

"Mr. Diamond."

Angela noticed the happy light dim in Clara's eyes for just a moment, and she didn't come forward to shake Sam's hand. Sam kept the smile on his face as he casually dropped the hand and looked at Angela.

"Sam's family is our biggest sponsor, Clara. His mother, Molly, sits on the board of directors. But his father's been ill, so in the meantime Sam has stepped in. He's been invaluable in getting the house ready for today."

As she said the words she knew they were true. Today couldn't have happened without him. She couldn't ever remember depending on someone so heavily. But she'd never taken on a project of this magnitude, either.

"It's an important project," Sam replied, and looked back at Clara again. "I hope you'll be happy here, Clara."

Clara lifted her chin. "I haven't been happy in a long time, Mr. Diamond. I'm looking forward to it."

Angela smiled at the fledgling confidence in Clara's voice. Yes, she'd do very nicely. Sam nodded at them both, picked up the bin and started up the porch steps. Angela followed at a slow hobble, wishing that Sam didn't look quite so good from the back view.

Sam was taking packages out of the bin when Angela arrived in the kitchen. He'd been unsure of what to say to Clara, especially when she seemed to withdraw into herself at his introduction. What should he have said? Was it better to address the issues plainly, or avoid the topic altogether? He was a rancher, no good at diplomacy, and today he was going to be put on the spot about Butterfly House. A few days ago he had considered today an annoying interruption in his schedule. But he felt differently now. He wanted to do and say the right thing. He wanted to be helpful. How could he when he couldn't even figure out the right way to speak to the women most affected by the project?

"Thank you, Sam, for bringing the food."

He put a tray of bakery muffins on the counter. "It was no trouble." He paused and turned to face her. "Delivering food is easy. But with Clara just now I didn't know what to say. I didn't want to say the wrong thing and offend her."

"You did fine," she replied, and the small half smile he was growing to look for tilted her lips. "You read the signs, which is good, and you didn't press her into shaking hands. It's a long process, Sam. When you've been abused, it stays with you forever. It's not surprising that she's not comfortable with close contact. Clara's come a long way and now she's ready to start over."

She sounded so logical, so professional. And perhaps a *little bit distant. This was her element, he realized.* She was more like her boardroom self today and he wasn't sure what to make of it. It was impressive, but he missed the flustered and slightly messed woman who huffed and puffed carrying furniture. Who sighed just a little when their lips touched.

Whose lashes fluttered onto her cheeks when she opened up just a little about her past. Sam felt his heart constrict. How any man could treat a woman badly angered the hell out of him. "My mother would be better at this sort of thing."

Angela looked up at him. She looked so fresh and lovely in linen trousers and a cute white top—all airy and summery. Her glossy hair was pinned up today, and he missed the way the waves fell over her shoulders as they had yesterday when he'd leaned in and kissed her. His body tightened just thinking about it.

"Maybe she would, but maybe not. It might actually be better if it's you. Molly would have set an example for the women of Cadence Creek and that support system is crucial, it's true. But you could make a real difference, too. Over half the businesses in town are owned by men. Men who look up to you, and to your father. Men who might just have employment opportunities."

His hand paused on a bag of chocolate chip cookies. He thought back to the conversation he'd had with Angela in the Diamondback yard—that his presence was important here today for PR reasons. Was that all he was to her, then? It surprised him that the idea bothered him, when weeks ago he hadn't wanted anything to do with her—at all.

"Angela? The first of the kids are here." Clara's voice came through the screen door.

"I should get them organized," Angela said, and his annoyance grew. He wanted to gather her into his arms and kiss her again to see if her cool and collected demeanor was genuine or if he still had the ability to frazzle her. Right now, despite the limp, she seemed implacable.

"I'll bring in the rest of the things. Mom wanted to help so she sent a batch of her taco soup and insisted that store-bought brownies couldn't compare to her recipe." Indeed,

Molly had seemed more than happy to take the time to cook for the event.

"Oh, how nice of her! I'll be right back to plate everything."

He watched her limp down the hall and frowned. Yesterday's kiss had done nothing less than fire something in him that he hadn't felt in a long time. And he discovered he was far from being done with it.

# CHAPTER SEVEN

ANGELA ladled out soup to the line of kids, every now and then glancing up to watch Sam speak to the local Member of the Legislature. He looked so comfortable in the situation, his weight resting on one hip and his shoulders down and relaxed. She envied how easy he made it all look. The idea of being in the spotlight just about made her blood run cold. She was so much better behind the scenes. It had been Molly who had pushed for an open-house day. She'd been right—the foundation needed the exposure. But it definitely put Angela out of her comfort zone.

Sam had been so great today. First with providing the food she'd needed, and then hanging around to speak with people while she spent her time supervising and organizing, all at a snail's pace as she hobbled about on her sore foot. She handed over another soup bowl and Sam looked over and smiled, gave a little wave. She fluttered her fingers in response and then tucked a stray piece of hair behind her ear.

She knew very well she shouldn't be so happy he was here. It was the reaction of the moment, it wasn't real. Her future was with the foundation and her plans, not with Sam. It was just hard to remember that when he was around.

Sometimes she wondered what it would be like to truly be a part of someone's world, rather than a series of people simply passing through. What would it be like to be part of *his* world?

The very idea sent a curl of warmth through her, tempered by a touch of fear. It would be easy to lose herself in Sam. He was so charismatic, so dynamic. His outgoing personality would swallow her whole.

"Ms. Beck?" One of the kids said her name and drew her out of her thoughts. "Can I have more soup? It's good."

She shook the troubling thoughts away and smiled. "Sure you can." The teens had worked up an appetite and Clara had kept them in line throughout the morning, trimming dead branches off shrubs and clearing out the old flower gardens at the base of the porch. A local garden center had donated some bedding plants—the season was ending and it hadn't been difficult to convince them to part with their leftover stock. Now flats of brightly colored geraniums, marigolds and petunias waited to be planted. One more thing to make Butterfly House home, to add some color and zip that was missing in so many of their lives.

She handed over the soup. "You've been a huge help. Thank you all for coming."

"It's been fun," one girl said, breaking off a piece of cookie. "I'd just be hanging around at home watching TV anyway."

The group of them belonged to an after-school club organized to keep local kids out of trouble. Now, in the summer months, they were left to their own devices more often than not. Giving them a project had been a good idea. Angela planned on speaking to the director again about partnering up. There was no reason why the two projects couldn't help each other.

"Yeah, me, too," said one of the boys. "Maybe we could take turns mowing the grass here or something. Whaddaya think, Ms. Beck?"

"I think it's a great idea. Tell you what. Come see me on Monday and we can set up a schedule."

"Cool."

She'd been so involved with talking to the group that she hadn't noticed Sam coming up the porch steps. "What plans are you concocting now?" he asked.

She wished she didn't get that jumped-up feeling every time she heard his voice. It didn't help that he was behind her and essentially blocking any escape off the veranda.

She began to lift her hands to her warm cheeks but stopped, dropping them to her sides. "The club is going to help out on a more regular basis. Isn't it great?"

"Sure it is." Sam smiled, but Angela sensed an awkwardness to his expression. He nodded briefly to the kids and then grabbed a paper plate.

His cool response seemed to have dimmed the enthusiasm, so Angela smiled broadly. "Hey, if someone is prepared to do my yardwork, I'll happily provide snacks." She grinned as sounds of approval came from the group. She looked at the lot of them. She knew their lives could be touched by a variety of problems—poverty, neglect, alcoholism—providing some home cooking was the least she could do. For some of them it might be the best meal they got all day.

"And have you taken time to eat anything?" Sam gave her elbow a nudge. "You haven't stopped all morning. A bird can't fly on one wing, you know."

His intimate smile was disarming and rattled her further. He'd noticed her movements even though they'd been doing different things. And his words weren't critical. Instead they felt caring. "Not yet," she replied, realizing her tummy was feeling a little hollow. "You?"

"Nope. And Mom's taco soup is one of my favorites. Let's get some before this crowd drains the pot."

While Angela got their soup, Sam loaded his plate with a

ham sandwich, a handful of potato chips and a selection of raw veggies. He led her away from the teens to a quieter spot on the porch steps. "What?" he asked, as they sat balancing the food on their knees. "I'm a growing boy."

She snorted. "Sam, if you grow any bigger you'll be…"

"Be what?"

She stared into her bowl. Even what was intended as easy banter flustered her beyond belief. She struggled to find a word and grabbed on to one she'd heard the kids use this morning. "Ginormous."

He chuckled. "You haven't met my father, have you?"

"No."

"My mom always said he was as big as a barn door." The warmth dropped out of his voice a little, replaced with sadness. "He's not as big as he used to be."

She wished she could say something to make it better, but she knew that there were times that words simply couldn't fix what was wrong. There was no other comfort she could give other than a paltry "I'm sorry, Sam. It must be so hard for all of you."

"Yes, it is. After yesterday…I talked to my mom. I think she's finally starting to realize she needs help."

Angela felt guilt slide down her spine. "I never meant that she should have to cook for today," she said quietly. "I know she has enough on her plate looking after your father." Sam had pushed and made it impossible for her to say no. If she'd known he was going to go home and foist it on Molly, she would have insisted on doing it herself. "Please thank her for me, will you? If I'd known that was your plan, I would have made a different suggestion."

"She wanted to," Sam replied easily. "She's been so wrapped up in Dad's recovery that it was good for her to focus on something else—something positive. I was going to go out and buy everything and she insisted she help. So don't feel the least bit bad, Angela. You were right. It's more meaningful when people put themselves into a project rather than just 'throwing money at it,' as you said."

She stared at her toes. Oh, how she wished she'd never said those words! "I'm sorry I said that to you," she replied quietly, putting down her empty bowl. He held out his plate, and she took a chip from it. "Thanks."

"No, you were right to. I've been like Mom. So absorbed in the issues at Diamondback that I couldn't see anything else. There are other things—important things—going on. I've enjoyed helping the last few weeks. I care about…"

Hope seemed to hover in the middle of her chest. After their first disastrous meeting she'd wanted him to appreciate what Butterfly House meant. That was *all* she wanted, she reminded herself. "You care about what?"

He popped a chip in his mouth, chewed and swallowed. "I care what happens to this place and feel invested in its success. That's new for me."

"I'm glad." And she was. The sinking feeling in the pit of her stomach was inconsequential. There was not a single reason why she should be feeling disappointed.

"That's what I told our MLA, and the reporter from the paper, too. That we as a community need to get involved."

Angela looked over at him. He was still wearing his Stetson and the way it shaded his face made him look mysterious and delicious. He was so different from anyone she'd ever known. No matter how confusing her feelings were regarding him, she was, for the moment, glad that Molly had stepped away *from the board and Sam had taken her place. If he meant* what he said, she'd managed to bring Sam around after that horrible first meeting when he'd been so dismissive. She remembered thinking if she could accomplish that, she could accomplish anything. Today was a victory in every sense of the word. But it felt hollow somehow.

"Thank you," she whispered. "For getting it. For helping."

"You're welcome."

There was a finality to the word that was a letdown. It occurred to her that after today she'd hardly need him around. Clara was here now and could help with the final touches to the house. The yard work was done. By the first of August, a few more beds would be occupied. Angela would be filling her days with the day-to-day management of the house and liaising with support programs. Sam would be back at Diamondback, overseeing the ranch and the new facility he was planning. It was as it should be. The sooner things got back to normal the sooner she could stop having all these confusing feelings. Sam Diamond was a distraction she didn't need.

But even as she knew deep down it was for the best, she was going to miss the anticipation of seeing him walk through the front door and hearing his voice challenge her.

"I'd better get back. I should make another pot of coffee and get those kids going again."

"They working out all right?"

She met his gaze. "Sure, why wouldn't they?" She realized he'd worn the same awkward expression when talking about Clara this morning. "Is there something wrong with having them here?"

He shook his head. "Of course not. I'm just not used to any of this. I don't know how to talk to people who..."

"Who weren't brought up by Molly and Virgil Diamond?"

He looked so earnest that her heart gave a little thump. "Maybe," he replied honestly. "I had a sheltered life, I guess, with advantages. I don't know what to say to people. You have a way that I don't, Angela. I admire that."

She was shocked. "But you handled the people part so well today—you looked totally at ease!"

He chuckled. "That's different. It's... Aw, heck. It's easier to put on an act when it's something official. But you—you're genuine. That's special."

Her? Special? He had no idea how much easier it had been to deal with troubled teens than face the press. "You played to your strengths today, Sam, and I appreciate it. As far as the kids go—they're just kids. There's no secret code. They just want to feel visible, important to someone."

She looked up and saw Clara waving her over. The photographer from the paper was standing close by and Clara's face looked absolutely panicked.

"There's something wrong with Clara, will you excuse me?"

Clara's eyes filled with relief when she arrived.

"Oh, good. I was trying to explain that I don't want my picture taken," Clara said to Angela in a low voice.

"Of course," Angela assured her. The last thing residents needed was their faces plastered over the media. "Why don't you get some lunch? I'll take it from here."

She spoke briefly to the photographer, who was undeterred. He wanted a picture for the paper to go with the story. Angela's insides froze when she thought about standing before a camera lens. After a few moments of strained diplomacy, she heard Sam's voice at her back.

"Anything I can help with?"

Sam was close by her shoulder and she looked up at him. "The photographer wants a picture for the paper."

"So what's the problem?"

"I don't do pictures, Sam."

Sam's brow puckered. "Will you excuse us a moment?" he asked the photographer pleasantly. Then, with a light hand at her back, he led her aside.

"You don't enjoy having your picture taken?"

If he only knew. She was so much better in the background. It was why she had wanted to be a director but not the face of the foundation. "It can be a fine line between starting over and trying to keep under the radar, you know? Worse for Clara. But I don't do photos. I just don't."

"Is that reasonable? You're the director here."

But the reasons went bone deep. There was the privacy thing, and perhaps she should be past it by now. But there was that horrible slap she hadn't expected, the one that had snapped her head around so quickly she'd dropped to her knees.

Steve had taken a picture of her and waved it in her face. She recognized the young woman in the photo all too well and she hated that person. "A reminder so you don't step out of line again," he'd said, taking a magnet and sticking it on the fridge. She hadn't posed for a photograph since.

She shuddered at the memory. "You do it," she suggested.

"But you're the director," Sam argued. "This is your baby. You should be in the picture."

Her throat constricted. "I can't," she whispered, her voice raw. That would make her public. It would make her feel... exposed. And she had no idea how to explain it without breaking down.

Silence spun out for several long seconds. Sam's gaze never left her face and she blinked rapidly. Then he put his hand on her shoulder, warm and strong. "Then let's do it together. We can both be in it."

As compromises went it was a good one. "I don't know."

"At some point you need to step out of the shadows, sweetheart. Otherwise he's still winning."

Sam was right. Nothing would sidetrack her from making this a success—not even her own fears. She was depending on Butterfly House to set the bar. A brilliant track record would follow her when she went to set up similar houses in other towns, maybe even other provinces. Maybe one day the one person she hoped would need help most would take that step. If her mother ever wanted to break free, a place like Butterfly House should be waiting for her.

"We just need to show a unified front for a few minutes. A couple of snaps and we're done."

A couple of snaps that would put her face in print. Angela wondered what Sam would think if he knew the real truth. She'd made it sound so *over* when they'd spoken earlier in the week. But beneath the businesslike social worker there was a victim still struggling to overcome her own issues. She was a complete fraud and terrified of being found out.

So today she would stop acting like a victim. "Okay," she agreed, feeling slightly nauseous but glad Sam was there beside her. "Let's do it and get it over with."

The photographer stepped in. "Are you ready?"

"Oh, yes. Sure." Angela pasted on a brittle meet-the-press smile. "This is Sam Diamond, one of our board members. He'll be in the photo with me."

"Mr. Diamond, of course. Thanks for sparing the time. Let's make it a nice casual shot, shall we? Maybe you can sit on the picnic table here, with Miss Beck beside you? That way the height discrepancy is minimized."

Sam shrugged and perched on the edge of the wood table.

"Right. Put your foot there, perhaps?"

Sam put his left foot on the bench seat of the table, while his right leg balanced on the ground. All it did was emphasize the long length of his legs.

"Now, Miss Beck, if you'll move in closer and stand beside him…"

Butterflies dipped and swirled and she fought to keep the professional smile glued to her lips. She moved closer to Sam until she was standing beside him. But not touching. Sitting beside him on the step during lunch had been close enough.

The photographer looked through his lens and then lowered his camera again. "Not quite right. If you could slide in a little, please. Maybe put your hand on Mr. Diamond's shoulder, Miss Beck."

Touch him? In a personal way? For a photo? Angela was suddenly at a loss as to how to express the inappropriateness of it without sounding offensive. This whole thing was growing more uncomfortable by the second. She scrambled to come up with an alternative. "What if I stand a little behind him, like this?" She moved in behind his shoulder and instead of placing her hand on his shoulder, placed it on the top of the table instead. The bulk of Sam's body hid her from the camera lens which suited her just fine. There was no doubt in her mind that he'd be the focal point of the picture.

"That's good," he replied, lifting the camera again.

She wasn't touching Sam but their bodies were close enough that it felt warm and intimate. His morning exertions had magnified the scent of his aftershave. It filled her nostrils, the clean, masculine scent making her mouth water.

She wanted to touch him. That was the heck of it.

"One more," the photographer said. "The Butterfly House team," he chattered on. Sam turned his head and looked up at her briefly.

"A team," he said, a grin lighting his face. "Imagine that."

His smile warmed her all over and she began to relax. "Pretty impossible if you ask me. You did drop a bed on my foot."

"You dropped that yourself, but nice try."

It really wasn't so bad after all, she realized. Sam's easy posture relaxed her as well. "Turn around and pay attention," she scolded.

He dutifully turned around. Angela couldn't hold in the little snort that bubbled up at his sudden obedience.

"All done. Thank you both." The photographer lowered his camera and smiled.

"That's it?" She looked up in surprise. It had been painless after all! She'd nearly forgotten that there was anyone behind the camera.

"That's it," he confirmed.

Sam's teasing had made Angela forget the awkwardness of being so close to him, but it came back tenfold when Sam leaned back against her for just a moment, his shoulder pressed lightly up against her breastbone. It was an odd moment where she suddenly felt very much like a part of a team, and something more. Intimacy. There was awareness, but there was also an increasing level of comfort with the way his body fitted against hers or the way his skin felt when they came in contact with each other. She'd never really experienced that kind of intimacy before and she wasn't sure what to do with it. She surely didn't want it—even if it did feel nice.

"Thanks for this," she murmured.

"My pleasure," Sam said, seemingly unaware of the turmoil he created within her. "Don't work too hard, now."

Hard work was just what she needed to forget about Sam—and her confusing feelings.

The flowers nodded their bright heads, perhaps a little unevenly but cheerfully nonetheless. The mess from the buffet lunch was tidied and Clara and Angela were packaging up the leftovers in the kitchen. The house was strangely silent after the commotion, and when Angela heard a distinct meowing, she went to the cat door and unlocked the flap. "It's safe now," she said soothingly as Morris stuck his orange head through the hole.

She'd locked him downstairs with full bowls of food and water shortly before Sam's arrival, knowing he'd hide in his basket anyway during the ruckus of people running in and out all day. She'd also worried about doors being left open in the chaos and him getting out. When Morris was out, he was a terror to try to get back. And the longer he was with her, the more Angela couldn't bear the thought of parting with him. He'd been her company on long nights. He never judged. He just did his thing and came for a cuddle when it suited him. Angela understood it perfectly.

Clara looked out the kitchen window and gave a little sigh. "Well, there's a sight."

Angela went to the window and looked out. Sam was working on the old woodpile that had been created when the previous owners had cut down a birch in the backyard. He'd taken off his cotton shirt and now wore a plain white T-shirt and jeans. Beside him were two of the boys from today's group, stacking the cut wood in even piles. One of them said something and Sam laughed, tipping back his head. For a guy who was so awkward around the teens, he was fitting in incredibly well.

"He likes you," Clara said quietly. "I can tell. It's in the way he looks at you."

"I'm not interested," Angela replied, turning away from the sight. But it was too late. She already had the picture of him in her mind, blended with the leftover reactions from their picture-taking episode. Sam was persistent, she'd give him that. And he'd seen the day through, which was great. But it was time he went on his way. It was time to take the next step—the day-to-day running of the house. The last thing she needed was Sam underfoot and distracting her with his slow swagger and sexy smile.

"Yes, you are," Clara contradicted. "What you are is scared."

Angela looked at Clara. The other woman's pleasant smile was gone. Instead she looked worried—and sympathetic. Clara seemed to understand things a little too well. And while she wanted to be friends with the women here, that couldn't extend to examining her own problems.

Angela forced herself to smile. "Which one of us is the social worker?"

Clara's shoulders relaxed and she resumed packing vegetables into a plastic container. "You know the saying about walking in someone else's shoes?"

"Sure."

"You've walked in mine. There's a big difference between appreciating how a man looks and acting on it. There's an even bigger gap between wanting it all and being brave enough to go after it."

*Amen,* Angela thought. Clara put it all so succinctly, summarizing the quandary in a way that Angela hadn't been able to because her emotions had gotten in the way. For the first time Angela admitted to herself that she had been flirting with other dreams. Dreams in which she had a perfectly normal happily ever after. But Clara was right. It was not the same as taking the bull by the horns and going after it. She wasn't even sure it existed in real life. She picked up a platter and opened a bottom cupboard, hiding her face from Clara. "I guess neither of us are there yet."

Clara shook her head. "I know I'm not. It's too soon. But what's stopping you, Angela? How long..." She paused. "Forget I asked that. It's not my business."

"I'm happy as I am. I made my choices and I don't regret a one." She grinned, determined to change the subject. "And now you're here. This is what I've been working toward all along. So don't worry about me. I'm exactly where I want to be."

Angela looked out the window as she passed by to the fridge. Sam was shrugging his shirt back on and she watched the play of the muscles in his shoulders. He shook the boys' hands before sending them on their way. Clara was right. She was scared. Of Sam. Of her feelings which seemed to grow stronger every day. Of everything. This job was the only place where she felt she had absolute control and confidence and that was how it was going to stay. She couldn't be rational about Sam, and she had to be. Her life depended on seeing things clearly.

Sam knocked on the back door and Clara let him in. "Do you ladies need anything else?" he asked.

Angela put Molly's slow cooker back in the bin. "No, I think we're good. We've washed up Molly's dishes and they're all here for her. Please thank her, Sam. Everything was delicious."

"Thank her yourself. She told me to ask you to dinner when things were through."

He had left his shirt unbuttoned and the tails hung around the hips of his jeans. Angela didn't know how to answer. An invitation to Diamondback! That hadn't happened before, even when Molly had worked with her on the project.

But it was different somehow. This felt personal, and it was crossing a line. Especially on the heels of Clara's observation. As much as Angela was tempted to accept, she knew she couldn't. "I'm sorry, but I can't. We need to get Clara settled and everything."

"Clara, you're welcome to come, too. It's just a barbecue on the deck. You both deserve a break after today. Surely you have all day tomorrow to get settled?"

Silence fell on the kitchen as Clara looked at Angela and Angela looked at Sam. He was making it awfully hard to say no. The idea of a dinner full of conversation and laughter— Molly and Sam both had such an easy way about them—was hard to resist. When was the last time she'd sat around a table with friends enjoying a meal? Relaxing? And she'd just determined that it was a good thing that they'd barely see each other after today. He was really hitting her in a vulnerable spot.

"It would mean a lot. Mom feels badly for leaving you in

the lurch and not helping more. And it would cheer her up to have people around. You know my mother, Angela." His dark eyes pleaded with her. "She is usually so outgoing, but she hardly leaves the house nowadays. It's so rare that she looks forward to anything. Surely you can spare an hour or two?"

Angela was still debating when Morris stalked in from the living room and halted a few feet from Sam as if to say *hey, what's he doing here?*"

Then, to Angela's great surprise, he came forward and rubbed on Sam's pant leg. Sam knelt down and stroked between Morris's ears. Angela could hear the purrs clear across the kitchen.

"Looks like your cat's had a change of heart," he said. He stopped rubbing and instantly Morris leaned against his hand, looking for more. For a moment Angela was transported back to yesterday, and the way Sam's hand had felt on her ankle, warm and reassuring. The way his lips had rubbed against hers. She couldn't blame Morris for wanting more—even if it did make him a bit of a traitor.

"So what do you say about dinner? If we had company, I think Mom would bring Dad outside to eat with us. He could use the change of scenery."

It was the mention of his father that tipped the balance. She knew Sam was struggling with the changes happening in his family and especially with his relationship with his father. She'd be small and insecure if she let a few misgivings keep a sick man from an enjoyable evening. "Oh, all right," she relented. It's not like it was just the two of them. There'd be other people around. Goodness, she'd hardly have to speak to Sam if she didn't want to. She could catch up with Molly, after all. She'd missed Molly, who'd been such a blessing during the early stages of the project. "We'll finish here and meet you at the ranch."

"Great."

He gave Morris one last pat and stood. "I'll take that with me." He held out his hands for the bin. Angela picked it up and placed it in his hands, careful not to touch him in any way. The earlier resolve stood. Dinner changed nothing.

"Tell Molly not to go to any fuss," she said, looking up at him.

"It'll just be casual, don't worry. See you in an hour or so."

She saw him to the door and watched him drive away until the sound of his truck engine faded. She sighed, wondering how on earth this had happened, and the bigger question: What on earth was she going to wear?

# CHAPTER EIGHT

For an hour Sam wondered if Angela was truly going to show up. It was nearly six o'clock and he'd had a fresh shower and changed clothes, helped move Virgil out onto the deck overlooking the valley, and now he turned the chicken over in the marinade even though it was already evenly coated.

He wrinkled his brow. Little things about Angela didn't add up in the usual way, and he wondered if there was more to the story than she was telling him. If? He was sure there must be. Nothing could be as cut-and-dried as she'd made in sound in a few short sentences.

Her lips were soft and sweet when he'd kissed her, but she'd pulled away first. She was fiercely dedicated to the project but panicked when it came to being the center of attention. She bantered easily with the teenagers but froze when it came to the press. And most miraculous of all—she'd managed to get him talking about himself. And yet she'd always kept the topic of conversation away from herself, only revealing what he suspected was the bare minimum.

All in all it made him wonder how best to proceed. The last thing he wanted to do was frighten her or come across as intimidating. He wasn't sure if a casual touch to him was equally casual to her. All in all, being involved with Angela in any way was a bit like walking through a minefield, not wanting to make a single misstep lest everything blow up in his face.

He was beginning to think he was in big trouble.

"Muss be sommme girrrl."

Sam looked over at his father. Virgil's speech was getting better but he still had trouble enunciating clearly, and often his words were drawn out. There was no mistaking the sparkle in his eyes, though, or the grin on his face—even if it was lopsided because of the lingering paralysis. It felt good to have the old, easy teasing between them again.

"I'm hungry, that's all."

The rusty laugh that came from Virgil warmed Sam's heart. It had been too long since he had heard his father laugh. Too long since they'd had a conversation without arguing, or lately, because of the speech difficulty, without disapproving grunts. "Uh-huh," Virgil replied.

"I know. Can't kid a kidder, right?"

A gleam of approval lit Virgil's eyes. Sam hadn't brought a girl home for a family dinner for years. If Angela knew what his parents had to be thinking, she'd be halfway to Edmonton by now. Sam had to tread carefully. "This isn't a date, so go easy on her, Dad. She's skittish."

"Like yrrr motherrr."

"Mom?"

Virgil nodded. "Shy when we met. Hard work."

Sam chuckled, then sobered. Without knowing the full details of Angela's past, Sam knew something terrible had shaped who she'd become. It was more than shyness.

In the end he wanted what his parents had. Virgil's illness had not only affected Sam's parents but Sam himself. Suddenly he was very aware of mortality. Molly and Virgil wouldn't be around forever. It wasn't just the responsibility of Diamondback that Sam worried about. It was the legacy. Things couldn't go on, fractured the way they were, with all the arguing and with Ty wandering all over the continent. Family needed to stick together. And it was Angela who'd shown him that.

"You warm enough, Dad?" He changed the subject, not wanting to delve into things any deeper. He hated that his father had to sit in a wheelchair. Physio was working with him with a walker, but he could only use it under supervision and for short periods of time. He looked so frail, unable to get up and take charge in his usual good-natured, blustery way. The stroke had altered Virgil in so many ways. He was short-tempered and while Virgil had always been stubborn, he'd also been open-minded. Not now. Sam was pretty sure that fear was making the old man hold on too tight.

"Isss thirrrty degrees. Fine."

The annoyance was back in Virgil's voice and Sam backed off, not wanting to cause any trouble when guests were expected. "Okay, okay."

A car door slammed, followed by another. His heart gave a leap.

He tested the grill and found the temperature just right and when Molly brought the ladies back through the French doors, he was busy putting chicken breasts on the grates.

"Virgil, this is Angela Beck and Clara Ferguson." Molly made the introductions as Sam turned around.

Angela had changed her clothes. Sam's mouth went dry looking at her. She was pretty as a picture in a floral linen skirt and a cotton sweater the color of the prairie sky as the sun came up. She kept her hair off her face with a simple cream headband, the dark waves of it falling gracefully to her shoulders. She looked so young and fresh it made him feel all of his thirty-seven years. And yet the nerves that centered in his belly made him feel like a teenager again. He'd never met anyone who could make him feel that way before.

Perhaps having her over for a family dinner was a mistake. He was afraid he was going to be horribly transparent, gawking at her the way he was right now.

Molly's speculative gaze lit on him and he went back to the barbecue, shutting the lid. Yes, a family dinner probably wasn't the smartest move. Molly had been pushing him for grandkids for years and would read more into it than it was. Sam knew Angela well enough by now to know that she could easily be chased away by well-meaning innuendoes. She reminded him of a skittish colt who needed a gentle and strong hand. He should have asked her out somewhere private. But where would that be in Cadence Creek? There was only the Wagon Wheel Diner and tongues would set to wagging the moment they walked in the door. She'd hate gossip. As would he.

"Mr. Diamond, it's so good to meet you. Thanks for inviting us to your home."

Sam schooled his features and stepped away from the grill in time to see Angela take Virgil's hand in hers and squeeze. Sam saw his father's eyes light up and she smiled. "Oh, goodness," she teased, "now I see where Sam got that wicked grin."

"Chip offf old block." His sideways smile was back. Angela laughed in response and Sam saw a touch of color bloom in her cheeks.

"Hmmm," she replied, raising a knowing eyebrow. "I see I'm going to have to watch out for you."

Sam's heart turned over at the happy expression on Virgil's face. She couldn't possibly know how much this one moment meant to his father—or to him. He'd watched over the weeks as his father's dignity—his manhood and vitality—had been stripped away. He'd been helpless to change it, and had made it worse at times with their arguments over ways to make the ranch more environmentally friendly. With one smile and a few words Angela had given something back to

Virgil. Did she have any idea how well she fitted here without even trying?

Sam put his hand on the deck railing. He was a fool. He kept telling himself that he was doing it for his mother, or that he was after friendship, but there came a time when a man couldn't lie to himself any longer. He was in the precarious position of falling for Angela Beck completely. All it would take was the slightest push and he'd be over the edge. The most shocking thing of all was that he almost welcomed the leap.

"Mr. Diamond, this is my friend Clara. She's the first resident at Butterfly House."

"Thank you for making me feel so welcome here," Clara said. She didn't move to take Virgil's hand, and Sam remembered what Angela had said about close contact. Sympathy for her mixed with respect for what Angela was doing. Whatever had happened in the past, Clara was getting a fresh start in Cadence Creek. Angela met his gaze and gave him a sweet smile. He knew it was a thank-you for including Clara in the evening. But for Sam, the smile meant more. It tethered them together as architects of something good. Angela was the driving force, but Sam had long stopped begrudging the time spent away from Diamondback. Somewhere along the way he'd started believing. In the foundation. In *her*.

"What do you do, Clara? What sort of job will you be looking for?" Molly spoke up.

Clara looked over at Molly, who was laying out napkins on a glass-topped table. "I'm a licensed practical nurse," she replied. "I'm hoping to find a job close by, maybe at a nursing home or clinic. I'm not sure how long my car can withstand a long commute, but right now anything would be wonderful."

"I see," Molly replied. Sam stared at Clara. She could be

the answer to his prayers. He'd been after Molly to hire some help with Virgil and Clara would be perfect.

But Molly would take convincing, and he needed to speak to her as well as Angela before any offer was made. Surely Angela would be pleased?

"And what do you have cooking there?" Angela left Molly and Clara chatting and came closer to the barbecue as he opened the lid and grabbed a pair of tongs to flip the chicken. She was still limping but not as badly as she had earlier in the day. She even smelled good, like outdoors and the soft lily of the valley that grew in the shade of Molly's weeping birch grove. He tamped down the wave of desire that flared and focused on brushing the meat with leftover marinade. "Mom's Greek chicken."

"It looks delicious," she replied lightly.

He looked down at her, staring at the top of her head. "You're late. You weren't going to come, were you?"

She shrugged, but still didn't meet his eye. "I thought twice about it."

"But here you are. And looking mighty pretty." He couldn't resist the compliment. Besides, he knew it would make her look at him, and she did. Her blue-green eyes met his and he felt the alarms go off all over again. Falling for her would be so easy. He should put an end to it right now. It hadn't been difficult in the past. The attraction he was feeling now was simply physical and would go away in time, wouldn't it?

The difference was that he wasn't willing to explore that attraction with her as he had been with other woman. She wasn't the sort of girl a man could be casual with. And so he looked away and absently flipped the chicken even though it didn't need flipping.

"I came because I thought it would be good for Clara to meet a few more people. Especially people who are supportive and not prone to judge."

"That's the only reason?"

She lifted her chin. "Should there be another one?"

It was his turn to shrug as he closed the lid on the grill again. "Not necessarily."

"Molly invited me. Isn't that enough?"

He didn't answer. Molly hadn't invited her at all. It had been Sam's suggestion. At his continued silence she grabbed his arm. "Sam, tell me you didn't foist us on your mother after all she did to help today?"

"She said it was a great idea." Those hadn't been her precise words, but the meaning was the same.

"What do you want from me, Sam?" She lowered her voice so that it was barely a murmur at his side.

He couldn't help it; his gaze dropped to her lips. They were full and a slight sheen of gloss made them look soft and supple.

"I don't want anything," he replied quietly. "I'm playing it by ear here, same as you. Maybe I just wanted to see you away from Butterfly House and get to know you better. Isn't that what friends do?"

There, well done. He'd played the friends card. That would help dial things back a notch. It was bad enough he was looking at her lips as if they were coated in sugar and he had a sweet tooth. She didn't need to be getting any notions of her own.

Her eyes cooled and her lips formed a thin line. "Butterfly House makes me tick. And that's probably all you need to know."

She turned away and went to join Molly and Clara who were setting the table. Sam caught his father's gaze and felt a flash of kinship as Virgil gave him a familiar look that said *you've got your work cut out for you with that one.*

As the meat sizzled on the grill, he watched Angela work her magic. The three women talked as they worked and the tired tension around Molly's mouth seemed to evaporate as her smile became more relaxed. Angela had a way about her that put everyone at ease, he realized, and she did it all effortlessly. She'd worked that skill on him, too, getting him talking when normally he held his problems close to his chest. There was a burst of laughter and Sam watched as Molly put her hand along Angela's back, a kind of pseudo-hug that spoke of comfort and affection. Angela's dark head was next to his mother's gray-streaked one, and a sense of certainty struck Sam right in his core.

Through the years he'd spent time on unsatisfying relationships without knowing why. Now it made sense. None of those other women could measure up to Molly. None of them had her grace, wisdom or strength. She'd led by example and set the bar high—a standard no one had been able to meet.

But Angela did. And the hell of it was she wanted nothing to do with what he had to offer.

The sun started its slow descent as they lingered over dinner. Angela couldn't remember a time when she'd felt this relaxed and hyped up all at once. There was something different here tonight. She was so used to being an outsider but tonight she had been welcomed and more importantly—she'd actively *accepted* the welcome. She'd opened her heart, just a crack, to the Diamond family. How could she help it? Her heart had gone out to Virgil the moment he'd teased her and his smile had shown her what Sam's would look like in thirty years. Still charming. Still powerful. It had grabbed her and had yet to let go. A lump formed in her throat as she watched Molly cut Virgil's chicken into tiny pieces because managing two utensils proved beyond his abilities. When she finished she patted her hand and the look they shared spoke of so much love it made Angela want to weep.

It was hard to believe such trust and devotion existed but

she had living proof tonight. It was rare. She knew that well enough. It would be easy to believe herself a part of it, but she wasn't. She was on the fringes, always the outsider looking in and wishing. For a moment she was angry with Sam. Didn't he realize how much he had here? How lucky he was? And he was determined to argue with his father over it. Molly and Virgil had given him everything a son could want while she'd been hiding in her clumsily mended secondhand clothes, scrimping and saving so that she could one day simply get out and choose her own life.

All the fluttery feelings she got when Sam was around couldn't disguise the truth. They were from different worlds and wanted different things. She should never have come tonight. It only made her wish for things that she would never have.

"Penny for your thoughts." Sam was seated across from her and his low voice sent shivers of pleasure along her skin.

"They're lovely, aren't they?" she replied, nodding at his parents and then meeting his gaze. Sam's dark eyes were watching her steadily and it made her pulse start knocking around like crazy.

"They've been there for each other as long as I can remember," Sam murmured. He glanced over at his parents holding hands while they chatted with Clara. "Even when my cousin came to live with us, there was no question or debate. Mom wanted to adopt him and Dad said yes without blinking an eye—even though Ty was a handful."

"Where's Ty now?"

"Here and there." Sam frowned. "He and Dad didn't see eye to eye and Ty rebelled by becoming a rodeo star." Sam gave a half smile. "He loves it but considers it a perk that it drives Dad crazy." The smile faltered. "He hasn't been back since Dad's stroke, either. I think it's bothered Dad more than he wants to admit. Especially since we've been at odds more and more often over the biogas thing."

"Why can't you let it go, Sam?" Surely it wasn't worth destroying their relationship.

His gaze never flinched. "Because I'm right. Because sustainability is important. And because he knows it and doesn't want to admit it. It isn't really about the development. It's about him, and how he's dealing with things changing. I'm trying to be patient, but I'm not doing a very good job."

She chuckled. "I confess I'm a bit relieved."

"Relieved?" He paused with his fork in midair.

"Your family was looking rather perfect, Sam, with a complete lack of dysfunction. It's quite intimidating for a social worker."

"Nothing to fix?"

She couldn't help but laugh at his wry expression. "Something like that."

He smiled. "You've already helped, did you know that?"

She felt her cheeks heat and she dropped her eyes to her plate, but his encouraging words warmed her during the rest of the meal.

Virgil tired as they sipped tea; Molly enlisted Sam's help to get him to bed while Clara and Angela insisted on clearing the table. Angela couldn't help but marvel at the state-of-the-art appliances, the solid pine cupboards and soaring ceilings. It was a stark contrast to the dingy kitchen Angela and her mother had kept in Edmonton, where the winter drafts froze up the kitchen window and nothing ever quite gleamed. She'd dreamed of having a place like this someday, dreamed of sharing it with her mother; the two of them living in peace. The shelters she had planned would never be this grand, relying as they did on donations and general goodwill. And her mother would never come, would she?

And yet Angela stared at the wealth around her and knew

she couldn't stop trying; it was just like Sam felt about Diamondback. To give up Butterfly House would mean giving up on her mom. And giving up would break her heart.

She was aware of Sam returning but he went out on to the deck as Molly joined them at the sink.

"Oh, thank you, girls. My goodness, you've got it all cleaned up."

"The least we could do after such a great meal, Mrs. Diamond." Clara folded her dishcloth.

"You call me Molly. Everyone else does."

"Molly." Clara hung the dishcloth over the faucet. "I noticed the quilt on the back of your sofa. It's beautiful."

"Do you sew, Clara?"

"I used to. I like doing things with my hands."

"I've got another one on the frames in one of the spare rooms if you'd like to see it. A wedding-ring pattern in wine and cream."

"That would be wonderful."

Molly looked over at Angela, but for once Angela was unable to read the older woman's eyes. "I think Sam wants to speak to you about something, Angela."

"Oh, are you sure?" There was something about being alone in the twilight with Sam that made her hesitate.

"You go ahead," Molly replied. "I'll look after Clara."

How could she refuse without looking desperate or like a coward?

She paused at the French doors, gathering her courage. She could do this. His commitment to Butterfly House was over and so she just needed to reset the boundaries. They could redefine their relationship. If it even was a relationship—it was really more of an acquaintance, wasn't it?

She stepped outside and held her breath.

Sam stood at the top of the steps leading down to the garden. His arms were spread, his hands on the rail posts and she watched, transfixed, as he stretched, the pose highlighting the lean muscle that made up his body.

For the first time in years, Angela felt the ground shift beneath her feet. After focusing on her career, on the lives of others for so long, she wanted something for herself. And what she wanted—*who* she wanted—was Sam. It didn't matter about the justifications or reasons or differences in their lives. Nothing stopped the wanting. The only thing holding her back was that it scared her out of her wits. She wanted to believe in him so badly it terrified her.

"Sam?"

He turned. "You came. I wasn't sure you would."

Her pulse hammered in her wrists, her throat. "Why?"

"You avoided me all night."

Her voice came out at a whisper. "I wish you didn't always have to be so honest."

"I don't make it easy for you, do I?"

She shook her head. An owl hooted in the distance, a soulful cry that echoed through the garden. The sweet summer scent of Molly's rosebushes filled the air. Somewhere in a pasture to the right, a couple of cows lowed mournfully. This was Sam's world. And for tonight she'd gotten a taste of it. A bittersweet taste.

"Let me make it easier." He held out his hand. "Come for a walk with me."

She hesitated, but he waited, holding out his hand. Finally she took it, loving the feel of his warm fingers encircling hers. She followed him down the steps one at a time, only feeling a twinge of pain in her toe when she put all her weight on it. She expected him to let her hand go once they reached the bottom. But he didn't. He kept it firmly in his grasp as they wandered through the garden with slow steps.

"You didn't mention Clara was a licensed practical nurse," he finally said, halting and turning to face her.

Clara? He'd brought her out here to talk about Clara? Angela was glad that dusk prevented him from seeing the rise of color in her cheeks. Thank goodness he couldn't read her mind and the romantic notions she carried there. It all became clear now. It should have made things easier but it didn't.

"No, I didn't. She only arrived this morning, Sam."

"Still, you've known her for a while. She would have gone through screening, right?"

"Of course."

"She's perfect, Angela. Mom was incredibly easy to convince."

Angela pulled her fingers from his grasp. She came back to earth with a crash. Of course. A man like Sam—a woman like her. She was building castles in the air that didn't exist. She had never had to worry. Her feelings were her own and not returned, and therefore easily managed. She schooled her features and struggled to move back into professional mode. "Perfect for?"

"You know Mom needs help with Dad. Clara needs a job. And Dad likes her. He said so when we took him back to his room. For once he didn't argue with us. It took me a long time to convince Mom that she needed to hire help, but after meeting Clara... Her qualifications are perfect for what we need. What do you think?"

It was a wonderful opportunity and she was happy for Clara, of course. It was exactly what the program was designed for, and Molly would be a wonderful boss. Angela had no reservations about that whatsoever, except the sinking sensation that Clara would be spending her days in the glorious house surrounded by the warmth of the Diamonds. She didn't begrudge it one bit—Clara deserved it after what she'd been through. But Angela couldn't help feeling the tiniest bit envious.

"I think it's a terrific gesture and very generous of you," she replied, staring out over the dark fields. "I'll talk to Clara about it tomorrow."

"Thanks. It's been a productive day, hasn't it? First the open house, now this. Your project is off to a roaring start."

It was true, so why on earth was she feeling so empty? *She should be happy, energized, raring to go. And instead* she was weary. The fulfillment she expected wasn't as bright and shiny as she'd hoped.

"Thanks to you and your family."

He took her hand again and his dark eyes were earnest in the shadows. She froze the image on her mind so she could recall it later. This was feeling very much like a cutting of the strings, and it was necessary. But now and again she'd like to remember how he looked at this moment.

"It's all down to you. Being able to help was an honor," he finished quietly.

"Sam…" Tears pricked her eyelids and she looked down at her feet.

"I want to stay on the board."

Her gaze snapped to his. He what? But today was supposed to be the end. Especially if his parents hired Clara, there was no reason why Molly couldn't resume her position. Why on earth would he want to stay? And how difficult was it going to be seeing him on a regular basis? She didn't have any experience with this type of longing. Surely it would fade over time, wouldn't it?

"What about Diamondback, and your own concerns?"

"I've managed so far. A lot of the worry has been about Mom. If she has help now, that will take a load off my mind."

"But what about the biogas facility? I know how much that means to you."

"I doubt it will happen now. Mom has Power of Attorney, but there's nothing wrong with Dad's mind. And even if she could, she wouldn't go against his wishes. I don't know how to convince him. I've tried everything. I don't want to give up, but I've stopped having a timeline about it. It's too frustrating."

"I'm sorry."

"You control the things you can and let go of the rest, right? You made me see that it's not worth losing my dad over. We need to look after him first and then perhaps revisit the idea. So, you see, I will have some spare time to give the foundation. I thought you'd be glad."

Glad? The idea that she'd see him regularly was sweet torture. She was smart enough to know he wasn't doing it for her. They had no future. They were committed to different things in different places. They needed things that they couldn't provide for each other.

"Of course. My first priority is the foundation, and the connection to your family has been so beneficial." She wondered if she sounded as cold as the words made her seem.

"Beneficial." The word was flat. "That's all you have to say?"

She fidgeted with her fingers, unsure of what he wanted her to say. "Today couldn't have happened without you. I just hope you're doing it for the right reasons."

*And not because you kissed me*, she was tempted to add, but didn't. The less they referenced that kiss, the better. Men like Sam didn't set as much store in a simple kiss as she did. He'd probably already forgotten it.

He reached out and took her fingers loosely in his. "I'm doing it because helping you this last month has changed me. I enjoyed it. I realized today that I am proud of what we've done. What you're doing is so amazing, Angela. I just want to be a part of it a little longer."

His fingers were warm and strong. "You thought I was a hoity-toity do-gooder," she whispered.

"I was wrong."

"Sam, I..."

"We make a good team, Angela. Admit it."

She took a step backward, needing to put a few inches between herself and his seductive voice. She bit down on her lip. Sam Diamond could convince her of nearly anything, she realized, and that scared her. It made her feel weak and malleable. But she could not admit to him just how much he meant to her. The idea of having him on the board, involved with the house, made her feel weak. There was no way to explain it to him, either, not without revealing her true insecurities and she'd rather die than do that. "But your mom. The board position was hers."

"The deal was that a family member must sit on the board. It doesn't have to be Mom."

The owl hooted again, the sound lonely and mysterious.

"What are you so afraid of?" he asked quietly, squeezing her fingers.

She inhaled, decided on the truth. "You."

The air around them seemed to pause until Angela realized she was holding her breath, and she let it out slowly. Sam hadn't released her hand. She was so very aware of his body only inches from hers and the urge to step closer fought with her long-time instinct to flee. She'd let him get too close already.

"Me? Don't you know by now I'd never hurt you?"

She didn't mean that way, though perhaps it was easier. After all, that sort of fear was a tangible thing. Admitting she was afraid of her own feelings would be like touching a match to paper.

"You d-don't understand," she stammered, pulling her fingers away again and taking a step backward.

"Then make me understand. Make me understand what

happened that night with the curtain rod. What happened yesterday when I kissed you? What's happening right now?"

He was asking questions that she didn't know how to answer, questions she'd spent years avoiding by not getting close to anyone. She shook her head. "I thought we were talking about board positions."

"Only if you're trying to avoid what's really happening here," he said, taking a step toward her and closing the distance once again.

"You said you wanted to be a part of Butterfly House."

"And I do. But not just that. Don't you understand? It's you, Angela."

"No." The word came out stronger than she expected. "You can't use the position to get closer to me. I don't come with the package."

"What has got you so terrified?" He reached out and laid his palm against her cheek. She wanted to trust him. She wanted to so much it hurt in places she hadn't let herself feel for years.

"I care about you," he murmured, taking one more step so that their bodies hovered a mere breath apart. "I didn't want to. You know that. But I do. I don't know what to do about it, but I know I don't want to stop. When I'm with you everything makes sense."

He was going to kiss her. She knew it even before he began to dip his head. Her lips started to tingle in anticipation and they parted as her eyelids drifted closed.

She would let him kiss her one last time. And then he'd walk away. She'd make sure of it.

# CHAPTER NINE

THE heat of his body warmed the air between them as he drew her closer, while the cool summer breeze ruffled the hem of her skirt. Hot and cold, light and dark. They were as different as two people could be, and maybe that was part of the attraction. Sam was all the things that Angela had never been—strong, confident, sure of his place in the world. It was no wonder she was drawn to him like a moth to a flame. As his lips grazed hers, she caught her breath and decided to enjoy the moment. She could always pull away before she got singed by the fire.

He cupped her face in his hands. So softly she could hardly bear it, he kissed the corner of her mouth, her cheek, her temple. His long fingers slid down over her jawbone and he paused. Angela put her hand on his shoulder and felt the tension vibrating there. He was holding back. The idea of all that leashed energy was vastly exciting and a very feminine part of her was wooed by the consideration that was costing him so much.

She wound her arms around his neck and placed her mouth on his.

Taking the initiative changed the dynamic of the contact instantly. After a heartbeat of surprise, Sam opened his lips and kissed her fully, wrapping his arms around her middle and lifting her off the ground until only the tips of her toes touched the grass. There was no hope of surviving unsinged now. Her whole body felt as though it was on fire, with the soft sounds of their kisses in the dark fanning the flames.

She let her fingers run through his short hair, adoring the silky warmth of it and feeling a jolt of desire as he made a sound of arousal deep in his throat. He held her against the planes of his workingman's body, long and lean and muscular, until she felt they must be imprinted on her own. It was the most glorious thing she had ever experienced. Even as she knew they had to stop, she didn't want to. Just a few seconds more before she had to give it all up. She was hungry and hadn't yet had her fill.

Slowly he lowered her to the ground so she was standing on both feet again. He linked his hands at the hollow of her back, holding her in the circle of his arms while he continued to sip from her lips.

Finally she broke away, knowing she couldn't let it go on any longer and still retain her dignity. She'd practically thrown herself into his arms, conveniently forgetting all the reasons why it was a mistake. Heat rushed into her face and she pressed her hands to her cheeks. Her heart drummed insistently against her ribs. His wary eyes watched her but the rest of his body remained completely still as she took a step backward.

He was too much, too powerful, too attractive. He made her want things, different things than she'd wanted for as long as she could remember. She'd known from the beginning he was going to be trouble. She just hadn't thought he'd be *this* kind of trouble.

"Sam," she chastised quietly. "We can't."

"Why?" He crossed his arms over his chest. The pose highlighted his muscled arms and she licked her lips. She wouldn't respond to his physicality. She had to keep her head. One of them had to.

"This is too complicated. There are so many reasons why we shouldn't."

"Is that right?" His voice was soft and seductive. "You know, I've been trying to figure out what it is about you that sets me off."

He put his hands in his back pockets, highlighting the breadth of his chest and shoulders. That restless energy that couldn't be tamed was sparking through the air again, making it come alive. Making *her* come alive, and she wasn't prepared for it.

"I don't mean to set you off," she replied in a small voice.

"But you do," he said softly. "You challenge me. You're *work*. You have firm opinions, and I respect you for them."

He took a step forward, relaxing his arms, treating her to a small, sideways smile. He reached out and ran a finger over her arm, raising the delicate hairs and goosebumps beneath his touch. "Something's happening between us, Angela. It started that night with the curtains. Don't deny it."

She stepped back. "Don't, please," she said, embarrassingly aroused and horribly tempted to give in. She imagined what would come next, out here in the soft darkness. She hadn't been intimate with a man in... She blinked as she stared into Sam's determined face. In a very long time. It had nearly cost her everything—and she'd nearly lost herself in the process. She couldn't do that again.

"It's not just wanting you, you know that, right?" His eyes gleamed at her. "It's the way you see the world. It's how you make me stop and think. Like with the kids today. I looked at them and saw trouble but you made me see something else—potential. With Clara, too." He smiled gently. "I never considered myself narrow-minded, but you make me look beyond the surface. That's why I'm fall..."

"Stop," she commanded, cutting him off before he could say any more. Her pulse hammered at her throat. She didn't know how to do this. She didn't know how to care about someone this much or—worse—accept that they might care about her. She was as emotionally stunted as any of her clients only she was able to give it a proper name and she'd had years of practice at covering it. He couldn't fall for her, and she couldn't fall for him either.

"You're afraid."

Sam knew nothing about what really drove her, and it took her breath away to realize how close she was to telling him the whole truth. To trusting him. Her heart told her she could but her head kept her mouth shut. She'd learned long ago that her heart had flawed judgment.

"I'm not afraid," she replied, forcing herself to stand tall as she lied. "What I am is leaving."

She turned to walk away and he reached out, his strong fingers circling her wrist. "Don't go. Talk to me."

This time there was no fear, only temptation to fall back into his embrace. A part of her thrilled to hear the words. But a stronger, more rational part had a bigger voice. She wrenched her wrist out of his grasp, panic rising at the dull pain that shot through her arm as she twisted it away. Panic that he would somehow see through her, leaving her vulnerable and exposed. He wanted more from her than she could ever give.

"I have to. I got carried away in the moonlight for a minute but it's over." She began to back away, feeling the cool grass against her toes as she stepped off the path. "Please, just let me go. Don't come after me and don't call, Sam."

"But, Angela…"

"Just don't." Her voice choked. "I can't, don't you see?"

"No, goddammit, I don't!" He ran his hand over his hair and heaved out a breath. "Tell me what you're so afraid of. Let me help you."

"I can't." She gave him one last desperate glance before

turning and fleeing. Not even the twinges in her toe slowed her down until she reached the steps of the back deck.

The glow from the kitchen lights filtered weakly over the grass and there was a muffled bark that sounded from inside—the Diamonds' dog was in for the night now that dark had fallen fully. Angela saw Molly's figure pass in front of the French doors and she hesitated, knowing she had to go in and collect Clara and her purse, needing to catch her breath first.

The motion light over the door came on as she climbed the stairs. She hurried to school her features into what she hoped was a pleasant smile before turning the handle on the door and entering the warm kitchen that still smelled of fresh bread and chocolate cake.

No one would ever know just how close she'd come to losing her head tonight. And even though she knew leaving was the right thing, she'd hold the sweet memory of this evening—all of it—inside during the months ahead. She was so used to being on the outside, staring longingly through the window at the perfect life she'd never have.

For one magical night, Sam had shown her what it could be like on the inside.

To Angela's surprise, Sam heeded her plea to leave her alone as July turned to August and Butterfly House became a buzz of activity. He was nowhere to be seen as three more tenants arrived and Angela's days were full with the day-to-day running of the project. Clara began working days at the Diamonds', looking after Virgil. She came home at night with stories about the family, tidbits that made Angela feel connected to Sam in some small way.

They also made her miss him horribly. She kept telling herself it was for the best, but there was no denying that she got an empty feeling every time a car turned into the yard and it wasn't him.

Then there were the handymen.

The first day the crew arrived Angela was in her office, conducting a session with her latest resident, Jane. She excused herself to see what was going on and found three men unloading scaffolding and paint.

"What do you think you're doing?"

"Mornin', ma'am. Just about to start working on your trim. We'll have it spruced up in no time."

She didn't want to sound rude but there was clearly some mistake. "But I didn't hire you."

"No, ma'am. Mr. Diamond did. We're to paint the gingerbread trim and stain the porch and railings." He put down the gallons of paint in his hand and straightened, wiping his hands on his coveralls. "Might want to use the back door until it's done."

She hesitated. Sam should have asked her first before going ahead with anything. The trouble was the trim did need a coat of paint and the porch, while sturdier since his repairs, made the house look shabby. A tiny voice inside her head asked her what she'd expected. Why would Sam ask her approval if she'd told him flat out to leave her alone?

Sending the men away would cause more trouble than it was worth. "All right then, go ahead. I'll be inside if you need anything."

"Yes, ma'am," he replied, and motioned to the others to begin setting up the scaffolding.

Angela had firmly believed that the whole out-of-sight, out-of-mind thing would work, but she felt Sam's presence constantly. After the workmen finished, one of the local teens came by to mow the grass and asked if he could put the new pushmower Mr. Diamond had provided in the shed when he was finished. The house and yard looked better than ever but, inside, her emotions were churning. Mr. Diamond this and Mr. Diamond that. Exorcising him from her thoughts proved harder than she'd expected. He'd helped with the fixing-up, and now it seemed that his handiwork was all around her, whether she asked for it or not.

The final straw was the feature in the local monthly paper. It had carried a wonderful spot on the project, but it was the *picture they'd used of her with Sam that made her heart catch.* It hadn't been one of the posed shots. Instead the black-and-white photo that stared up at her from the newsprint was one where Sam was looking back at her and she was grinning down at him—when they'd been teasing each other. He'd been a royal pain in the behind and a bright light in her life all at once, and now everything was gray and dull in his absence.

She folded the paper and put it in a desk drawer. The feature was good, though she wished it had focused more about the foundation and less about her. Sam had done a bang-up job singing her praises and her name was everywhere. She told herself she shouldn't worry. No one in Edmonton even cared where she was now. And the two people who might—well, Angela had stopped deluding herself long ago. The chances of Jack Beck actually reading a small-town rag were slim to none. The anxiety was natural, she supposed, but not necessarily rational.

But the picture of her with Sam was branded on her mind. She lay awake one hot summer night, her window open as she listened to the sounds of the peepers in the nearby slough and the rustle of the leaves. Coyotes howled, the sound so plaintive and lonely that she felt like howling along with them. She flipped over, punching her pillow, but her eyes remained stubbornly open. She couldn't erase the image of Sam in the moonlight, his lips still slightly swollen from her kisses. She had to do something, so she got out of bed and went downstairs in her pajamas. When she couldn't sleep, she baked. And when she was this twitchy, only one recipe would do.

She was careful to be quiet as she whisked together the cream, sugar and cocoa over the burner for the chocolate silk filling. A baked crust cooled on the counter as she stirred, wishing she could stir away her thoughts as easily as the whisk smoothed away the lumps in the mixture.

She poured the thickened filling into the crust and scraped the sides of the pan with her spatula. She gave the plastic surface an indulgent lick—the secret was in the melted dark chocolate—and then put both pot and spatula in the sink before turning back to the fridge and sliding the pie in to set. She stretched and gave a huge yawn. Baking always did the trick. Tomorrow morning would be time enough to whip up the cream for the top and they could all have a treat.

She was just wiping the pan dry when there was a horrible pounding on the door.

For one terrified second she couldn't move, flooded by a hundred memories crowding her consciousness all at once. This was the reality she knew—that no amount of therapy or time ever completely erased the fear, especially the reflexive reaction in that moment before rational thought took over. The pounding persisted and she forced her feet to move, grabbing the handset to the phone on the way by. Just in case.

Steps echoed behind her as Clara, Jane, Alyssa and Sue rattled down the stairs. When Angela reached the door, she turned and looked at the women standing behind her, their eyes wide, cheeks pale. Whatever Angela was feeling, it had to be a hundred times worse for them. It was fresher for them and they were looking to her to set an example. She squared her shoulders and peeped through the Judas hole.

What she saw turned her knees to jelly.

She flipped the locks and opened the door, her stomach

turning and heart pounding as she looked down at the woman on her knees on the front step.

"Mom?"

Beverly Beck lifted her head and Angela's soul wept at the sight of her. One eye was so swollen it was closed, while the opposite cheek sported an angry red bruise. Her bottom lip was cracked and when Angela knelt and touched her arm, she started to cry.

Angela felt an anger so profound she thought she might explode out of her own skin with it. This woman—this kind, caring woman who had done nothing but give blind devotion to her husband—had been repaid with *this*.

"Come inside," she whispered, going out carefully. "Let me help you."

Gently she helped her mother get to her feet and led her inside. She shut the door and locked it and nodded at the group of women still standing in the kitchen. "It's all right," she said, trying to sound reassuring while the conflicting mass of emotions tied knots in her belly. "We'll be in my office," she said, leading Beverly into the small room off the entry.

Beverly was still crying quietly and Angela led her to a small couch. They sat side by side and she simply waited for her mother to speak. When Beverly was ready, she patted Angela's hand and sighed.

"Help me, Angie," she said.

Angela had waited her whole life to hear that simple request, and her heart seemed to burst hearing the words.

No matter the hurt or blame that she had held inside over the years, this was her mother. The woman who had cut flower shapes out of sandwiches with cookie cutters when she was a child, the one who had taken her on weekly trips to the library until Angela was old enough to go on her own. She was the one who, no matter what, tucked Angela into bed at night and promised that tomorrow would be better even if she never kept those promises. Somewhere inside this broken body that beautiful woman still existed, and Angela opened her arms. "Of course I'll help you," she murmured, kissing her mother's graying hair. "It's all I've ever wanted."

There was a discreet knock on the door and Clara poked her head inside. "I made a pot of tea," she said quietly. "I thought you might like some."

"That'd be lovely—thank you." Angela sat back, wiping her fingers under her eyes and then took Beverly's hands in her own. She noticed that her mother's nails were short and chipped, her hands chapped. How many horrors had she suffered in the years since Angela left? Not for the first time, she felt unbearable guilt for leaving her mother to face things on her own.

Clara returned with a tray containing a teapot, mugs, milk and a plate of toast with a jar of jam. "In case someone would like a bite," she offered.

"Thank you, Clara." She offered a small smile, wanting to inject as much normalcy into the evening as she could. "Is everyone okay?" Clara was turning out to be a truly nurturing soul. The Diamonds were lucky to have her.

"A little shaken, but okay. They're going back to bed now."

"I'll see you in the morning, then."

Clara shut the door with a quiet click.

The new silence was deafening.

Angela poured two cups of tea and added milk to each. "Here," she offered, holding out the cup. "Drink this. You'll feel better and you can tell me what happened."

Beverly offered no resistance as she wrapped her hands around the warm mug and Angela wondered if she'd simply been used to obeying for so long that she didn't know how to do anything else. For the first time since becoming a social worker, Angela felt as though she was in over her head, flying by the seat of her pants.

The tea was hot and reviving, and she caught her mother's gaze focused on the toast. Angela wondered when she'd eaten last. She knew very well that there wasn't always money for groceries. "Jam?"

She spread a triangle with saskatoonberry jam and handed it over.

When the piece was gone, Angela sat up straighter. "You're not here for tea and toast. Can you tell me what happened?"

Beverly nodded. "I left your father."

"After he did this to you." The words came out tightly, like the string of a bow held taut, ready for release.

Another nod.

"Have you left him for good?"

Angela held her breath. The answer had to be yes. Beverly couldn't come this far and then go back, could she? But Angela knew she could. How many times had they talked about packing a bag and disappearing? It was always too good to be true. She had to attempt to keep her own feelings out of the mix right now. She had to if she were truly going to help.

Fear widened Beverly's eyes but she nodded once more. "I packed a bag tonight when he was at the bar. I took the car and came here."

Oh, Lord. Beverly hadn't had a driver's license for over fifteen years. If she'd been stopped she would have ended up right back home again. And Angela wouldn't put it past her father to report the vehicle stolen. Wouldn't it be ironic if the police were the ones to deliver her back to her doorstep? Angela looked at Beverly's downturned head and said slowly, "Does he know *where* you've gone?"

Agonized eyes met hers. "I don't know."

Something in the tone, and the way her mother's eyes dropped once more to her lap, made a line of dread sneak down Angela's spine. There was something more. "What set him off this time? What changed?"

Beverly's gaze skittered away again. "It doesn't matter."

"Mom."

Beverly's fingers picked at the frayed hem of her blouse. "I cut out that picture of you in the paper. I couldn't believe it was you, honey. You're so grown-up and pretty. I read all about this place and I was real proud, you know?"

Everything came crashing down. This was her fault, wasn't it? She hadn't realized the story had been picked up by the city paper. The words were like little knives cutting through Angela's skin, sharp and stinging. Why couldn't this have happened years ago when she'd begged and pleaded? Maybe they could have done this together. Maybe...

But Angela knew that the world didn't run on maybes. She forced the useless wish aside. "And?"

"Your dad, he found the picture and got right ugly."

"And he took it out on you."

There was no answer to give. They both knew she was right. Ever since the day Angela had left, there'd been no one but Beverly for him to use as a punching bag.

And ever since that day Angela had worked so hard, trying to atone for it.

"He told me to remember my place, and..." Her throat worked but no words came out for a moment. "When he was done with me he took off to the usual watering hole. I wasn't going to come, but he said he should have made you pay years ago. I was so scared, Angela. Afraid of what he might do. Afraid that he'd...he'd use me to get to you again."

Another thick silence fell. Neither of them needed to say the words. They both knew he'd already used Beverly to get to Angela.

"So he knows where I am. What I do?"

"It made him some mad."

A cold finger of fear shivered down Angela's spine, followed by anger. She couldn't let him have this power over her anymore. Not just her, either. There were four other women—five counting Beverly—looking to her for strength and leadership. She couldn't let them down. She didn't know what to do—everything seemed to be crumbling inside. Beverly put her hand over her face and started weeping again, the sound full of despair and hopelessness.

Angela's insides were quaking and she knew she couldn't do this alone.

Her first call should be to the police, but she couldn't make herself dial the number. The very thought of it was exhausting and left her emotionally drained. There was only one thing—one person—she wanted. It probably wasn't wise, and it definitely didn't make sense after their last conversation, but right now she would give anything to see Sam's strong face.

She got up from the couch, went to the desk drawer and pulled out a scrap of paper that she'd kept since the day she'd dropped the box spring on her toe. *If you need anything,* he'd said, *call me.*

With a tangle of nerves in her stomach, she dialed Sam's cell number.

# CHAPTER TEN

THE shrill ringtone of his cell dragged him out of a dead sleep and set his heart pounding. He reached for the phone beside the bed and fumbled with the buttons. A sane person never called at this hour unless something was wrong.

"Yuh, hello," he said into the phone, rubbing his hand over his face.

"It's Angela."

His eyes snapped open. There was something wrong. It was in the tight, odd sound to her voice. Like she was trying to sound normal but there was an edge to it that hinted of hysteria. He sat up in bed, fully alert, and reached over to turn on the bedside lamp. "What's going on?"

"Can you come over?"

There was a quiver in the last word as her voice caught. No preamble, no explanation, no wasted words, just a plea that put a cold shiver into his heart. The Angela he knew would have been rational and explained. She never would have been so raw and vulnerable. Or afraid. He was sure she was afraid for some reason. "Are you all right?"

"I just…I need you."

Goddamn. The last time they'd spoken she'd told him to leave her alone and he'd granted that request. For her to turn to him now had to mean something was desperately wrong. "Give me ten minutes," he replied, hanging up at the same

time as he launched himself out of bed and reached for his
jeans.

He drove far too fast in the dark, trying to think of plausible scenarios for why she'd call him in the middle of the
night. Running the sort of place she did, his first reaction
was that an ex-husband or boyfriend had caused trouble. He
swallowed, putting his foot on the gas. Was someone hurt?
Angela? Or Clara? She'd been such a bright spot around the
house. Clara's help had made such a difference with Virgil.
The very thought of her being in trouble was horrible. But
when he thought of Angela, it was different. There was fear
for her, but something more. A desire to protect her. Even
though weeks had passed since they'd kissed in the garden,
it was far from over. Not for Sam. It was time he admitted
the truth to himself. He'd fallen in love with her, he'd blown
it and he had no idea what to do next.

He was there in seven minutes flat. He knocked on the
door and then tried the knob. It was locked, so he knocked a
little louder. A strange car sat in the driveway and he set his
jaw. If someone didn't answer soon, he'd break in the door if
he had to.

Clara answered, wrapped up in a housecoat and slippers.
Her face was pale but she offered Sam a weak smile. "She
called you. I'm glad. Come in, Sam."

He followed her inside, glad she was clearly unhurt.
"What's going on?"

Angela's office door opened and she stepped into the hall.
For a moment all he could see were the tearstains on her
cheeks. In the next heartbeat she was in his arms.

He took a step backward as the force of her embrace took
him by surprise. He closed his eyes and put his arms around
her. Lordy, she felt like she'd lost weight, she was so small
and fragile. Her shoulders rose and fell and he heard her snif-
fle against his shirt. She was not a woman who surrendered

easily; now she was crying in his arms. He held her tighter, wanting to protect her from whatever was pulling her apart at the seams.

There was no sense denying it now, no sense fighting what he'd been trying to ignore for weeks. He'd do anything for her. And right now he sensed that what she needed was a gentle touch. "Shhh," he offered, rubbing her back through her thin T-shirt. "What's wrong, Ang? You have to tell me what's wrong."

She lifted her head. "I..." She drew in a shuddering breath. "I shouldn't be so glad to see you, but I am."

A woman stepped out of the office, peering timidly around the corner. Sam saw the cracked lip and bruises and felt as though he'd been punched in the gut for the second time in as many minutes. She looked startled as she met his gaze and went back inside, but she turned a little, showing her profile. A profile that was remarkably similar to the woman in his arms, if she were a few decades older.

He ran his hand over her hair, suddenly understanding why she was so upset. "Is that your mom?"

Angela turned her head quickly but the woman had already gone back inside, shutting the door with a quiet click.

"Yes," she answered. "Yes, that's my mother. She showed up tonight after my father lit into her. For the last time, if I have anything to say about it."

Shock rippled through him as she admitted the truth. He knew how passionate she was about Butterfly House, how committed she was to ending abuse and helping these women start over. But her own mother... She had to be devastated. He was gutted just looking at the bruises. How must she feel as her daughter? How would he feel if it were Molly? Questions zinged through his mind, piling one on top of the other. Had she known? Had it been going on all through Angela's child-hood? Had she been a victim of her father's abuse, too? His stomach turned. How much had she suffered? And then there was the relationship she mentioned. How did that fit into everything? How much had she truly hidden from him?

But the answers would have to wait. They had to deal with the right now first.

Angela wouldn't push him away this time. No matter what it took. No matter how much she might fight him on it. The days of her standing alone against the world were done.

"Tell me what you need," he said, tipping up her chin with a finger and meeting her gaze. "Tell me what I can do to help and I'll do it."

Angela lost herself in his dark gaze for just a moment. Never before had she let herself need someone this much. Not just need—but she'd willingly placed herself in the hands of another and it was terrifying and a relief all at once.

It was scary to surrender when she'd spent her whole life avoiding that very thing. But also terrifying in how *right* it felt. It filled her with a sense of certainty that she'd never experienced before. She knew that Sam would be there. She'd known it the day he'd given her his cell number and told her to call if she needed anything. It had gone beyond items on a grocery list. It had even gone beyond a kiss in the moonlight.

She reached up and circled his wrist with her fingers, drawing his hand away from her face. Right now she was just happy to have him there. "I need your advice."

She wanted someone objective to look at the situation, someone whose life hadn't been colored by abusive situations. It stung her pride to know that she'd lost her objectivity. But some things were more important than pride. Like safety for all of them.

He looked startled, uncomfortable as he drew back a little and furrowed his brow. "Are you sure I'm the right person to ask? I have no experience with this."

She didn't share his doubts. "I can manage my mom. I think. But it's my father." She filled him in on the events of the evening. "And so you see, she took the car. She has no license, no insurance. He could report the car stolen. He'll be angry, Sam, and I'm not sure what to do next." She fought against the finger of fear that trickled down her spine and the backs of her legs. "He'll be really angry. And…" She swallowed. "He knows where I am. Because of the article and my picture."

"This is my fault," he murmured, his face flattening with shock. "I pushed you into being in that photo. You didn't even want to do it. Oh, Angela."

"It's not your fault, I promise."

"But…"

Things became very clear for Angela in that moment. Sam was blaming himself just as she'd blamed herself for years. "Look at me," she said, her voice stronger than she thought possible. "It's easy to blame yourself. You play the 'if only' game. 'If only I had done something differently.' 'If only I hadn't said that.' But the truth is abusers like my dad don't really need reasons. It is not your fault, Sam. It's his, and his alone. I promise."

There was freedom with the words, but she also felt her energy being sapped from the high emotion of the events. "But that doesn't change what we're dealing with." She pressed her fingers to the bridge of her nose, feeling the beginnings of a headache. "It won't take him long to figure out where she went."

"Did you call the police?"

"I've only called you. He won't realize she's gone until he gets home from the bar, maybe not until he wakes up with a hangover."

She couldn't help the bitterness that flavored the words. She knew the routine well. Jack would come home smelling like tequila and cigarettes and pass out. It was the next morning that was the worst. When the shakes set in along with the anger.

"But he needs to be arrested."

Nausea turned in Angela's stomach. "I…"

Her voice abandoned her and she looked at her feet.

Sam didn't speak for several long seconds. Finally he said the words down low. "Are you still afraid of him?"

"I left, didn't I?"

"Oh, honey. It's not the same thing, and we both know it. Look at me, please."

She lifted her head and met his gaze, hot shame filling her as she bit down on her lip.

"It's one thing to accept you're not to blame, but quite another to look down the barrel of the gun, isn't it?"

She didn't want to agree, so she kept silent. There were too many years and too many scars. She wanted to say she didn't care, that she wasn't afraid. But she was.

"If this were any other woman, would you hesitate to call the police?"

They both knew the answer. She'd made the phone call many, many times over the years.

"I can't," she whispered. "Oh, Sam, I'm such a hypocrite. I run this place and pretend I'm all whole and everything. But when it comes down to it, I'm still…" Tears clogged her throat. "A victim."

"Those women have you as their champion. But you had no one." He cupped her chin in his fingers. "Until now. You have me. And you are not going to do this alone."

She wouldn't cry. Not anymore. She needed to be strong and deal with what needed to be dealt with. And right now her first priority was her mother.

"I've got to be with her," she murmured. "She's so fragile right now. So scared."

"You look after your mom and I'll look after the rest," Sam said, drawing himself up to his full height. He was an imposing sight, her protector. She had never wanted to admit she needed a guardian, but she was glad to have him tonight. There wasn't a spare ounce that wasn't solid muscle and the glint in his eye and angle of his jaw spoke of determination. She'd pegged him as being stubborn before, blindly so. But now she knew he was not. He simply fought for those things he believed in. And tonight she was fortunate he believed in her and Butterfly House.

"I need to get her settled. This isn't the place for her. In the morning I'll need to get her to a different kind of shelter. It's a different sort of help here. And she's going to need me beside her."

"You do that and I'll make some phone calls. Don't worry, Ang. I won't let him hurt either of you. I promise."

She swallowed past the lump in her throat. Sam always made good on his promises. She knew that by now.

"You'll wait for me, then?"

He nodded. "Of course I will."

"There's tea in the kitchen."

His lopsided smile nearly popped a dimple. "I think I could use a whiskey, but I know the rules. Tea will do."

She stepped away from him and took three shaky steps back to her office before turning back.

"Thank you for coming," she murmured, her hand resting on the door frame. "I don't know how I would have gotten through this without you."

Then she turned away before she could hear his response. Because the look in his eyes was so tender and caring she suddenly felt at risk of exposing everything.

And that was something she just couldn't do.

When Beverly was settled in the last unoccupied bedroom, Angela shut the door gently and finally let her shoulders slump. If they could get through this first night it would be better. For a few panicked minutes her mother had insisted on going home, saying that it would be better than Jack's fury when he found out what she'd done. That he'd forgive her—as if she somehow needed forgiveness. Jack—Angela had long ago stopped thinking of him as Dad—was the one who should be on his knees. It had taken all of Angela's energy to stay calm and logical when she still felt her own fear and anger.

But she bit her tongue and was soothing and rational and all the other important things she needed to be, knowing that Sam waited. She might be weak but she would do this. They hadn't come this far to mess it up now.

She had tended to Beverly's wounds and helped her to bed, assuring her mother it would all be fine, while inside she held no such guarantee. This wasn't the end. It was only the beginning. And she still listened with one ear, wondering if Jack would come along and pound on her door and start making demands. That couldn't happen. Not just for Beverly but for the other women. This was supposed to be their safe place. She leaned back against the bedroom door and closed her eyes. That open house was supposed to be such a positive thing. Something to build awareness and support. And now because of her, it could all come tumbling down.

When she entered the kitchen, she was shocked to see Sam casually washing up the dishes from the tea and toast. A dish towel was slung over his shoulder as he washed out the teapot and rinsed it beneath the hot spray. There was something both masculine and nurturing about it and she knew she was in horrible danger of falling in love with him despite all her precautions. The phone call and embrace had been simple reactions to an extremely stressful situation, but even Angela, in her emotional state, realized that she never would have done either if something deeper weren't at work.

Love. A lump formed in her throat. It was impossible.

"I can do those in the morning," she said, wrapping her arms around her middle. She was still in the pink boxers and T-shirt she'd worn to answer the door and while perfectly modest, felt quite exposed beneath his dark gaze.

He slid the dish towel off his shoulder, gave the pot a wipe and put it down on the counter. "It was no trouble. I needed to do something while I waited."

"I kept you a long time."

His gaze was far too understanding for her to be comfortable. "You had a good reason. Do you want tea? I can make a new pot."

She shook her head. At the moment, his earlier suggestion of whiskey sounded just about right, but she had a policy about alcohol on the premises. "No, I'm fine. I had some earlier."

"Is your mom asleep?"

Angela shrugged. "I don't know. I figure she'll either lie awake a long time, or she'll be so exhausted she'll conk out completely." She moved farther into the room, forcing deep breaths to keep from feeling overwhelmed. "She's here, and that's the main thing."

"Well, no one's going to bother you tonight."

There was an edge to his voice, a defiance that sent a little fizz through her veins. "You don't have to stay, Sam. You've done so much already." She felt obligated to say it even as the thought of him leaving made an empty hole form inside her.

"You can't get rid of me that easily," he replied. He hung the dish towel over the oven-door handle. "I called a friend of mine. The car's been towed and it'll be delivered back to Edmonton like it had never gone missing. Then I called Mike Kowalchuk. He was here at the open house, remember? The constable. He's aware of the situation and he's contacted the police in the city. Someone's going to be watching the street until your dad is picked up. No one will get within a hundred yards without Mike knowing."

Relief swamped her. "I had no idea…"

"We take care of our own around here."

And he included her as one of them. The fact that he'd gotten people out of bed and into action with a few simple phone calls wasn't lost on her. When Sam wanted something done, he didn't stop until he made it happen. It was intimidating—and embarrassing that he'd had to do what she normally would have done in this situation. She was thankful for the support even as she felt like he was taking over.

She didn't like being the one not in control.

"I don't know what to say."

"Don't say anything." He stepped forward and cupped her face in his palm. "Keeping you safe comes first," he said simply.

She stared at his lips, wondering if he was going to kiss her, wondering if she even truly wanted him to.

Instead he pressed his lips to her forehead. They were firm and warm and reassuring. "You must have been so scared," he murmured.

"Not the first time. Or the worst," she said quietly.

He uttered a curse and ran a hand over his jaw. "I didn't know."

She took pity on him then, not liking the awkward silence that had fallen over the kitchen. "How could you? I've never told anyone. Don't worry about it." She sighed, feeling so much older than her years. "My mother has been in the same situation for as long as I can remember."

"I'm worried about you. You're pale and exhausted. You should rest."

"I'm fine. Everything's fine now." She pushed away and

wished she had a housecoat, a hoodie, anything to make her feel less naked.

"If you're fine, why do you look like you're about to collapse?"

He had her there. She wasn't fine. She was nowhere near fine. And she wouldn't be for a long time. Most days her energy went into current projects and she could forget—or ignore—those very real incidents that had shaped her past. But tonight she'd come face-to-face with her demons again. And relived every moment when she'd opened the front door and wondered what she'd find inside.

She blinked rapidly as his shape blurred. All the adrenaline abandoned her and exactly what had happened truly, finally, sank in. The life she had left behind had caught up with her. But her mother was out and had made that important first step. It shouldn't hurt this much to get what she'd always wanted.

"It's okay," she heard him say gently. "Aw, baby, come here."

He opened his arms.

She went to him because now that it was over she was fragile. He hugged her close and she drank in his smell—a bit woodsy, a bit like citrus and the blankety-soft scent of sleep because she'd dragged him out of bed.

"Come sit down before you fall down." His breath was warm on her ear and made her body shiver in an instinctive reaction. She had no energy left to fight him with, and, her hand tucked inside his, they went into the living room and sat side by side on the sofa.

"It's so hard," she confessed, and it felt so good to finally confide in someone. "It's not the same when it's your own mother, you know?" She closed her eyes and leaned against his shoulder. "At one point I thought she was going to get up and walk back out the door. I wanted to beg her not to go. I wanted to get down on my knees and plead with her not to let it happen again. But I learned a long time ago that begging doesn't work. So I sucked it up and put on my best social-worker hat. I was very professional on the outside," she continued, chancing a look up at him.

She realized for the first time that his shirt was buttoned incorrectly. She stared at the uneven buttons and her heart melted just a little. She'd frightened him that much, then, that he'd rushed into his clothes and raced over here without a second thought. She hadn't deserved that, not after the way she'd treated him. Not after the way she'd treat him before this was all over.

"And on the inside?"

She sighed. "On the inside I'm a mess. I'm supposed to be *objective and smart and helpful. And you know what I am?*"

He shook his head.

She looked down at her hands, not wanting to see disappointment in his eyes. "I'm a coward."

"You're the bravest woman I know," he replied, putting his arm around her shoulder, cuddling her in more as he leaned against the arm of the sofa. "Look at all you've accomplished here. Look at Clara, and the other women you're helping. Ang, at one time they arrived somewhere looking very much like your mother does tonight. Now look where they are."

Tonight was the first time he'd ever shortened her name. No one had ever called her Ang. Not ever. Not friends, not her mom, not even Steve when he'd been at his charming best and had sucked her into a controlling relationship. She liked the way it sounded when Sam said it, maybe too much.

"You don't understand."

"Then help me to."

Why did he have to be so wonderful? The last time they'd spoken she'd left him standing in the moonlight and told him to leave her alone. He'd followed her wishes to the letter, but he'd been taking care of her all along, she realized, helping her project when she refused any other sort of contact. He couldn't do that forever. At some point the emergency would be over and they'd have to get back to their regularly scheduled lives.

"Sam, what you saw tonight—that was my life, too. It was my daily existence from my first memories until I finished high school. I got a scholarship, packed my bags one night when my father was passed out, and never looked back."

"I wondered," he said quietly. "Tonight I was shocked, but not really surprised. There is something about you. A distance, a protective layer you never let down. You are always so determined to stand on your own two feet, never to back down. Like you have something to prove."

"Maybe I do." He was being rather insightful and she wasn't sure if she was glad at not having to explain or unsettled that she was so transparent.

"The only other time you let your guard down was the day before the open house."

Yes, the day she'd seen all her plans crumble before her eyes when that cursed box spring dropped on her foot. The day he'd turned her into a puddle of feminine goo and scared the hell out of her when he'd kissed her. "I felt safe, I suppose. Doesn't mean it was easy."

His hand rubbed along her arm, warm and reassuring, anchoring her to the present. After a few minutes, he spoke again. "He beat you, too, didn't he? That's why you were too afraid to make the call tonight."

"I don't want your pity," she warned. "There are a lot of ways to hurt a person, and not always with fists, though I had my share of those, too. I went to school and was around other people so Jack was careful not to leave any marks where they'd show. Those bruises healed faster than the hateful words and names he called me."

Sam didn't answer. She knew it was a lot for him to take in, but maybe now he'd finally understand why things could never work between them. "A father is supposed to be a provider and protector, you know? He broke trust with my mother and with me."

"Yes, he did."

"And I left rather than confronting him about it. He was my father. I thought I should love him. That he should love me. But love isn't supposed to be like that. It was easier to leave than to deal with it. With him."

He seemed to consider for a moment. "But when you studied, when you became a social worker…"

"You mean that I should have figured this all out then, right? Fixed myself?" She gave a short laugh. "I thought I had, but that was before I really understood what…"

She stopped. She'd been about to say *what real love feels like*. It would have been a slip that was tantamount to a three-word declaration. And a big mistake. Maybe she was in love with him. And maybe it did change everything. But it didn't mean it would ever work and it was better to leave the words unsaid.

"Before I really understood," she repeated, hoping he wouldn't pursue the *what*.

"You must be happy that your mom has taken this step, then."

She sighed. "Of course. But that's not easy, either. I don't want to be angry with her but I am. She broke trust with me, too, Sam. *I needed her to stand up. To leave. To put me first.* She stayed, insisting that he loved her. I've been so angry, so helpless." Her lip wobbled. "So guilty."

"Guilty? What on earth do you have to feel guilty about?" He twisted a little so that he was looking down at her face. "That's crazy talk."

She shook her head. "I left her there, Sam. I left her alone to deal with Jack all by herself. How many beatings did she endure when he realized I was gone? How many since?" She put her head in her hands, feeling the awful truth wrapping its cords around her neck. "I was angry and I gave up on her."

"You listen to me," Sam said, taking her hands in his and removing them from her face. "Look at me."

She couldn't. She was this close to falling apart and looking at him would ensure it. Nothing he could say would convince her that this wasn't her fault. It was all true. She had given up on her mother. She'd written her off. She'd dedicated her life to helping abused women and she was an absolute farce.

"I said look at me."

She looked up.

He looked angry, she realized, but not in a frightening, threatening way. In a way that made her heart take a ridiculous leap. "You did not give up on her. What you did was survive."

"I sacrificed her for myself, Sam. It was utterly selfish."

"That's garbage and you know it. You just got finished telling me that it was not my fault. Well, it's not yours, either, and deep down you know it. You relied on her to protect you and when she didn't, you protected yourself. That's courageous and smart, and don't let anyone tell you differently. You were a *kid*. You dedicated your life to helping women like your mom. And I'm guessing there are a lot of people out there thankful for whatever selfishness, as you call it, that you demonstrated. You've saved lives, Angela Beck. So do not sell yourself short because you are human."

"My penance," she whispered.

"You started Butterfly House because of her, didn't you?"

"I had to do something or go crazy. She wouldn't let me help her. Oh, Sam, she wouldn't help herself. I couldn't go back there. I thought about sneaking back and trying to convince her, but I couldn't get within two blocks of home without feeling sick to my stomach."

"Then this relationship you spoke of..."

"Classic pattern. Steve seemed wonderful at first, and I was young and alone. And then I started losing myself bit by bit, molded into what he wanted. I became a carbon copy of my mother until the day he hit me and then took my picture and stuck it on the fridge so I would remember what would happen if I put a toe out of line. That was my moment. I *packed my things and walked away.*"

She'd conquered the demon by getting her degree in social work and proving time and again that she was stronger than the fear. But all the while she knew in her heart she was a coward. An imposter.

"I'm going to tell you something and I want you to think about it, Angela." He squeezed her fingers. "What you did back then made today possible. Every decision you've made brought you to this day, in this place, and put you in the position to give help when she finally decided to seek it."

"I want to believe you." It sounded so good, so logical, so exonerating. But was it true?

"You can't force someone to do what they don't have the strength to do. You can't force them to feel what you want *them to feel. What you can do is be ready, so that when the* day comes, you're there with open arms."

That sounded to Angela like the voice of experience. Sam was thirty-seven. Had he been waiting for someone to come to their senses all this time?

"And who are you waiting for, Sam? Who broke your trust?"

For a long moment he looked into her eyes, as if deliberating whether to speak. Finally he relaxed a little, his lips curving just the tiniest bit. "I'm not waiting for anyone."

And that was where he stopped. All kisses and tender moments aside, he finished his sentence there and said no more. Angela had turned to him tonight because she'd needed him. And he was there because they were...what exactly? More than friends? But he'd had chances to kiss her tonight and the closest he'd gotten was a peck on the forehead, like a brother might give a sister. She'd screwed it up big-time at Diamondback when she ran away.

Because she'd lied. She did want him. She did care and the truly astonishing thing was that she trusted him. With anything. With her life. And she could tell him so or she could let him walk out the door.

# CHAPTER ELEVEN

WHEN Angela woke, sun was streaming through the kitchen windows. The throw from the back of the sofa was soft against her skin and a cushion had been placed beneath her head. She felt as though a weight had been lifted even though she knew there was so much heartache to come. But it was going to get better. She just knew it.

She rolled slightly and looked toward the kitchen. Sam. He was standing at the counter in front of the coffeemaker, staring out the window at the backyard as the coffee brewed. Had he slept at all? His jaw was darkened with a layer of stubble and his hair was usually a bit messy so it was hard to tell if he'd slept or not. But she noticed his shirt was now buttoned correctly, and she gave a small smile.

He'd stayed all night. Looked after her in a way no one ever had before. Listened to her, and she'd opened up and let him see all the dark, hidden corners. And yet here he was, making coffee, humming tunelessly, completely oblivious to the changes he'd wrought in her.

She would be okay. She'd be more than okay and so would her mom. Because they would face what needed facing and she wouldn't be afraid.

She shifted on the sofa and he turned and smiled. The sight of him grinning at her made her warm all over, and if the wattage of his smile missed any spot, his easy greeting found the shadows. "Hey, sleepyhead."

Oh, my. Sam's morning voice was husky with the rasp of sleep. "Hey yourself," she replied, trying to keep her pulse under control. "How long have I slept?"

"A few hours. We were talking and then I looked down and you were out like a light."

The idea of falling asleep curled up against his side made her feel all hot and tingly. "Sorry about that."

"Don't be." The coffeemaker beeped and he held up an empty mug. "Want some?"

She pushed herself up to sit, leaving the blanket over her bare legs. He was trying to keep things easy and she needed to follow his lead, even if she was feeling a bit shaky. She didn't quite trust it, but had to admit it felt amazing to let someone look after her for a change. She smiled up at him. "Love some. Black's fine."

He brought her a cup along with one of his own and sat down. "I thought you'd want to know right away that I heard from Mike. They picked up your dad just south of Leduc. He was hitchhiking, on his way here."

She sipped her coffee, trying to sort out her feelings. Relief, certainly, that Jack would not show up. Hope that Beverly was truly on the road to a new life. And simple sadness. This was what her family was reduced to. And it was a mess. It would be for a long time, until things with both her parents got sorted. It certainly wasn't fair to drag Sam into it. He'd done enough last night.

"Mike wants to see you and your mom this morning. They need to interview you both if they're going to press charges. He can only stay in the drunk tank for so long before they have to release him."

"I know." She would face this—face him—after all this time. She had to.

"I can go with you if you want."

The offer was unexpected and generous but unsettling. She knew he was trying to help but couldn't escape the fear of being smothered by his involvement. She ran her finger around the rim of her cup. Didn't he trust her to see it through? She had needed him last night, but she was made of stern stuff. She stopped circling her finger and looked up at him. "To make sure I go through with it?"

He frowned. "Of course not. For support. I know this is going to be very difficult and painful."

Her hands felt cold and she curled them around the heat of the cup. "You're a strong person, Sam. You see a problem and you fix it. You aren't afraid of anything. And it would be easy for me to let you fix this for me, but if last night showed me anything, it's that I need to fix it for myself."

"I wasn't planning on fixing it for you." He sounded put out about it. "It was for moral support, but if you don't want me to go, I won't."

The gap that had narrowed last night started to widen again.

He put his cup down on the table and then took hers and put it down as well. He clasped her fingers in his hands and met her eyes. "But for the record, I do get afraid now and again. I'm not always as strong as I should be."

She doubted it. He was so very perfect, so masculine and approachable with his chocolate eyes and hint of stubble and wrinkled shirt. It wasn't fair that she should find him so attractive when she needed to gather the wherewithal to keep her distance. It would be too easy to let him take the lead.

At that moment Morris jumped up on the couch, stepped carefully across the cushion and curled up on Sam's lap. He started purring instantly while Sam's surprised gaze met hers.

"Well, I'll be," he murmured, letting go of one of her hands and dropping his to stroke the soft orange fur.

He'd won over Morris. Her timid, cranky boy hadn't just accepted a touch but had sought it out. He hardly ever sat in her lap, let alone curled up in a contented ball. And here he was cuddling with Sam. Traitor.

It shouldn't have irritated her but it did, adding to her sense of feeling alone. She was used to being the one who made things happen, but when it counted she'd frozen. It all came so easily to Sam. Even Morris seemed to have forsaken her this morning, choosing Sam instead.

Sam rubbed his wide hand down Morris's back. "Will you at least promise to call me if you need anything? Or just let me know how it goes later? I'll be worried."

"I appreciate it, Sam, but there's no need for us to take any more of your time. I know you have your own concerns." She would be strong. She would prove it—first to herself, and then to everyone else who had ever doubted.

"There's every need," he contradicted.

Something in the warm timbre of his voice set off alarm bells. "Why?" she asked, trying to pull her fingers away but he held them fast.

He seemed to consider for a moment, then relaxed as if he'd come to some silent decision. "When this is over, we need to talk."

The bells were ringing madly now. "I don't know if that's a good idea. I need to get my mother settled and there'll be legal matters to sort out...not to mention the running of Butterfly House." Nerves flickered in her voice but she was determined. If she relied on Sam now she would never know if she had it in her to defeat her own demons.

"Angela."

The soft but firm way he said her voice cut off her babbling.

"I understand you need to do this by yourself. I really do.

*But I will worry about you whether you want me to or not.* That's what happens when you love someone."

Oh, no, he hadn't just said it. Hope slammed into her chest quickly, followed by despair. His gaze never left her face and time stood still for just a second as she absorbed the words. No one had ever said them to her before. And she knew Sam well enough that she knew he wouldn't say it if he didn't think he meant it. Hearing the words filled her with a momentary, glorious happiness. It was a revelation to know she was loveable.

But they were both going to be so hurt at the end of all this. He wanted to care for her and shoulder her burdens. And what she needed was someone who could step back and let her fight her own battles. When she'd thought it was only her feelings involved it had been better. But now he'd gone and said it out loud without even hesitating or choking on the words. He couldn't take it back even as a small part of her acknowledged that she didn't really want him to.

"You..." She couldn't bring herself to say it, but she *couldn't look away from the honesty and emotion in his eyes.* She knew he meant it even before he spoke the confirmation.

"I love you, Angela. You drove me insane the first time we met and you haven't stopped. I didn't know what to do with you and your sharp tongue and tidy little suit. I wanted to throttle you and kiss you senseless at the same time. But then something changed. I kept telling myself my feelings were all wrong and you told me to stay away and I thought that would solve it. But when I heard your voice on the phone last night I was so afraid and I knew. Your past doesn't matter. I love you. I just do."

She was without words. Never in her life had she been the recipient of such a speech. And he meant every word. She didn't doubt that for a second.

*He leaned in and touched her lips with his and she felt him* tremble beneath her hands. She curled her fingers around the cotton of his shirt and held on, absorbing the taste of him so that she could remember. He was always so unspeakably gentle. So gallant and courteous. And she deserved none of it, because she was letting him kiss her even though she knew in the end she'd turn him away.

Morris got cramped and with a meow of complaint jumped off Sam's lap. Sam slid a few inches closer until their bodies brushed. Angela gave herself this moment to cherish because even though she refused to say the words in return, she *knew in her heart that she did love him back. She loved his* loyalty and strength and the compassion that he sometimes kept hidden behind his hardworking exterior. The hands that worked the land and branded cows and broke horses were as gentle as a butterfly's touch on her skin. And yet she could not give in to it all the way. Because she would ask things of him that were not fair to ask. Things he could not give. She would ask him to stop being himself, and there was no way she could ask that of anyone.

And perhaps—just perhaps—she was afraid that if she forced him to make a choice between Diamondback and her, it wouldn't be her.

She pulled away from the tender embrace and sighed. "Oh, Sam."

The words were wistful and sad and needed no explanation or elaboration. The betrayed look in his eyes said it all for him. She hadn't said it back. They both knew that his declaration was not the beginning of something but the end.

The moment dragged out until he got to his feet, took a few steps, squared his shoulders and turned back to face her.

"This is why I didn't want to talk right now. You've got too much on your mind, too much you have to focus on. Once the dust has settled…"

"It won't change anything." She folded her hands on her

knees and looked up at him. He had done so much for her. She'd needled and accused him of some unjust things and in the end he'd come through, every single time. He deserved better than what she had to offer. He was looking for a wife who would move into the position of chatelaine of the ranch. That was his history and legacy. He needed someone who would put his needs—and Diamondback's—first, and that wasn't her. Because Butterfly House was *her* legacy and it was just getting started. She couldn't do both. And if the last twelve hours had taught her anything, it was that she had a lot of work left to do—both personally and professionally. *She wasn't ready for what a committed relationship would mean.*

"So you don't love me," he said, challenging her.

Could she lie? Could she look him in the eye and say *No, I don't love you, Sam*? She couldn't do it. He would see right through her.

"Where do you see this going?" she asked instead. It was an important question. A flicker of hope still burned. There was a chance she was wrong, after all, a chance that he might say the sorts of words that would give them a chance.

He came closer and squatted down in front of her, the denim of his jeans stretching taut across his long legs. She longed to reach out and lay her hands on his knees, just to feel connected to him again. She clenched her fingers tighter together to keep from doing it. She had to be strong.

"I saw you at the ranch the night of the open house, remember? You and Clara and mom all together in the kitchen, laughing. It felt so right, Ang. It's never been that way before. For a long time now it's been like living in black and white. And then you walked in and everything was in color again. I want you there, with me. I want you to make a life with me. I want us to face those challenges together."

Angela could think of a half dozen women who would give

their right arms to hear such a speech from Sam. What he had to offer any woman was a fine life. A beautiful, stable home, a prosperous living, and an incredible man capable of a lot of love. It was a dream come true. Except it was his dream and not hers.

She shrank back against the cushions. She was horribly afraid that if she said yes she'd end up losing the very best part of herself in the process, making them both miserable. They wouldn't make it. While she knew that Sam would never mistreat her the way Jack and Steve had, she was terribly afraid of losing the part of her she was just beginning to find.

In the end losing Sam would be so much worse than leaving Steve. That hadn't been about love at all. But Sam—he was unfailingly honest and deserved someone who could be as open with him. This time her heart was well and truly involved.

"I'm sorry, Sam. Your life is Diamondback. And mine is not. And that leaves us at a bit of an impasse."

He stood up, looked down at her and made her feel very small. "You'd have me walk away from the ranch?"

"Of course not. Diamondback is who you are. That's what I'm saying, you see?" She couldn't stand being on the sofa anymore and got up, letting the blanket drop to the floor. "You have built your life there. You are a part of the ranch and it is part of you. You need someone to be there by your side, to have a big family. I know you want that; I can see it every time you speak of your parents or your cousin. Family will always be at the center of your life—it's what drives you. And this foundation drives me, don't you see? You can't imagine walking away from the ranch so you must understand how it would be for me to walk away from this."

"You could still help," he offered. "You wouldn't have to give it up." But he looked away, knowing it was a paltry solution next to the absolute truth she spoke.

"I've dreamed of this foundation for most of my life," she said quietly. "If I walk away from this now, I leave the best part of me behind. I leave behind the part that makes me *me*. If you love me at all…"

"You know I do."

Her heart thudded. This was so hard. "If you love me at all," she continued, "you love me because of this place. Because of who it makes me. Because of who it will allow me to become. What is left if you take that away?"

"I would never want you to change who you are!" His eyes blazed at her. "You know that."

"I know you wouldn't mean to. But I have plans. It hasn't ended because of my mother, you know. Yes, I'm hoping this provides us with some healing and closure, but I believe in this project more than ever. I still want to expand and open up other shelters. And you need a wife who won't be traveling around all the time putting something else ahead of you. That's no way to run a relationship. I'd hurt you in the end, Sam, and that's not fair to either of us."

A door opened and shut and shuffling footsteps echoed in the hall. Beverly appeared in the doorway of the kitchen and Angela's heart hurt just looking at her. Dressed in an old nightie and a borrowed housecoat, she looked old and stooped and the fresh wounds on her face had deepened, giving her a tired, battered appearance.

"Mom. I hope we didn't wake you."

"I smelled coffee." The woman tried to smile but her cracked lip started to split and halted the smile in mid curve. Instead she moved to the coffeemaker and took a mug from a hook on a cup tree.

"I can't deal with this right now," Angela whispered to Sam, not sure if she was relieved by the interruption or not. Once he was gone it would truly be over. But sending him away was as close to breaking her heart as she'd ever come and she wasn't sure she was prepared for it. A part of her wanted to put it off as long as she could.

"Of course," he answered, but she detected a chill in his voice that hadn't been there before. Perhaps he was accepting the truth in what she said. It was an impossible choice for either of them to make. She was glad now that she hadn't said the words back to him. It would have made this even more unbearable.

"Mike will be expecting you at his office later this morning. And perhaps you can tell Clara that we can manage today without her. You need her more."

He grabbed his keys from the table and nodded at Beverly while Angela looked on helplessly.

"Mrs. Beck," he said, "I'm Sam Diamond. If you need anything, my family's here to help. Angela's going to take really good care of you. You can trust her to do the right thing."

Oh, the sting in those words, especially now that doing the right thing was costing them both so much. She blinked back tears and walked him to the door.

He paused for a moment on the steps, putting his hands in his pockets. Angela held on to the edge of the door, putting off shutting it, knowing it meant goodbye. Finally he looked up.

"You won't reconsider?"

She swallowed. "I can't," she whispered, looking down at her feet so he wouldn't see the glistening in her eyes.

"I want you to know that I meant what I just said to your mother. Same goes for you. If you ever need anything, I'm a phone call away. Got it?"

She nodded dumbly, still unable to look up at him. Her willpower was hanging by a thin thread. "I've got it."

He spun and jogged down the steps to his truck. Angela shut the door and locked it, then leaned her back against it. She couldn't bear to watch him drive away this time.

\* \* \*

Virgil was sitting in the late-August sun, a magazine in his lap. He hadn't even turned the cover. Instead Sam found him staring out over the pasture. Sam followed the path of his gaze and took a deep breath. Angela was right. This was more than home. Diamondback was something he felt through the soles of his feet straight to his heart. He and Virgil both did. And because of their love for the ranch, Sam was determined to give it one last try. There had to be a way to bring his vision for the future and the family all together.

"Dad."

Virgil started at the sound of his voice and Sam smiled wistfully. His father was improving slowly but there was no denying how much he'd aged since his stroke.

He pulled up a chair and sat beside his father. "Where's Clara?"

"Told her I wanted to sit outside for a while. No more fluttering."

Sam chuckled. Virgil's speech was improving, still slow but with fewer slurs. "She's good for you."

"Gives your mother a break. And she's a good woman." Virgil threw Sam a meaningful glance.

"Sorry, Dad. Barking up the wrong tree."

"I know." Virgil nodded. "You and Angela."

Surprise made Sam's mouth drop open. "How did you…"

"I see things. Slow. Not blind."

Sam sat back in his chair. Had he been treating his father as if he was blind? Had he underestimated how sharp his father's mind remained while his body betrayed him? He blew out a breath. "Of course. I'm sorry, Dad."

"I know that, too."

The dry August breeze blew across their faces, bringing with it the smell of fresh-cut grass and manure and the hundred other aromas of a ranch at its seasonal peak. For a few minutes Sam was quiet, gathering the words he needed.

Hoping that this last time he could break through and make his father understand.

"Dad, I need to say something and I want you to hear me out. Without jumping all over me." Virgil gave him a skeptical look and Sam's lip curved a little. "Okay, at least wait until I'm done."

"Say your piece."

He took a breath. "I think you're afraid, Dad. I think you hate what's happened and you're frustrated and you feel like you're losing control." Virgil's eyes blazed but Sam pressed on. "I think it has got to be hell on earth having to let go of your life's work and I think the fights we've had this summer have been a way for you to make sure you are not forgotten. That you are still a vital piece of Diamondback."

Virgil remained silent. Sam took that as a good sign, an affirmation without Virgil having to say the words.

Encouraged, he leaned forward. "Dad, you *are* Diamondback. I know it's been in the family for generations but you are the one who built it into what it is today. You are the one who took chances and became a leader in this industry. You are the fearless one. And it kills me to see that fearlessness taken away. I don't want to be the one to do it."

A magpie chattered beneath the caragana bushes and Sam watched it bob awkwardly along the grass, weighted down by its cumbersome tail. "I could never cut you out of Diamondback. I want us to do this together. And I know in my heart that this is the right thing. The right thing for right now and the right thing for the generations to come."

"What generations? Don't see any wives or babies runnin' around here."

Sam crossed an ankle over his knee. "Not for lack of trying, okay?" Irritation clouded his voice. The truth was, he hadn't been able to stop thinking about Angela. The bits and pieces he'd got from Clara over the past weeks were paltry crumbs. It had taken all his willpower to let Angela handle the changes in her life on her own, but he'd done it. Because he knew she needed to, for herself.

Besides, she hadn't even said she loved him. And that drove him crazy, because he could see her here, by his side. See their children running around in the hayfields. See himself teaching his son or daughter how to drive a tractor, ride a horse. For years he'd viewed children as a practical necessity, but not now. For the first time ever he could see it all and it wasn't his for the taking.

"You ask her?" Virgil reached out and touched Sam's arm. "Can't say yes if you don't ask."

"I told her I loved her. But it didn't make any difference."

Virgil started laughing. It was wheezy at first, rusty-sounding, and after a few moments he coughed, gasping for air. Sam started to feel alarmed once he got over the shock of seeing Virgil laugh. But Virgil grinned, sat back in his chair and sighed, catching his wind.

"Son, you can be so smart. And so stupid." He took a deep breath, unused to speaking so much. "What's really important here? You pestered me all summer like a dog with a bone. Now at the first sign of trouble with a woman, you run away with your tail between your legs."

"My tail!" Sam burned with indignation. "You don't know, Dad."

"I know enough. I know you gave up. Sad excuse for a Diamond."

Dammit. Sam hated to admit it but Virgil was right. He had given up. Angela had sent him away and he'd let her. He never wanted to seem pushy or overbearing because of her past. But the truth was, he'd been ornery before he knew anything of her history and she'd risen to the challenge, not cowered.

If anything, he'd let her down by not showing her how a man should stand by a woman.

"This project appears to be more important to you anyway," Virgil remarked. "So maybe it's best."

Sam sat back in his chair. He knew exactly what his father was doing and wanted to call him on it. But the truth was smack between his eyes. He'd fought for this but he hadn't fought for her. He thought back over all the reasons he'd just given his father for fighting the ranch development, and realized he could have been speaking to Angela about Butterfly House. She *was* afraid. She had been the one to realize her dream and now she was terrified of losing control. Of losing the most vital part of herself. She'd said it and he hadn't been listening.

"Sam, I'll sign the papers if you want me to. I know you'll do right by Diamondback. But I want you to remember something. This place—this life—means nothing without your mother. Make sure you make the right decisions and for the right reasons."

Virgil was giving Sam all he'd wanted and the victory felt hollow. What stretched before him was a cutting-edge, prosperous future and an empty one. It had taken him thirty-seven years to fall in love and he knew it was going to stick. So what was he going to do about it? Let her go without a fight? Spend the rest of his days at Diamondback, a man of property but with a hole in his soul?

He got up and put his hand on Virgil's shoulder. "Appears I have some thinking to do."

Virgil nodded. "Yessir."

"I'll send Clara out if you like."

"I don't mind sitting a little longer."

Sam gave the shoulder a squeeze before heading inside. An idea was beginning to form, the seedlings of a plan to bring the family together *and* have the woman he loved. Virgil wouldn't like it, but it might just get him the daughter-in-law and grandkids he'd been harping about for years.

# CHAPTER TWELVE

THE house seemed horribly quiet. The Cadence Creek Rodeo was on and Clara and the other girls had gone to enjoy the festivities, including entering their own pot of chili in the chili cook-off. It had been a bright spot, seeing the women come out of their shells as they got further acquainted. Angela had heard them giggling over the chili-making, speculating on how many employers they could entice with their secret ingredients.

Angela felt lonely listening to them. She was on the outside yet again and by her own choice. They'd invited Angela along, but she wanted the time alone. Moments of quiet were fewer and farther between these days and she was seldom in the mood for company.

A week had passed since Beverly had moved to a different shelter in another town. While Butterfly House helped women ready to start over, the assistance Beverly needed was different. And as much as Angela wished she could help her mother all on her own, she was wise enough to know she couldn't be objective. Leaving Beverly in someone else's care had been very, very hard. But wounds were healing. They'd hugged and cried a little as Angela had promised to be back to visit soon.

She wished she could say the same about Sam, but she hadn't spoken to him. The only time she'd seen him was when Jane had invited her to go along to church one Sunday. Sam and Molly were in the fourth pew from the front and she'd caught her breath at the sight of him in dress pants and a freshly pressed white shirt, open at the collar, his face smooth from a recent shave but with his hair still the same *sexy, unruly mess.*

She hadn't gone back to church the next Sunday.

So this afternoon she was spending the afternoon cleaning her room and listening to Patsy Cline. The wistful music suited her mood perfectly. She'd gotten what she wanted, hadn't she? So why did she feel so empty? Maybe it was time to start looking into the next project, scout new locations.

And then Sam's words came back to haunt her. That once he met a challenge he got bored and moved on to another. Was that what she was doing? Except instead of boredom she was running away from her problems.

She didn't have a magic solution, so she put her energies into the job at hand. Her sheets were on the clothesline and she was dusting off her dresser when his voice behind her scared her out of her skin.

"Busy?"

She nearly threw the duster at him as he laughed. Her heart raced from the shock. She'd been thinking about finally decorating this room and listening to Patsy singing about "Walkin' after Midnight" and then there he was. "You should know better than to sneak up on a person like that."

"May I come in?"

She lifted an eyebrow. Mercy, he looked good in new jeans and a crisp Western shirt, his customary Stetson atop his head. *"You're going to anyway."* She flourished the duster. "Go ahead."

Sam stepped inside, as calm as you please, removed his hat and held it in his hands. Her bedroom was the smallest of the six and he seemed to fill it with all his larger-than-life glory. Why did it seem as if nothing had changed? Maybe he'd realized he was wrong about his feelings. Surely if he still thought he was in love with her it would be more awkward, wouldn't it? Instead it felt as if he'd done this hundreds of times before.

He looked around the room. "You didn't decorate this one like the others."

She shrugged. "The money is allocated for the residents. Those rooms had to come first. I've been thinking about it, though..." She let the thought trail off. The truth of it was Butterfly House didn't feel like home. She wasn't sure where that was—or what it would feel like when she got there. But she'd put off decorating a room for herself just the same.

The CD shifted and "Crazy" started playing.

"Nice music choice." Sam waved his hat in the direction of the turntable. "My mother would approve. She loves Patsy Cline. Bit melancholy for a summer afternoon though, isn't it?"

"There's never a bad time for Patsy," Angela replied, putting down the duster and ignoring his observation about her state of mind. "Are you going to make me ask why you're here, Sam? Is this official Butterfly House board business? Because I figured you'd be at the fairgrounds with everyone else in town."

"I was, for a while." That explained his "dress" Western clothes, then. "My cousin's retiring after this season. But bull-riding's the last event of the day and he's not up for a few hours yet. I ran into Clara and the ladies in the church tent surrounded by Cadence Creek's finest chili. They told me you were stuck at home."

She'd stayed home because the thought of running into him at the rodeo put knots in her belly. Avoiding him wasn't the answer, but she figured one day it would get easier.

"That still doesn't tell me why you're here."

For a long moment he seemed to consider. Finally he said, "How's your mom?"

It touched her that he asked that first thing. "She's doing okay. We filed a report with Mike, and she's in a different place now getting the help she needs. The court date isn't going to be much fun, but we're going to be there together." She smiled a little. "She's going to be okay, and that's the main thing."

"And you? Are you okay?"

"I'm getting there." The truth was she couldn't have done this without his help that first day. It wasn't a magic solution, but she was working on making peace with things. With people.

The music changed, and the opening notes to "I Fall to Pieces" filled the room. Slowly Sam took a step forward, then another. He put his hat back on his head and held out his hand. "Care to? Since you're missing the festivities?"

"Sam…"

"Please, Angela. I've worked myself up to coming here all day and you're not making this easy. Dance with me."

She only complied because she knew how difficult it had been doing without him the last while and didn't want to make it any worse for Sam. She stepped tentatively into his arms, placing one hand in his and the other on his broad muscled shoulder.

His hand rested firmly on her waist as he pulled her close. In the tiny floor space his feet shuffled in small steps, but it was enough that she felt the movement of his thighs against hers, the rise and fall of his chest as he breathed, the warmth of his lips next to her hair that was shoved carelessly in a ratty ponytail.

"I'm sorry." He whispered it next to her ear, sending shivers down her spine as they swayed to the music.

It was not what she'd been expecting. "What do you have to be sorry about?"

"That I gave up."

"I told you to, remember?" Her heart started beating abnormally. She'd been the one to send him away. And she'd been the one to cry into her pillow at night because of it. Her reasons had been right, so why had it felt so wrong?

"You were scared and you should have had a friend by your side. Not to go through it for you, but with you. Instead I let you push me away, and I'm sorry I wasn't stronger."

Her lip quivered. "You scare me, Sam. You make me doubt everything."

"Why?"

His feet stopped moving for a moment and he drew back, looking down into her eyes. She gathered courage, knowing she'd faced her demons alone and she'd been strong enough to do it, but that she'd also missed him every moment. She'd been very wrong to push him away when she should have trusted him. "Because of the intensity I feel when I'm with you. I'm so afraid of getting lost in it."

"I know you are."

"You do?" She looked up at him with surprise. He hadn't understood before. He'd had his eye on a perfect Diamondback life where she could "help" with the Butterfly Foundation. The fact that she'd been at all tempted still frightened her to death. Was she so weak that she'd trade in her dream so easily?

"Of course I do. When you open yourself up to someone, then you allow them the opportunity to hurt you. To disappoint you. And you've already been hurt enough, sweetheart."

His feet started moving again, but slower, and she had the weirdest sensation that they were snuggling. He'd called her sweetheart again, she realized with a sigh. And despite trying to hold her feelings inside, she knew that she'd shared things with Sam already that she'd never shared before with another person. She trusted him, believed in his goodness. That was a brand-new feeling.

"By the way—Dad signed off on the biogas project."

She furrowed her brow, confused at the abrupt change of subject but willing to follow along if it meant she could stay within the circle of his arms. "How did you convince him to do that?"

"I was honest with him. I finally realized that he was afraid of being invisible, afraid of losing all he'd worked so hard to build. Holding out was the one thing he could still control when everything else was flying to pieces. But I told him that he would never be unimportant or ignored. Because we're in it together. That's what people who love each other do, you know?"

"No, Sam. I never had a family like yours so I don't know."

But he persisted. "I think you do. Look at what you've done for your mother. You are standing beside her even though she hurt you. You do the right thing, Angela, always. You give people a voice who otherwise don't have one. And yet your voice goes unheard."

*Their feet stopped and her throat swelled.* How could he see all of that? How could he know? She stumbled back, out of his arms, but he caught her fingers and held on.

"I didn't hear you." He captured her gaze and held it. "I didn't listen to what you were saying. It wasn't until I understood my dad that I got it."

He reached over and cupped her cheek. "You're a butterfly that needs to fly, not be shut up in a jar somewhere. I hear you now," he said softly, "and it's high time someone fought for you. I love you so much, Angela. And I was a fool to let you push me away. I told you the morning after your mother arrived, do you remember? That you can't force someone to feel what you want them to feel. What you can do is be ready,

so that when the day comes, you're there with open arms."
His forehead touched hers. "My arms are open now, Ang.
Hoping you're ready."

The floodwaters broke and she went into his embrace.
Oh, he felt so good, so strong, so right. His shirt smelled
like detergent and the outdoors and the spicy scent that was
distinctly Sam. "I love you, too," she said, her voice muffled
against the cotton.

This man—this gorgeous, humbling, incredible man before her—was offering her the moon. How could she not take
it? As her eyesight blurred through her tears she realized that
surrendering to her feelings only made her more, not less.
That over the last few difficult weeks she'd wanted him by
her side not to bear the burden for her but to share it with her.
Somehow, by some miracle, he'd restored her faith.

She leaned back and laid her hand on his tanned cheek. "I
do love you, and it's hurt me so much to hold it inside."

"I never wanted to hurt you." He put his hand over hers,
holding it there against the warmth of his skin, turning his
head a little so he could kiss the base of her palm. His eyes
closed for a second and his thick lashes lay against his cheek.
Angela was swamped by a love so whole, so complete, she
knew she'd remember this moment forever.

"I know that," she whispered, and he opened his eyes.

"I have a plan," he said. "Would you hear it? Please?"

Staying away from him hadn't solved a thing; she'd been
utterly miserable. Besides, Sam wasn't the kind of man who
said please often. He was used to having his own way. He was
the kind of man who took charge rather than be at anyone's
mercy. And that strong, forceful man was holding her in his
arms saying please. Hope glimmered as she nodded just the
tiniest bit, encouraging him to go on.

"I spent my whole life focusing on Diamondback. It meant
everything to my mom and dad and then to me, too. It defined

the Diamond family. I remember when times were tight. How we were looked down upon rather than up to. When things started to change, when the years of careful management paid off, I got cynical."

He squeezed her fingers. "I'm getting to the romantic part, I promise. I saw the love between my parents and knew I could never settle for anything less than the example they set. No one ever measured up—until I met you. Angela..."

*Oh, lord. His dark eyes were wide and earnest and her heart was pattering a mile a minute.*

"You really don't know, do you?" A soft smile touched his lips. "You walked into that benefit and it was like someone hit me right here and stole my breath." He pressed a hand to the middle of his chest. "And when you get talking numbers and figures and demographics it's a sight to behold. But it's not just that, either. You're compassionate, and strong."

She swallowed past the tears thickening her throat. But he wasn't done yet.

"*And then I thought maybe you did care for me. I could* see our life together. But it was still about me. It wasn't until I talked to Dad that I truly understood. He said something to me that day that brought it all back to one. He said that Diamondback and his life would have been nothing without Mom. And I realized he was right. I've been miserable. I holler at people and spend too much time brooding in the barn. I'm no quitter but I'd given up on us. I had to be willing to fight for us. And that meant putting us first. The only way to do that is to share your dreams with you. Because Diamondback be damned, Ang." His dark eyes shone down at her. "My dream is you. The rest of it doesn't matter if I don't have you."

He lifted her hand to his lips and kissed it, the gesture so chivalrous and tender that if she hadn't before, Angela would have lost her heart completely.

"I was looking for a way to put my family back together, and I couldn't see that you are doing it just by being you."

"I am?"

He nodded. "You made me see things from my dad's side. You helped my mom ask for help, became her friend. The only thing missing now is Ty—he belongs home rather than roaming the country. And now even he has a reason to come back."

"He does?" She was trying hard to keep up, but she couldn't see how she'd had anything to do with Sam's cousin whom she'd never met.

"I'm asking you to compromise," he said. "Make Diamondback the home base for something extraordinary. You don't belong running one single house, Angela, you deserve to be heading up the whole foundation. Hire a director for here, and oversee the start-up of each and every house built to help those who need it. I don't want you to give up your dreams. I want to share them with you, be with you every step of the way. And I hope that in the end, you'll share mine. Make a home with me at Diamondback. Maybe raise a family. A ranch is a good place to have kids. Hard work and open spaces and two parents who love and respect each other."

"You want to marry me. And have babies." Her mind was spinning, with the words he was saying tumbling about like little miracles and bubbles of possibilities she hadn't even considered before.

He tucked a piece of hair behind her ear, smiling softly. "Yes, I want to marry you." He grinned. "And have babies. Maybe I'm not great with teenagers but I'm guessing I'll learn, especially with you there beside me. What will it take to convince you?"

The CD had long since run out and the room echoed with expectant silence.

"I know you want to make this happen, but, Sam, you

can't be gone from the ranch all the time and your father is in no shape to go back to work." She wanted to believe him. Wanted it desperately.

"This is the best part. My cousin is retiring and coming home to run Diamondback with me. A full partnership. That means that I don't have to be at the ranch 24/7. I know that I can go away from time to time and the ranch is in good hands. It's where he's belonged all along anyway. The family all together."

"Your cousin?" she asked. "But I thought he was estranged from the family."

Sam grinned. "Convincing him to come back wasn't easy. He and Dad haven't seen eye to eye in a long time. Peas in a pod, that's why if you ask me. But Ty's sharp and he's a hard worker. If it hadn't been for one big blow-up I don't think he'd have gone in the first place. Even so, it took my trump card to make him say yes."

She risked a smile. "Of course you have an ace up your sleeve. You always do."

His lips curled in a sexy, private smile. "A long time ago we made a pact that we'd never lose our heads over a woman. I told him I had fallen in love and wouldn't have as much time to dedicate to the ranch. He said he didn't believe it and that it was something he needed to see in person. But it's just an excuse. I think he knows it's time he came home."

Sam had turned his life upside-down to make this happen. All for her. It was everything she wanted and it made her want to weep.

She put her hand on his chest and tipped her face up to his. "I had to face some things on my own, had to prove to myself that I was strong enough to be me and come out of the shadow that's been hanging over me for so long. But I missed you the whole time, Sam. I wish I could have done that without sending you away. I don't feel like I deserve you. I asked too much, I…"

"Hush." He placed a finger over her lips. "You taught me that it's about what you give, rather than what you get. You deserve far more than you think, and I'm going to spend my life showing you—if you'll say yes."

There was no other possible answer to give. He was offering her everything—the Butterfly Foundation, a home, brown-eyed and dark-haired babies to call her Mama. She just had to be brave enough to trust, and believe and reach out and grab it.

She cupped his face in her hands and kissed his lips. "Yes," she whispered. "Yes."

# EPILOGUE

THE fall day was gilded in hues of gold—the ripe harvests in the field, the drying grasses in the meadows, the gold coin-shaped leaves rustling on the poplar trees. The guests sat in rented chairs on the lawn while Sam stood at the top of the newly painted porch, where he'd shared lemonade and those first confidences with Angela in the twilight.

Sam watched as she made her way up the path, walking slowly in a simple white dress with her hand on Virgil's arm as he took small steps behind a rolling walker. When they'd announced their engagement, Virgil had insisted on walking her down the "aisle," and he and Clara had kept it a secret as they'd worked over the past weeks. Sam's throat thickened at the sight and he ran a finger between his neck and the tight collar of his new shirt. Angela smiled up at him and the world stopped. It was just the two of them now as she took the steps with her small train gliding behind, the long veil floating in the fall breeze.

"I, Samuel, take you, Angela…"

"I, Angela, take you, Samuel…"

She smiled at the use of his full name and he smiled back, full of a happiness he hadn't known existed. Within minutes it was done—the ring was on his finger where he planned to keep it forever.

The reception was held at Diamondback in a huge tent set

up in the garden. The asters, chrysanthemums and dahlias were still blooming, their spicy scents mixed with the delectable smell of Diamondback's finest prime rib.

Clara, Angela's only bridesmaid, came to offer her last congratulations before taking Virgil inside after the excitement of the day.

"I'm going in now, but I wanted to say happy wedding day to you both." She gave Angela a quick hug. "I'm going to miss you around the house, but you're going to have a wonderful time."

Sam had booked them in a chalet in Quebec's Eastern Townships for a week's honeymoon, to be followed by a week in Ottawa where they'd be in meetings about federal funding for the Butterfly Foundation. A new director of the Cadence Creek house had been hired, and a temporary office had already been set up at Diamondback for Angela to use until construction finished on their new house. He intended to keep his promises.

Sam hugged Clara as well—she'd gotten over her physical shyness with him shortly after their engagement. "Have you met Ty yet?" he asked. "Your paths will be crossing a lot from now on as he'll be staying in the house. Hang on."

He waved his cousin over. "Ty, come on over here."

Ty looked out of place in his suit. His jaw sported a faint bit of stubble and the suit coat hung awkwardly on his rangy frame. Sam hid a smile. Ty was back but he was still determined to do things his way. Thankfully that didn't mean butting heads with each other. But Sam had his doubts where Virgil was concerned. Ty and Virgil seemed to set each other off without trying. The next few months would be interesting. Still, he was convinced they'd work through it.

"Ty, this is Dad's assistant, Clara."

"Mr. Diamond," she said, and Sam saw the defiant set of her jaw as she held out her hand. It was more than she'd done with him at their first meeting, and Sam shared a look with his new wife. It was good progress.

"It's just Ty," he replied, taking her hand and shaking it. Sam saw Clara's eyes widen at the contact before she pulled her hand away. "Or Tyson if I'm on your bad side."

"Right. Well, I'd better get your dad inside. Goodnight everyone."

When she was gone, Sam saw Ty's gaze following her to the house.

"Go easy," Sam warned.

"Did I do anything?" There was a hint of belligerence in Ty's voice. Boy, he did still have a chip on his shoulder.

"Of course not," Angela stepped in with a smile. "Clara was our first Butterfly House resident, that's all. Sam just wants you to respect that."

Ty's gaze narrowed as he watched Clara's sage-green skirt disappear through the deck door. "Her husband abused her?"

"They weren't married, but yes," Angela confirmed. "But we know you'll be considerate, Ty. Don't worry."

Ty hesitated a moment, then to Sam's surprise excused himself and started toward the house.

Sam started forward but Angela stopped him with a hand on his arm. "Let him go. She'll put him in his place if need be. I'm not worried, Sam. Ty's a good man underneath all his cockiness." She grinned. "Like his cousin."

"Like your husband," he corrected, pulling her into his arms.

"Don't worry," she said, standing up on tiptoe and touching her lips to his. "I know how lucky I am. There's no other Diamond like you, Sam."

"Damn right," he confirmed, and picked her up, spinning her in a circle of happiness.

\* \* \* \* \*

*A sneaky peek at next month...*

# Cherish™

**ROMANCE TO MELT THE HEART EVERY TIME**

*My wish list for next month's titles...*

**In stores from 18th May 2012:**

❏ A Cold Creek Reunion – RaeAnne Thayne

& A Weaver Proposal – Allison Leigh

❏ The Nanny and the Boss's Twins & The Nanny
 Who Kissed Her Boss – Barbara McMahon

**In stores from 1st June 2012:**

❏ The SEAL's Promise & The Marshal's Prize
 – Rebecca Winters

❏ Mendoza's Return – Susan Crosby

& Fortune's Just Desserts – Marie Ferrarella

**Available at WHSmith, Tesco, Asda, Eason, Amazon and Apple**

*Just can't wait?*

# MILLS & BOON® Book Club

## 2 Free Books!

## Get your free books now at
### www.millsandboon.co.uk/freebookoffer

## Or fill in the form below and post it back to us

**THE MILLS & BOON® BOOK CLUB™—HERE'S HOW IT WORKS:** Accepting your free books places you under no obligation to buy anything. You may keep the books and return the despatch note marked 'Cancel'. If we do not hear from you, about a month later we'll send you 5 brand-new stories from the Cherish™ series, including two 2-in-1 books priced at £5.49 each, and a single book priced at £3.49*. There is no extra charge for post and packaging. You may cancel at any time, otherwise we will send you 5 stories a month which you may purchase or return to us—the choice is yours. *Terms and prices subject to change without notice. Offer valid in UK only. Applicants must be 18 or over. Offer expires 31st July 2012. **For full terms and conditions, please go to www.millsandboon.co.uk/freebookoffer**

Mrs/Miss/Ms/Mr (please circle)

First Name

Surname

Address

Postcode

E-mail

**Send this completed page to: Mills & Boon Book Club, Free Book Offer, FREEPOST NAT 10298, Richmond, Surrey, TW9 1BR**

Find out more at
**www.millsandboon.co.uk/freebookoffer**

*Visit us Online*

0112/S2XEA/REV

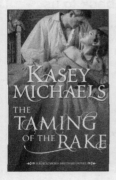
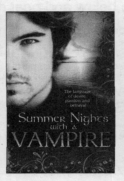
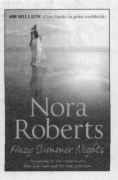

# The World of Mills & Boon®

There's a Mills & Boon® series that's perfect for you. We publish ten series and with new titles every month, you never have to wait long for your favourite to come along.

---

*Blaze*®
Scorching hot, sexy reads

By Request
Relive the romance with the best of the best

*Cherish*™
Romance to melt the heart every time

*Desire*™
Passionate and dramatic love stories

*Visit us Online*
Browse our books before you buy online at
**www.millsandboon.co.uk**